Charlotte Greig is a journalist, editor, songwriter and performer. Having worked with various rap crews in the early 1980s, she is now writing songs with a view to a solo career. She lives in London.

To P. & S. Greig

will you still love me tomorrow?

GIRL GROUPS FROM THE 50S ON

CHARLOTTE GREIG

VIRAGO PRESS

Published by VIRAGO PRESS Limited 1989
20–23 Mandela Street, Camden Town, London NW1 0HQ

Copyright © 1989 Charlotte Greig

A CIP catalogue record for this book is available from the British Library

Designed by Lone Morton

Printed in Great Britain by
Butler & Tanner Ltd,
Frome and London

'Maybe' (R. Barrett) © NOM Music Inc.; 'Mr Sandman' (P. Ballard) © H. Edwin Morris & Co.; 'A Girl's Work Is Never Done' (Barrett, Raysor); 'Tonight's the Night' (L. Dixon, S. Owens) © 1960 Ludix Music Corp., USA, reproduced by permission of EMI Music Publishing Ltd London WC2H 0EA; 'Will Power' (G. Goffin, C. King) © 1963 Screen Gems-EMI Music Inc., USA, reproduced by permission of Screen Gems-EMI Music, London WC2H 0EA; 'Will You Love Me Tomorrow?' (G. Goffin, C. King) © 1960 Screen Gems-EMI Music Inc., USA, reproduced by permission of Screen Gems-EMI Music, London WC2H 0EA; 'Then He Kissed Me' (P. Spector, E. Greenwich, J. Barry) used by permission of Carlin Music Corporation, 14 New Burlington Street, London W1X 2LR; Warner Chappell Music; 'What Does A Girl Do?' (Townsend) © 1963 Shelby Singleton Music Inc., used by permission; 'Uptown' (B. Mann, C. Weil) © 1962 Screen Gems-EMI Music Inc., USA, reproduced by permission of Screen Gems-EMI Music Ltd, London WC2H 0EA; 'He Hit Me' (G. Goffin, C. King) © 1962 Screen Gems-EMI Music Inc., USA, reproduced by permission of Screen Gems-EMI Music Ltd, London WC2H 0EA; 'He's A Rebel' (G. Pitney) © January Music Corp.; Intersong; Warner Chappell Music Ltd; 'He's Sure the Boy I Love' (B. Mann, C. Weil) © 1962 Screen Gems-EMI Music Inc., reproduced by permission of Screen Gems-EMI Music Ltd, London WC2H 0EA; 'Chapel of Love' (P. Spector, E. Greenwich, J. Barry) used by permission of Carlin Music Corporation, 14 New Burlington Street, London W1X 2LR; Warner Chappell Music Inc.; 'He's So Fine' (R. Mack) © 1963 ABKCO Music Inc., USA, reproduced by permission of Peter Maurice Co. Ltd, London WC2H 0EA; 'You Don't Own Me' (J. Madara, D. White) © Unichappell Music Inc., lyrics reproduced by permission of Warner Chappell Music Ltd; 'Leader of the Pack' (G. Morton, P. Spector, E. Greenwich, J. Barry) © R. Mellin Music; Tender Tunes; EMI Publishing Ltd; 'Give Him A Great Big Kiss' (G. Morton) © Trio Music; Warner Chappell Music; 'I Can Never Go Home Any More' (G. Morton) © Warner Chappell Music; 'Long Live Our Love' (Barnes, Jackson) Leiber Stoller Songs Ltd.; Warner Chappell Music; 'Out In the Streets' (E. Greenwich, J. Barry) © Country Music Inc. Helios Music Corp.; Warner Chappell Music; 'I Hate Men' (J., T. and B. Beverley) © Warner Chappell Music; 'Some of Your Lovin'' (G. Goffin, C. King) © 1965 Screen Gems-EMI Music Inc., USA; 'The Boy From New York City' (Taylor) used by permission of Leiber Stoller Songs Limited and Carlin Music Corporation, 14 New Burlington Street, London W1X 2LR; 'Please Hurt Me' (G. Goffin, C. King) © 1963 Screen Gems-EMI Music Inc., USA, reproduced by permission of Screen Gems-EMI Music Ltd, London WC2H 0EA; 'One Fine Day' (G. Goffin, C. King) © 1963 Screen Gems-EMI Music Inc., USA, reproduced by permission of Screen Gems-EMI Music Ltd, London WC2H 0EA; 'Needle in A Haystack' (N. Whitfield, Wm Stevenson, E. Holland), 'Nowhere to Run' (Holland-Dozier-Holland), 'Really Saying Something' (N. Whitfield, Wm Stevenson, E. Holland), 'You Can't Hurry Love' (Holland-Dozier-Holland) © Jobete Music Co. Inc.; 'Want Ads' (Johnson-Perry-Perkins), 'While You're Out Lookin' For Sugar' (Dunbar, Wayne), 'The Day I Found Myself' (Dunbar-Wayne-Johnson) © Heath-Levy Music Ltd/Gold Forever Music; 'Dirty Ol' Man' by Leon Huff and Kenneth Gamble © 1973 Mighty Three Music/Island Music Ltd, used by permission. All rights reserved. 'At Peace With Woman' by Kenneth Gamble, Joel Bryant and Herb Smith © 1980 Mighty Three Music/Island Music Ltd. Used by permission. All rights reserved. 'The Player' (N. Harris, A. Felder) © Golden Fleece/Nickel Shoe/Six Strings/Mighty Three/Silk Music. 'He's the Greatest Dancer', 'Lost In Music' (N. Rogers, B. Edwards) © Warner Chappell Music. 'How Long (Chick on the Side)' (A. & B. Pointer, D. Rubinson, J. & R. Pointer) © Kathy Horton, Dave Rubinson and Friends; 'Marry Me (If You Really Love Me)' (B. Cooper); 'Funk U Up' (C. Cook, G. Chisholm, A. Brown) © Sugar Hill Music Publishing; 'Roxanne Roxanne' (The Real Roxanne, Howie Tee, Full Force) © Zomba Music Publishing; 'B Boys B Ware' (Rodriguez, Smith) © Sugarscoop Inc.; 'I Wonder If I Take You Home' (Full Force) © Chrysalis Music Ltd; 'I'll Take Your Man' (H. Azor), 'Chick on the Side' (H. Azor), 'Tramp' (H. Azor) © Next Plateau/Turnout Bros Music; 'Stealin' Love' (Hayes, Porter); 'When Tomorrow Comes' (Hayes, Porter); 'Best of My Love' (M. White, A. McKay) © Pam Jokeen/Steel Chest/Saggifire Music; 'A Long Way to Go' (B. Mann, C. Weil) © 1970 Screen Gems-EMI Music Inc., USA, reproduced by permission of Screen Gems-EMI Music Ltd, London WC2H 0EA; 'Candy Man', 'Prove It', 'All Night Long' (Rick James) © Stone City Music; 'Nasty Girl' (Vanity), 'He's So Dull' (Vanity, D. Dickerson), 'If A Girl Answers, Don't Hang Up' (Vanity 6, Terry Lewis) © Warner Chappell; extract from Quant by Quant © Mary Quant used by kind permission of Pan Books, London.
    Photographs by kind permission from the following collections: cover (Chantels), pp. 10, 15, 19, 20, 38, 63, 65, 68, 70, 73, 78, 80, 83, 87, 100, 102, 107, 111, 113, 119, 122, 126, 128, 129, 132, 176 Malcolm Baumgart; pp. 23, 32, 35, 42, 46, 51, 53, 56, 58 Mick Patrick; pp. 10 (Chordettes), 155 Ace Records; p. 89 the Beverley Sisters; cover (Ronettes), pp. 41, 93, 96 Morning Star; pp. 136, 163, 170, 196 Blues and Soul.

contents

ACKNOWLEDGEMENTS

First of all, I would like to thank Virago Press for publishing this book; my thanks go to Ruthie Petrie, who commissioned it, to my first editor Jane Parkin for her perceptive comments on my initial draft, and to my present editor Lucinda Montefiore for all her hard work and encouragement. Thanks also to Gil McNeil, Karen Cooper and Amanda Cohen. I am also very grateful to Lone Morton for her imaginative design of the book, and to Richard Thornton for his beautiful cartoon illustrations.

I had a great deal of help from different sources in my research, firstly from the women I interviewed: Arlene Smith of the Chantels, Beverly Lee of the Shirelles, Ellie Greenwich, Dee Dee Kennibrew of the Crystals, Darlene Love, Jiggs Allbut of the Angels, Mary O'Leary (alias Reparata) of the Delrons, the Beverley Sisters, Vicki Wickham, Gladys Horton of the Marvelettes, Carolyn Gill of the Velvelettes, Cindy Birdsong of the Blue-belles and the Supremes, Valerie Holiday of the Three Degrees, Glodean White of Love Unlimited, Jeanette Hutchinson of the Emotions, Debbie Sledge of Sister Sledge, Shirley Jones of the Jones Girls, Keren Woodward of Bananarama, Bernadette Cooper, and Cheryl James, Sandra Denton and Dee Dee Roper of Salt 'n Pepa. I am also grateful to Eddie Holland and Pete Waterman for the insights they gave me in interviews. Those who also contributed help, information and advice, included: John Abbey, Aly at Rhythm Records, Tony Barratt, Frances Bentley, Alan Betrock, Simon Carter, Stuart Coleman, Sue Davis, Helen Falconer, Carol Faucet, Charlie Gillett, Malu Halasa, Mike Hart, Malcolm Imrie, Bob Killbourne, Nick Kimberley, Patrick Lacy, Ian Levine, Miles, Brian Raymond, Lester Sill, and Sylvie Tata.

Special thanks must go to Malcolm Baumgart, girl-group archivist extraordinaire, and Mick Patrick, editor of *Philately* and *That Will Never Happen Again*, without whom this book could not have been written. They read through my drafts, filled me in on many unfamiliar aspects of the subject, helped with the captions and provided nearly all the photographs here free of charge. Many music experts would not have been so keen to share their knowledge and their collections with an upstart on the scene, but the girl-group fraternity in Britain could not have been more generous.

I would also like to thank my colleagues at Verso and Miquette Giraudy for giving me time off from other projects; my aunt Phillida Viest and my cousins Nick and Richard for their hospitality in New York; my mother, father, sister and brothers for their encouragement; and my son Henry. Finally, I owe a great debt to John Williams: for finding me endless books, magazines and records, for discussing the book with me, and for maintaining my belief in it; thank you for loving me, as the Sapphires would have put it.

PREFACE

When people asked me, whilst I was writing this book, what it was about I at first replied confidently, 'girl groups in pop'. 'Ah, you mean all-women bands' came the response, or 'I see, women in rock'. As time went on I tried to be clearer about my subject matter by calling it 'girl vocal harmony groups', but that seemed to provoke an even more mystified reaction. It soon became clear to me that although anyone who takes even a passing interest in pop is familiar with the girl-group records of one period or another, very few people have a clear picture of what a girl group actually is, let alone a sense of girl groups as forming the central female tradition within mainstream pop.

In this book, I take the term 'girl group' to mean a group of three or more young women singing pop tunes in vocal harmony together, using a style which originated in fifties' teenage American rock 'n' roll. Girl groups on this model – from the Chantels and the Ronettes to the Supremes, the Three Degrees and Bananarama – have been swarming all over the charts in full view of everyone for over three decades, but for some reason their presence as anything more than voices on disc has been virtually ignored. This book sets out to explain why.

What I have not set out to cover is the story of the relatively few all-female rock bands during this period: from Goldie And The Gingerbreads in the sixties, to punk groups like the Slits or the Raincoats in the seventies, to post-punk groups as various as Girlschool, Fuzzbox and the Bangles in the eighties. It seems to me that these groups belong to a quite separate tradition, one which is decidedly 'rock' rather than 'pop', in which self-contained bands play their own instruments and write their own songs; and that moreover, this tradition has long been the focal point for critical attention (for instance, a cultish London white rock group like the Slits is discussed far more widely than an enormously successful contemporary black pop group like Sister Sledge); in this book, I have tried to redress the balance a little.

Also, I believe that the girl vocal harmony groups have their own distinct history as the central female genre in pop, and that they cannot simply be lumped in with other female musical traditions – whether in rock, folk, country, jazz or anything else – and labelled 'women's music' as a job lot. There is currently a strong tendency to concoct these generic terms in pop music, mostly for marketing reasons – witness the vogue for the term 'world music' which might just as well be 'foreign music' for all its descriptive usefulness – and the idea of collapsing women's immensely diverse contributions to contemporary music into one genre on grounds of sex alone seems equally ludicrous.

My aim in this book, then, has been to overturn some of the prejudices with which many people, whether general punters or music buffs, approach the girl groups. The stereotype is that of an entirely passive group of young women who are called in by a male producer to make real his musical fantasies, and who have no part to play in the whole business beyond donating their services as so many sets of vocal cords. There is an element of truth in this picture, but it is not the whole truth, as this book tries to show. Firstly, as is well known, there were in fact several highly successful women producers, songwriters and arrangers behind the early girl groups, notably Carole King, Ellie Greenwich (who gives a fascinating account of her life as the 'super ace' of girlie tunes in chapter 2) and lyricist Cynthia Weil. Secondly, as nearly all the artists interviewed for this book tell, there was songwriting and production talent within the girl groups themselves, although this was not for the most part encouraged or credited. Thirdly – and this is perhaps the most important point – the fact is that male producers were not entirely at liberty to indulge their fantasies on disc in their work with the girl groups. As Eddie Holland, co-composer of so many hits for the Supremes, points out in chapter 5, girl-group producers were writing to a female audience and therefore had to some degree to adopt a female persona, composing songs that expressed women's concerns – particularly with regard to sex, love, romance and marriage. For good commercial reasons they had, as he says, to listen to women; otherwise the records they put out simply wouldn't have sold. Also, as Joni Sledge and Shirley Jones point out, these male producers were often inspired by the girl artists they worked with and wrote songs in tribute to them (Sister Sledge's 'We Are Family' is the classic example here), so that the songs are in a sense an aural image of the girls who sang them. Thus, in all these ways, the girl-group artists did have a central role to play; and the songs they sang, even when written by men, told stories for and about women.

As a result, the girl groups' songs are a fascinating and accurate expression of the changing aspirations and preoccupations of women over three decades. The song lyrics faithfully reproduce popular attitudes amongst women to various issues of the day (from marriage in the sixties, to feminism or 'women's lib' in the seventies), whether those attitudes were coherent or wildly irrational and contradictory. For that reason I have given the song lyrics more space than is usually accorded them; but the other reason I have quoted so extensively from them is because I like them. For me, far from being trivial, the lyrics of the best girl-group songs are an intensely evocative and accurate reminder of how young women have thought and felt about those weighty issues of sex, love, romance and marriage that have defined their lives.

My focus throughout has been on the most popular of the girl groups, those who have been commercially successful in the mainstream charts but who have for the most part been critically ignored. Sadly, this has often meant leaving out some obscure but fascinating groups; for instance, lack of space forced me to ditch a section on surf girl groups, and to delete all mention of such arcane girl-group heroines as the Rev-lons, the Ribbons, the Joys, the Darlettes, the Pin-ups, the Delicates, the Teardrops, the Thrills, Patty Lace and the Petticoats, the Pandoras, the Charmettes . . . the list is endless.

Many people reading this book, especially aficionados of the girl-group sound, will be surprised to find that it doesn't end in 1964, when, as received wisdom has it, the boy beat groups of the British Invasion hit the American scene and drove away the girl groups for ever. I hope these readers find that the last two chapters of the book, which look respectively at the increasingly musically sophisticated black girl groups that emerged in the seventies in the wake of the Supremes and at the rise in the eighties of girl groups and crews in punk, funk and hip hop, shed new light on what happened to the genre after the sixties; and help to answer the question the girl groups have asked over the years, 'Will You Still Love Me Tomorrow?', by affirming the continuation of a great musical tradition.

① tonight's the night

The year is 1957. The place, 49th Street, New York. Hanging around outside Loew's Theatre is a gaggle of schoolgirls waiting to catch the ear of a record producer. He eventually appears, and they strike up in unison, sounding as sober and polite as young girls in a school choir – which, as it turns out, is exactly what they are.

After a few minor local hits, the Chantels, as the girls named themselves, released a song written by producer Richard Barrett that proved to be a smash. It was called 'Maybe' and featured the high, searing voice of a fifteen-year-old black girl called Arlene Smith, backed up with sweet vocal harmonies from the rest of the group. Arlene sang:

> *May-ay-be if I pray every night, he'll come back to-o-o me*
> *And may-ay-be if I cry every day, he'll come back to-o-o stay*
> *Oh, oh, oh, oh, oh maybe.*

There was more than a hint of teenage melodrama to this, but Arlene's voice gave the track a dramatic intensity and innocent sincerity that made it different from run-of-the-mill love songs. It was the incongruity of a young girl singing such grown-up, desperate stuff that made 'Maybe' so gripping; Arlene was clearly in the throes of a passion she was too young to understand. As she later observed, 'I was singing about the kind of love I didn't know ... I loved my parents.' Taught by a nun, Arlene's vocal style was derived from singing Gregorian chant and Latin hymns in a Catholic school choir rather than from the experience of being in love, from praising the Lord rather than the boy next door. 'That nun,' she says today, 'really brought it home to me that you had to sing with a fineness of tone and an honesty that will stand with you. To this day, I still have the same sensitivity to those qualities in music.'

In the fifties, the Chantels pioneered the new sound of girl-group pop, but it was the more traditional groups like the Chordettes (inset) who hogged the limelight.

The Chantels' style, a blend of devotional love lyrics and simple rhythm 'n' blues backing with youthful yet heartfelt wailing from the girl lead singer and cooing, sweet harmonies from the chorus, formed the basis of the girl-group sound that was to hit America and Britain in the sixties. In 'Maybe', a girl seemed to be talking to her friends; their voices followed her story, emphasizing their agreement, their interest, their shared emotions in a private female world. It was the first time that this had been done so effectively in a pop setting. In the adult world of gospel, women often sang in a call-and-response pattern, the powerful lead singer telling her story, baring her soul, seeking affirmation from the choir and congregation; but the Chantels' high, ethereal harmonies and purity of tone, which derived from an altogether different strain of church music, added a totally fresh element, one that seemed to chime perfectly with an emerging pop sensibility amongst teenage girls.

Even when, at a later period, girl groups reached the heights of bubblegum romance and teen schlock, the bedrock of their appeal remained the honest, emotional intensity of that lead voice and the girl-talk intimacy evoked by the chorus. The basic elements, except for waltzy string arrangements, were all there in 'Maybe', even if the balance was not yet quite right: you could hardly hear the chorus on the record, the drums and piano crashed along a bit too cheerfully, and only Arlene's impassioned lead vocal pulled it all together. Yet despite – or perhaps because of – the rather home-made feel of the track, it became immensely popular in the New York area, and even hit number fifteen on the national pop charts. For an unknown group of girls on a tiny label, this was a tremendous start.

Today, Arlene Smith sits in the plush Broadway offices of the management company she has just signed to (entitled – ironically enough for an artist who has spent a lifetime struggling to fulfil her early promise – 'Fast Break'), a tall, glamorous woman in her early forties. She speaks in a soft, tentative voice that still sounds surprisingly young, and remembers how it all began:

> When I was about seven I became a member of the St Anthony of Padua Cherub choir. We were all trained in music from a very early age; we all took piano and voice lessons from the same nun. By about '53 or '54, just as we were coming up to our teens, we started to be interested in pop – and boys, of course. At that time, I played basketball because I was tall. I was second string so I had a chance to sit on the bench and fool around with my friends. We grouped together and sang; and a sound kept evolving.

In their early days, the Chantels adopted a style of unaccompanied vocal harmonizing that went back to the forties and that had more recently become all the rage as a new wave of teenagers – mostly young black, and Italian boys – took it up. The Chantels brought a new and dist feminine sensibility to this male teenage craze but it wasn't they who introduced moon-in-June romance into it (girl talk was a much more serious business than that). The hearts and flowers were already there; the mostly all-male groups (very occasionally they featured a girl singer like Lilian Leach of the Mellows) would call themselves romantic names such as the Moonglows, the Charms and the Valentines, and would indulge in intensely dramatic renditions of popular ballads, crooners' songs, silly novelty tunes, their own compositions and anything else that took their fancy. They represented a move in popular music in the mid fifties towards a younger audience, towards a more delicate teenage sensibility perhaps; 'doo wop', as their music has since been called, was sweet-sounding, charming and tuneful, in contrast to the sweaty excesses of a Screamin' Jay Hawkins or a James Brown. Yet, for all its pleasant sweetness, there was an edge of lunacy about the music, an ecstatic emotional yodelling that made one wonder if the romantic sentiments expressed were quite serious, and if they were, whether the singer expressing them was quite sane. And if it was difficult to tell how normal these guys were from all those 'doo-wop-shoo-bop-a-doo-bas' coming out of the radio, live, everything became clear: they dressed with an attention to detail bordering the obsessive, sported greasy conked hairdos, executed spins, turns and splits on stage that were as elaborate as their harmonies, and generally created mayhem in the audiences they played to. Doo-wop groups like the legendary Cadillacs were every bit as flash and wild as the older kings of rock 'n' roll, and those like the Penguins every bit as crazy; maybe teenage sensibilities weren't so delicate after all.

To Arlene and her cohorts, these boy groups represented the pinnacle of glamour at the time:

Our role models were really the older guys. We would listen to them at the after-school programmes in the gym. The elementaries and junior highs would open up at night and have what they called centres. The fellers would play recreational games, and there'd be dances. You had to have a centre card in order to belong, and you had to get good grades to get out a couple of nights from home to go there. The guys would usually separate and go play basketball, and the girls would dress up and gossip and listen to music. There was always a group. There was one called the Sequence, I think they later became the Cadillacs, and everyone would gather round while they sang. That got to me, I enjoyed it. We were in love with those guys, because they were so handsome. They would come to the centres dressed in these really wonderful suits, doing nice steps, looking so showy . . . and we were just little girls watching them.

Doo wop was essentially street music; its great appeal to the hundreds of black teenagers in the cities who became involved with it was that it required no instruments at all. The 'doo wops' and 'shoo-be-dos' had come about as singers tried to imitate the sounds of bass guitars and pianos; a group of four or five people taking different parts could layer sound on sound like a whole band. All you needed was a street corner and a few friends. This was a simple, democratic and communal way of making music; using the harmonizing skills learnt in church, in school and at home, the groups would meet, practise and sing, out on the street or in the school playground, for the pure pleasure of it. Rival groups would compete with each other, and the neighbourhood would echo with the piercing cries of 'Onleee Yooooo!' or 'Earth Angel, earth angel, will you be mi-i-ne?'

The best of the groups might be rewarded with the chance of making a record; this usually meant putting a simple R&B backing behind the voices and recording the song in a matter of minutes. There were small labels who put out this sort of music, like George Goldner's label End, which eventually released the Chantels' songs. The labels distributed records to the local stores and often paid local radio DJs to play them. However, if a record sold a few thousand locally, the artists wouldn't usually see the profits; even if it went national, one way and another they would seldom manage to get any money out of it. Despite hearing a record all over town, artists would be told that it just hadn't had the sales, or studio costs, payola, musicians' fees and a hundred other things would be cited as the reason for that inexplicable but ever-present condition of life for young hopefuls in the music business: no money.

However, the small labels did at least provide teenagers with a constant supply of their kind of music. Arlene recalls:

> We bought records by label colours. Bruce label was on a blue/purple label. Even if you'd never heard of the act, you knew it was good, that you'd have something to listen to when you got home. We'd have to save our allowance. The pink was Josie records, and so on . . .

In addition to the radio and records, songbooks were another essential source of supply for teenagers with a musical addiction, particularly the girls:

> We weren't allowed to read *True Love Confessions*. But I used to buy the magazines with all the lyrics to the songs. I had loads of them. I was a *Paper Doll* person. A new book with a new song was almost as exciting as a record itself; we'd all get together, learn it and sing it . . .

This was the music scene, then, as the Chantels found it in the late fifties. Despite their own by now considerable vocal abilities, Arlene and her friends remained for some time in awe of the older boy groups, worshipping them from afar and impressed by their conquests of the mysterious world of radio, until one day Arlene made a discovery:

Alan Freed came on the radio and played Frankie Lymon and the Teenagers singing 'Why Do Fools Fall in Love'. It was a lovely high voice and a nice song. Then Freed announces that Frankie is just thirteen! Well! I had to sit down. It was a big mystery, how to get into this radio stuff. I thought if he could do it . . . It seemed so far removed, but I made a conscious decision to do the same.

I don't know if Alan Freed mentioned it on the radio, or if it was the gossip that just happened to come up to the Bronx, but it seemed Frankie was involved with one of the Valentines. When we saw that the Valentines were appearing in the city, we went and saw the show. We went backstage to see this Richard Barrett who we heard managed Frankie. We had also gone over to Frankie's block before that, on 162nd Street; we'd met some of his friends, but we hadn't had a glimpse of Frankie. Well, anyway, we went backstage. When the group came out, they were mobbed by

Frankie Lymon and the Teenagers: high voices, hearts and flowers, just like the girls.

WARNER BROS. present
THE KING OF ROCK 'N' ROLL
ALAN FREED IN
"ROCK, ROCK, ROCK" (U)
FRANKIE LYMON and the TEENAGERS
CHUCK BERRY · LA VERN BAKER
AND A HOST OF ROCK 'N' ROLL FAVOURITES
A DCA RELEASE   A VANGUARD PRODUCTION

girlfriends and fans. We caught up with one of the members. I said I wanted him to hear my group, but he said he was really too busy. When Richard came out, I did the same thing again, and he listened; we sang 'The Plea', a song that I'd written. It was beautiful. Richard was impressed and took my number. He came over to meet my parents who reluctantly agreed to let me sing with him.

He took 'The Plea' and another song of mine, 'He's Gone', and arranged them. Then we went down to George Goldner at 1650 Broadway and stood in his office. We sang 'The Plea'. He just jumped up and said, 'I have contracts for you!' In a month or so we were in the studio.

When 'He's Gone' reached the charts that year and 'Maybe' became a hit the following year, the Chantels looked set for the top:

We were the first girls to be on a national hook-up. There were girl groups on R&B stations, like the Cookies and the Deltairs. These were prototypes of the guys, but they just happened too early. We were the first girl group to record a ballad and get over. I was singing in a key that was considered unrecordable, that people supposedly wouldn't listen to. Everyone else was singing mid-range to low – I came out screechy and high. I remember hearing Carla Thomas singing in my register just after we got started, and I was outraged! People were really catching on to my thing.

Rose and Betty Collins: teen sweethearts of the fifties.

As Arlene points out, the Chantels were not the first black girl group to hit the airwaves. In the early fifties, there had been the rather more adult all-female groups like the Miller Sisters, the Three Tons of Joy and Shirley Gunter and the Queens. In the late fifties, a pair of sisters called the Teen Queens added the now essential element of youth to the image of the female vocal group, although musically their style was not particularly modern, harking back more to old-fashioned jump blues than to teenage rock 'n' roll. Also, amongst the male doo-wop groups that had so influenced the Chantels, there were the girl singers: New York boasted Lilian Leach of the Mellows and Pearl McKinnon of the Kodaks, whilst in Los Angeles there were Trudy Williams of the Six Teens and Rosie Hamlin of the Originals. There were even a few all-girl teen groups amongst the Chantels' contemporaries, like the Cookies, the Deltairs and the Dreamers. Moreover, a month or so before the Chantels' success with 'Maybe', a group called the Bobbettes had hit with a tune called 'Mr Lee'. Yet the Chantels stood out from all these groups as unique, because they had clearly staked out a female zone in the male territory of doo wop, bringing into it the peculiar emotional preoccupations and obsessions of the teenage girl, rather than simply adding a pleasant female variation to the male themes of the music.

However, despite the Chantels' distinctive sound, disappointments were in store after the girls' first hit record. For a start, there was virtually no media coverage:

> There were no PR folks in those days doing stories on a group of black girls from the Bronx. They played the record, and that was the end of it. We did Alan Freed tours. We got involved in the race riots in Boston, about '57. There was a fight, and we had to get out of the theatre. I thought it was fun! We did clubs, but we were really too young, though we managed a few southern spots. During that time, there really were not a lot of places for five little girls to work. The real harsh places our parents would object to.

Apart from a TV appearance on Dick Clark's American Bandstand, which was just starting out at the time as a kind of Ed Sullivan Show for popular music acts, the Chantels had very little publicity. There were only their appearances on the rock 'n' roll tours of the day. Tours like the ones Alan Freed mounted were notorious for the wild antics of their stars, but the Chantels didn't get to join in the fun. On the contrary, life on the road was for them a kind of purdah:

> I was miserable. We had tutors and a chaperone, who happened to be my father. He was really diligent, I can tell you; but the more he cared, the more the resentment built up. There was a distance between me and the other girls because of him. And then, Richie kept us pretty locked up too. We were very well protected. People were instructed not to speak to us. I became very shy.

Life as a singing star was not, after all, that much fun. But there were more serious problems gathering on the horizon:

> We weren't getting our money. We were supposed to get royalties. We didn't get anything that was satisfactory. Our lawyers are still working on that! We got our cars and tuition paid for. We all lived at home, of course, so it didn't hit us as hard as it would if we were twenty-one or so and independent, but even so ... You're talking about adults doing these things to children. We were five little girls and they were rippin' us off. That's exploitation. I could be really bitter. I've had my moments.

Small record companies at the time had a very casual attitude towards their artists, to say the least, both in terms of paying them properly and in respect of building an artist's career over the long term rather than releasing one-off singles only – what would now be called 'career development':

> There was never a true accounting for the sales of records. 'Maybe' became popular because Dick Clark got involved, so it went national.

The business was young, we were young. While we were working, a couple of other acts came through like the Isley Brothers, the Miracles. It was Little Anthony and the Imperials that finally made the company dump us.

But couldn't the girls' parents have done something about the way they were being treated? Arlene:

Our parents didn't want to say or do anything that hampered our success. They were proud of us, they wanted us to be happy. They were too nice ... and nice means foolish. My mother was most concerned about what was going on, and we did have meetings with an attorney. But you know, black families in those days usually only dealt with a lawyer in times of death – we weren't noted for divorce in our community. And this lawyer presented the business as something no upstanding individual would want to participate in. But my position was clear. I wanted to sing. Period. The others hummed and hawed. Finally, they decided they didn't want to sing any more.

In 1959, after the release of the Chantels' next two singles, 'Every Night' and 'I Love You So', which both charted, Arlene left the group. Another member, Lois Harris, also left, to pursue a career in nursing. The other Chantels, Sonia Goring, Rene Minus and Jackie Landry, finally did decide to continue singing, so their manager Richard Barrett simply substituted lead singer Annette Smith from another of his girl groups, the Veneers, for Arlene. The Chantels went on making records, without much success until 1961 when 'Look In My Eyes' and 'Well I Told You' both reached the pop charts. Arlene herself embarked on a solo career at Big Top records, where she soon encountered a very young producer named Phil Spector:

When I met him, he was wonderful. I thought he was so cute. We'd sit together at the piano and giggle and laugh. We wrote a song together called 'Pretty Face' which was kind of a compliment to me. Usually when I rehearsed with people I was scared. But he was really open and friendly. I guess he changed; he hit on his style later and he fought to protect that. I was too young and too silly to realize I had to fight too.

Unfortunately, Arlene's career did not take off at Big Top. She puts it down to the wrong kind of production. Although she admired Spector, she felt swamped by his arrangements:

Phil had so many instruments. I've never seen so many at one date! We had no place to sit! We had kettle drums, a viola section – it was fabulous. But all I need is a piano and a bass. It could have been that simple.

I recorded 'He Knows I Love Him Too Much' with Spector. It sounds

The Bobbettes created their hero 'Mr Lee' in 1957, only to bump him off later with a subsequent single, 'I Shot Mr Lee'.

very much like other singers of the day, Tony Orlando stuff. It was 1961, by that time everyone was using big string sections. I ended up sounding just like everybody else.

Arlene was herself a highly trained musician; she had proved her skills as a writer, vocal arranger and a singer on her earlier discs. Yet ultimately, the studio system of the period ensured that her talents were overlooked; in a pattern that was to become familiar amongst girl groups, she became merely a voice, an instrument added to the producer's battery of sounds. It wasn't Spector's fault that Arlene's talent was being wasted; evidently, he did his best to get a hit for Arlene and she enjoyed working with him. But it seems that neither she nor he realized the importance of her own contribution to her early success. In those days it was apparently unthinkable to let a young black girl anywhere near the producer's side of the desk, and that for Arlene meant no real opportunity for her to build on the unique, popular sound that she and her friends had developed from the beginning in the school yard:

> In reality what was popular was the uniqueness of the Chantels' individual style – not churchy, not gospel, but Gregorian chant. It's easy to say it's 'church' because it's black. We should have been classified as pop. If they had gone with what we gave them, we would have been a fabulous group . . .

Today, Arlene Smith teaches in elementary school in the Bronx. She still sings and is about to launch herself once again on a solo career. After our interview, I went to see her perform at Sweetwaters, a Manhattan club; she was taking part in a benefit there for Mother Hill's home in Harlem for the children of drug addicts. She is at present highly involved in her work within the city's black community, both as a teacher and a singer; she speaks with a confidence that comes from knowing her own worth as an artist; and she is calmly philosophical about her past as a teen star. But there is a quiet anger in her final comments on the Chantels' career:

> I don't think the females had an exclusive on this exploitation business. If you're talking ethnically, the blacks got ripped. Everybody was getting it. Most of the fellers sold their songs for flat fees. We at least got credits for our songs – but when you go to get your royalties, it doesn't count.
>
> Today's youngsters are in a better position than we were. Now we know it's a money industry. We didn't then. It wasn't such a big deal in those days.
>
> Looking back, the disappointment wasn't that devastating. We just wanted to sing. If you know there's not anybody as good as you are at what you do, and when you sing you prickle all over and knock yourself out, then sure, somebody should hear it ... that was our motivation. It still is today. All they cheated me out of was money.

*   *   *

The Chantels, popular as they were amongst a small, city teen subculture, were light years away from what the majority of Americans in the late fifties would have thought of as 'girl groups'. The well-known girl groups of the day were decidedly white, and they were part of a tradition that went back before the war, which included groups like the Boswell Sisters and the Andrews Sisters. At their best, these groups had come up with light-hearted songs of social satire and snappy little novelty tunes, many of which were culled from black R&B, delivered in a neat, crisp vocal harmony style derived from the black 'barbershop' quartets who had been popular with white audiences in the 1940s. However, the genre could also give rise to songs of unbelievable idiocy, sung with a wooden, almost military precision that made them even more unbearable. By the late 1950s, groups like the Chordettes, the McGuire Sisters, The Fontane Sisters, the Lennon Sisters, the Shepherd Sisters and the DeMarco Sisters were at the height of their popularity; yet after 1956, when Elvis broke through the mire of mediocrity in the pop world and unleashed rock 'n' roll on an unsuspecting public, it became clear that their days were numbered. At a time when the Chantels were the precursors of a host of rising girl-group stars, the Chordettes and groups like them were about to become, together with a host of crooners and novelty song starlets, the dinosaurs of the pop world.

The ability of the white girl groups to sustain their position well after

The Shepherd Sisters, who continued to sport their bouffant wigs and dresses well into the sixties, after their first hit 'Alone' in 1957.

rock 'n' roll had hit the headlines was largely a result of the workings of the television system of the day. By the late fifties, television had become part of most Americans' everyday life; as a TV yearbook of the period put it:

> The biggest story of the 1957 TV season is the television industry itself. In a little over ten years it has grown from the faltering experiments of a handful of performers and technicians (remember the 'Please Stand By' signs, the 'snow' and the ten-inch screen?) into a multi-million-dollar business. Colour has become a reality – albeit an expensive one – and big-name stars walk into your living room at the twist of a dial.

Yet in its short history, the role of television as arbiter of public taste had changed dramatically. The early days of television had reflected the variety of families living in America's cities, but by the middle of the decade, this eclecticism had been replaced by a standardized version of the typical American home. Early sitcoms had often been based around stories of immigrant and ethnic urban families: The Goldbergs, Amos and Andy, Life with Luigi and Life of Riley, for instance. Yet, once the big American corporations began to advertise their products on TV, and also to foot the bill for many of the shows, the public began to be presented with a single, highly idealized image of American life. Tremendous efforts were made to persuade consumers that any normal American could, indeed should, live like the white, suburban families pictured in sitcoms such as Father Knows Best. In the process, the notion of variations in the racial and social background of American families was inevitably wiped off the nation's screens.

The new, identikit version of the modern American family unit applied as much to women on the screen as it did to men. Female TV personalities were presented, for the most part, as pretty, stay-at-home housewives who had somehow wandered into their careers by accident. In the TV magazines of the day, they were often pictured with their children and husbands, delivering little homilies to their female readers about how important it was to put family before ambition. Girl-group singing stars like the Lennon Sisters ('four girls whose singing ability captivates audiences on the Lawrence Welk Show', as one TV mag described them) were part of a bevy of female TV personalities, from actresses and singers to glamour girls, whose roles were virtually indistinguishable, since they all tended to make records; on the whole, they all came over as low-rent Hollywood starlets. Only a few women performers, like actress Lucille Ball, managed to transcend the prototype of the all-purpose showbiz female on screen, and emerge as well-loved stars with unique personalities.

The TV music shows were a continuation and extension of what had been going on in the record business and on radio for years. Shows like

Your Hit Parade were very much the vehicle of the professional songwriters of Tin Pan Alley (originally the name given to a particular area in New York centred around the music business), where songs were written, published as sheet music and released as records. The shows tried to ignore the rising tide of rock 'n' roll as far as possible, since the large record companies who backed them as yet had no financial interest in the new music; they were, indeed, doing their best to stave off the moment when they would have to sign rock 'n' roll's uncouth young stars to their labels. Elvis Presley finally appeared on TV, not on a music show, but on Steve Allen's and Ed Sullivan's talk shows as a kind of conversation piece. Despite electrifying the nation with his first TV performances, Elvis was not invited to participate on the more staid music shows until later, when all the fuss had died down; in the meantime, to pacify the public, TV music programmers attempted to replace genuine rock 'n' roll acts with more presentable and respectable substitutes.

With a few notable exceptions, such as Dick Clark's initially local show, Bandstand, there was no rock 'n' roll on TV, at a time when the country would have been riveted by it. This had more than a little to do with the fact that many of the music's artists were black, and at that time, there were virtually no black people to be seen on the screen.

In record companies and radio stations, entrepreneurs and businessmen had in the past been able to get away with presenting black singers as white because nobody actually saw the performers. Very often, black artists were not pictured at all on record sleeves, particularly if they sold to a white market. Moreover, artists were expected to sing in a white style, with a particular kind of diction, so as to fool the listener. Darlene Love, who in the sixties became one of the biggest voices behind teen pop, was singing in recording studios around Los Angeles towards the end of the fifties with her back-up group, the Blossoms, who were renowned for their ability to sing 'white', according to the demands of the time:

> We had a very unique sound. They liked us, because nobody knew whether we were black or white. If they wanted a soulful sound, we'd give them that; or country and western, we could do that, or gospel. We were singing with Jan and Dean, people like that. Pop records.

Television, of course, presented a problem. On TV, it was not possible to use the voice without the face. There was tremendous resistance to showing black performers on screen at all, except in the most fleeting way. Black acts made one-off appearances on white shows, but there were very few regular black performers on television until as late as 1965, when the Blossoms made history by appearing as the house back-up group on the TV pop show, Shindig:

Bandleader Johnny Otis with the Dreamers: these girls formed the nucleus of many West Coast girl groups of the sixties, including the Blossoms, the Girlfriends and Bob B. Soxx and the Blue Jeans.

Mitch Miller had Leslie Uggams on his show. Nat King Cole had his own show, and Diahann Carroll had a show called 'Julia'. When we did the pilot of Shindig, the TV people loved the show, but they did not want the three black girls on it. As far as seeing three black faces every week on a national television show, they just couldn't deal with it; they said the markets wouldn't buy the show, or whatever. But our producer, Jack Good, put his foot down and said, 'I want these girls. If I can't have the Blossoms, I'll take my show somewhere else.' After that, it became the in thing to have three black girls singing vocals, for everybody. They'd used them on records before, but never in public, on personal appearances.

Back then, the civil rights movement was going, you know, and although I don't think it had a whole lot to do with it, the ground was broken. It was just a little easier. Not a whole lot, but just a little. Up to that time, black people didn't even do commercials. There used to be a running joke, 'Don't black people clean their teeth? Don't they use soap?'

Against this background of racism in television, which proved to be just as insidious in the new industry as in the older radio and record businesses, the white TV singing stars of the fifties, many of whom patterned themselves on the radio stars of the decade before, were given a virtual monopoly of the media.

One of the most popular white girl groups of the day were the Chordettes, who had a run of hits between 1954 and 1961, beginning with 'Mr Sandman':

Mr Sandman, bring me a dream
give him a pair of eyes with a come-hither gleam
give him a lonely heart like Pagliacci
and lots of wavy hair like Liberace

This cheerful, up-tempo ballad stayed in the chart compiled by the music industry's trade paper, *Billboard*, for seven weeks, and the Chordettes followed up their success over the next few years with a number of hits like 'The Wedding', 'Eddie My Love' and 'Born to Be With You'. The group's outstanding feature was their vocal harmony style; they sang with an unusual degree of professionalism and accuracy which singled them out from others, and which gave their songs a limpid, sweet quality that was sometimes very pleasant to listen to. However, they too often combined this with the air of forced gaiety and funloving wholesomeness that female singers of the period seemed to feel it was de rigueur to adopt, so that today many of their records sound embarrassingly, not to say irritatingly, hearty and enthusiastic.

The Chordettes were from Sheboygan, Wisconsin, a place synonymous with nowheresville as far as most US citizens were concerned. Their publicist, one Dave Sprankel Jnr, wrote this glowing description of the group's rise to fame:

> In 1949 from one of those pine-scrubbed homes lining the neat streets of Sheboygan, came the dulcet, maple-syrup sound of a barbershop quartet that was to put this sleepy burg on the showbiz map in big, bold letters: THE CHORDETTES. Not a bunch of whiskered males whispering 'Sweet Adeline' and the fogey-old days of the turn of the century. No siree! This quartet consisted of four vivacious and curvaceous lasses who put out the most modern harmonies of this atomic age, lacing their music with loveliness.

The Chordettes were picked up by Arthur Godfrey's talent show on national networked radio, and became radio stars before they hit the nation's television screens. On the national radio stations as well as later on TV, they were always favoured over the black groups; and their often rather feeble cover versions of songs by black artists sold in their thousands while the originals, in many cases, remained unknown. This was common enough in the fifties, when pop was all about getting acceptable white faces to cover – and in the process, sanitize – black songs. Pat Boone had done it with Fats Domino's 'Ain't that a Shame', Bill Haley with Joe Turner's 'Shake, Rattle and Roll', and Gail Storm with Smiley Lewis's 'I Hear You Knocking', to name but a few.

In the same way, another girl group, the McGuire Sisters, made a career out of a cover version. A 1957 magazine gave this plug for the McGuires:

> The McGuire sisters were talking about ambitions. Phyllis, the one in the middle, was the spokesman. 'We want to remain inseparable and have a hit record.' Her sisters, Christine and Dorothy, nodded agreement.

This conversation took place two years ago when the girls were just making their mark in show business with Godfrey. It proves to have been prophetic. The girls have had not just one hit record but many, with their waxing of 'Sincerely' topping the million mark. Besides making records, they've been breaking them in nightclubs all over the country. They have discovered that working in a nightclub is very different from preparing just one song for TV. They've had to learn how to dance, walk – even smile. Most important, they're still inseparable.

The article neglected to mention that 'Sincerely' was first sung by a black vocal group, the Moonglows, and had been a smash on the streets of New York well before the McGuires or the rest of the public had heard of it.

The Chordettes, however, had the edge on their rivals like the McGuire Sisters. They, more than most of the mainstream girl groups of the time, attempted to adapt to the new rock 'n' roll teen culture that was threatening their species with extinction. They soon saw a niche for themselves amongst the preppy white teen combos who were beginning, by the end of the fifties, to become popular on college campuses. In 1959, they covered 'Charlie Brown', Leiber and Stoller's classic teen-whine anthem with the plaintive refrain 'Why is everybody always picking on me?', a favourite with the college teen set. Their version of 'Lollipop' the year before, a song that mainly consisted of the words, 'Lollipop, Lollipop, oh lolly lolly lolly lollipop' was a poppy little record which almost ranks with the teen girl group singles of the sixties. Yet, finally, there was rather too large a gap between their early image as bright young singing housewives and their new role as cute, naive high-school girls for them to be entirely credible.

A track that the Chordettes recorded in 1956 called 'A Girl's Work is Never Done' pointed up this problem. It was sung, with great gusto and jollity, to the strains of a honking sax à la 'Yakety Yak' by Leiber and Stoller:

wash up the windows and the blinds
oh heck, the rain, a waste of time
And now the kids are home from school
They're tracking dirt from room to room ...

and now my father's home from work
with fifteen hundred dirty shirts
you think he'd help me clean the house
he says he's tired and knocked out

Never done! Never done! A girl's work is never done

The lyrics of the song blurred the matter of whether the girl singing was a big sister in the household or a young wife. Evidently, the Chordettes were somehow trying to appeal both to adult women and to their daughters.

In a sense, this was not such a hopeless undertaking at a time when the teenage girl had not yet really emerged in popular culture as having a separate identity from her mother. Most obviously, teenage girls tended to dress like older women, particularly for evening wear. Nearly all the singing stars of the day, from the Chantels to the Chordettes, wore strapless evening gowns for their public appearances and publicity shots. The formality of their dress often made the younger artists, used to dressing for high school or college by day, look awkward and ill at ease.

The rather ambiguous styles of dress for teenage girls in the fifties, which seemed to dodge between childish innocence and adult sophistication, reflected the fact that, during the fifties, more than before the war, girls were being subjected to intense pressure to grow up quickly. In a sense there were no real teenage years for girls, only a sudden leap from being children to having children, from leaving home to making a home. For a variety of reasons – not the least of which was that the boom in consumer goods required an army of housewives to tend its labour-saving gadgets and maintain a steady increase in standards of cleanliness around the home (even to the extent of washing windows and blinds between rain showers, as the Chordettes assumed the good housewife did!) – there was an over-whelming emphasis in the media on marriage and the family. It became a matter of pride for girls of all classes to marry young. The teenage housewife was, after all, becoming a reality. No wonder the Chordettes were a little hazy about exactly who the heroine in their song was: daughter or wife.

Even so, the image peddled by groups like the Chordettes and the McGuires was by this time a bit too corny, a bit too 'tupperware' for the average hip young girl, who was beginning to come under influences other than those her parents had planned for her. No one summed up the female teenager's new preoccupations better than Chuck Berry when he wrote 'Sweet Little Sixteen'; on the surface of it, the teenage heroine of the song longed to be grown-up, what with the tight dresses, lipstick and high-heeled shoes she wore outside class. But it was beginning to become clear that 'grown-up' did not mean to her quite what her mother had had in mind. By the end of the decade, the teenage girl was no longer simply chasing autographs, but beginning to carve out her own persona in rock 'n' roll, transforming all the conventional ideas of love, romance and marriage that she had been given into visions of a steamy teenage paradise throbbing with emotion and sexual desire, fantasies which had very little to do with the notions of adult responsibility, motherhood and domesticity that her elders had vainly hoped to instil in her during her early years.

*   *   *

Until the national TV and radio networks and the big record companies in the US slowly began to realize that massive profits were to be made out of rock 'n' roll, the nation's teenagers had to look to sources of entertainment outside the mainstream. There were rock 'n' roll tours, like Alan Freed's 'moondog parties' which attracted such enormous crowds of teenagers, both black and white, that in many cities they were banned. There were also many local black radio stations dotted all over America, in particular clustered around New York, Los Angeles, Chicago, Detroit and Cleveland. In New York alone, stations like WINS, WLIB, WNJ and WWRL were flooding the airways with rock 'n' roll, which meant anything from the black vocal harmony groups to the southern rock sounds of Elvis. These, too, began to attract alarming numbers of white teenage listeners.

Obscure local radio stations, like the ones who played the Chantels' first records, gave affluent suburban teenagers access to an arcane culture of street life in the big cities which had nothing to do with the world of the white picket fence that they were familiar with. A mass of young white high-school and college kids, mostly boys, became obsessed with the strange music they could find on the radio dial; and each kid tuning in believed himself to be uniquely initiated into the mysteries of an esoteric subculture all his own. Philip Groia, a New York teenager at the time, describes the shock of finding he was not alone in his tastes, in his book *They All Stood On the Corner*:

> While privately digging the Moonglows, sports shirts with the collars worn up over black turtle necks, 1955 Olds 88s and pegged pants, my sissy classmates, as I believed in my adolescent certainty, were into white button-down shirts, the Franco–Prussian war, perpendicular lines in geometry and pluperfect tenses. But then, the meeting of minds occurred! One afternoon when our French teacher asked us to reply in French to the question 'What is your favorite song?', Franco–Prussian Steve answered 'Earth Angel' and button-down Barry offered 'Shtiggy Boom'. Wow! These guys with the big vocabularies who read the *New York Times* and got 99 on algebra tests had listened to Freed and Smalls too!

The next shock came when Groia, having gone to one of Alan Freed's shows, then tracked down DJ Tommy Smalls's show at the Brooklyn Paramount:

> When we walked into that huge auditorium, the contrast was astounding. The predominantly black audience, much older than Freed's adolescent following, barely half-filled the theatre. In retrospect this was the first evidence for me that this music belonged to the black people of the great

cities of America: a music that expressed frustration, happiness, sadness and just plain good talk about girlfriends and getting high.

At this stage, rock 'n' roll was still a very male preserve. But a mass of teenage girls were about to make the same discoveries about music and life as Groia and his pals, and moreover to participate in rock 'n' roll themselves: through one of the most popular shows in American TV history, Dick Clark's American Bandstand.

The first national broadcast of American Bandstand was on an August afternoon in 1957. The show had actually been running since 1952, however, and had started life as a tacky afternoon fill-in on Philadelphia's local WFIL TV, with host Bob Horn presenting film clips of performers like Patti Page and Bing Crosby. When Horn left the station in disgrace after various drink and sex scandals, a smart young radio DJ called Dick Clark took over. Many years later, in an interview in *Rolling Stone* magazine, he described how the show had begun:

The studio was at 46th and Market Street, it was out of the way. The only people in the area were the girls who went to West Catholic High School. So the only people that came by that first Monday or Tuesday were little girls in their Catholic school uniform who sat in the studio bored to tears. And the music came up and they said, 'Can we dance?' So the two girls would dance together. A bright-eyed cameraman said, 'That's interesting' and punched it up. Couple of people called in and said, 'That's fun, let's watch the kids dance while the films or the records play.' By the end of the week, the response was overwhelming. And then they remembered that in the movies, people never really sang, they did a lip synchronization. So they brought artists in and they would mime their records. And the format never changed in twenty years.

When Dick Clark joined Bandstand, he immediately began to book the rock 'n' roll acts that hit town, like Fats Domino and Jerry Lee Lewis. This was the real thing, and the teenagers loved it. Not only were the acts a main attraction, but so too was the studio audience; the set was overrun with teenage girls, dancing with boys, shrieking with excitement and generally looking as though they were having the time of their lives. The audience was also mixed race, which was unusual, especially after Alan Freed's TV show in New York had been taken off the air when black teen star Frankie Lymon was spotted on it dancing with a white girl.

Very soon the Bandstand 'regulars' in the audience, particularly the girls, were becoming stars in their own right. Their hairstyles, their dance partners, their clothes and of course, their dance routines, all had Philadelphia's teenagers glued to the screen. In Detroit, Santa Barbara and

Baltimore Bandstand imitators sprang up. By the time the show went national, becoming American Bandstand, the 'regulars' were getting more fan mail than the acts, at the rate of 15,000 letters a week. There was a special Bandstand committee, and a magazine, *16*, where the girls wrote their own columns and were pictured wearing fluffy jumpers and slacks, sitting on the living-room floor with their scrapbooks.

The overriding feature of the Bandstand girls was that they were all Italian Americans from Philadelphia's large immigrant community. As such, they seemed to exist in a world somewhere between the white suburbs and the black urban ghettos. For the teenagers watching the show, they seemed to represent a channel of communication between the performers and the viewers, black or white, promising an easy passage between the two worlds for future generations. There were the 'girl-next-door' types like Arlene de Pietro and Barbara Levick and the glamorous bleached blondes like Justine Carrelli, Pat Molittieri and Frani Giordano. Pictures of them filled the pages of *16*, along with teen starlets like Nancy Sinatra and Shelley Fabares, Sandra Dee and Connie Stevens. Annette Funicello, who had made her name as a child star in Walt Disney's *Mousketeers* and who went on to make endless forgettable teen records and films, was the most important of all the Italian girls, except for Connie Francis, the 'big sister' who presided over everyone, constantly dishing out advice in the agony columns of *16* between hit records.

Not only did the Bandstand regulars style themselves as stars, but they confidently aired their opinions on everything from Problem Hair to the question of whether Elvis Should Marry. Bandstand's host of pretty-boy Italian teen idols, who usually seemed to function for the girls in the studio as decorative sex objects, were also subjected in the pages of *16* to in-depth psychological investigation by the magazine's young columnists: 'Is Paul Anka Afraid of Love?' demanded the girls; 'In Defence of Bobby Rydell' they defiantly cried; while poor Fabian, the Nick Kamen of his day, begged them all to leave him alone – 'Let Me Be Myself', he pleaded.

The pin-up boys of Bandstand, like Frankie Avalon, Paul Anka, Fabian and Bobby Rydell, to name but a few, were more important than the girls as performers. Only Annette proved as big a star as the boy teen idols. But the ethos of American Bandstand, which gave its teenage audience, especially the girls, as high a profile as its acts, had by the early sixties helped to provide the nation with a specifically feminine idea of the teenager, and one which was fairly close to reality. The Bandstand girl, ordinary yet fascinating, with her sprayed hair and her dance routines, had proved herself to be at the heart of rock 'n' roll. It was only a matter of time before she and her girlfriends took the stage.

*　　*　　*

In 1960, the Shirelles appeared on American Bandstand. Four young girls from Passaic, New Jersey, they performed a song written by group member Shirley Owens and producer Luther Dixon. 'Tonight's the Night' was a wonderfully atmospheric story of romantic anticipation, backed with a mass of plush swirling string arrangements. In the song, a young girl wonders what's going to happen on her first date; she knows that she's going to have some kind of sexual encounter, but it's not the boy's advances that worry her; the strength of her own feelings is what makes her apprehensive: 'Well, I don't know, I don't know, I might love you so . . .' She fears that, 'I may want you so much, that all my dreams might fall apart'; if she does get carried away, what will become of her ambitions, her hopes for the future? Finally, she decides, 'Let's take a chance, it's gonna be a great romance.' Despite the song's youthful teen appeal, this was as frank a discussion of the pros and cons of sex as any on disc, and indeed was seen as fairly risqué at the time.

What made the Shirelles unique was that they were spelling out, in an uncompromising way, the dilemma of a young woman contemplating her first romantic attachment. Far from being coy, the song was quite straight-forward. But if for the Shirelles, sex didn't mean the saccharine and soft-focus romance of the Chordettes' white pop, neither was it the raunchy bump-and-grind of black R&B. Like the Chantels, the Shirelles were something new; they were romantic, but they were honest. Doris Coley, who took the lead on the song, was the unmistakable, plaintive voice of innocence and inexperience, all the more intense and passionate for that.

'Tonight's the Night' reached the top forty late in 1960; but it was the Shirelles' next hit record that really set off the girl-group explosion. If 'Tonight's the Night' had had its heroine anxiously wondering whether to succumb to her lover's charms, 'Will You Love Me Tomorrow?' represented the next episode in her affair. This time she was asking, not 'Should I?' but 'What Now?':

Tonight with words unspoken
you tell me I'm the only one
But will my heart be broken
when the night meets the morning sun?

Here again were the dilemmas of sex and love, of anxiety and elation, of rationality and passion so familiar to all girls growing up, and yet usually so carefully glossed over in pop. Shirley Owens, who took the lead this time and was to remain the Shirelles' usual lead vocalist, sang with a directness that could not fail to engage teenage girls everywhere; yet the song also voiced the hopes and fears of the boys. Pete Waterman, now a producer of the eighties' girl group Bananarama, remembers what the record meant to him back in 1960:

> I was just coming up to puberty. I wanted a girlfriend, but I didn't know how. I was naturally shy, I couldn't find words to chat up a girl. But that record sent shivers down my spine; 'Will You Love Me Tomorrow?' said everything I ever wanted to say.

If the girls, once in their lover's arms, wondered whether they'd done the right thing, so did the boys; but for them, the question meant something different: would the girl still love him once his sexual inexperience had been revealed?

The Shirelles were go-betweens, emissaries between the sexes, summoning up their emotional courage on behalf of teenage boys and girls too shy and inarticulate to speak directly to each other. They were the first group to clearly fulfil this role, and they were dearly loved for doing so. The Shirelles spoke for as well as to their audiences in a way that Waterman still sees as essential in pop music:

> Every song should tell a story; it should say things that boys and girls can't say to each other. It's about teenagers giving each other messages. After years of being in clubs and watching what happens, I've realized that when you make a record, it's got to give out a message, something that a girl can sing to a boy she fancies standing at the bar, while she's out there with her mates dancing round her handbag.

'Will You Love Me Tomorrow?' was the first record to lock into this basic function of pop, which is to provide girls with a way of approaching, admiring and commenting on boys in a socially accepted fashion. As the Shirelles asked in a later song, 'What Does A Girl Do?':

> *When a boy meets a girl that he wants to get to know*
> *He just walks right up to her introduces himself and tells her so*
> *But what does a girl do when she meets a boy*
> *who makes her feel the same way too?*
> *Tell me, what does a girl do?*

In a sense, the girl groups of the sixties yielded the answer to that question: put on a record.

② then he kissed me

WELL HE WALKED UP TO ME AND HE ASKED ME IF I WANTED TO DANCE...

WHEN HE DANCED HE HELD ME *TIGHT!*

AND THEN HE *KISSED* ME ...

By the end of 1960, Shirley Owens, Doris Coley, Beverly Lee and Micki Harris were topping the US pop chart with 'Will You Love Me Tomorrow?'. Here was an extraordinary development; four young black girls had over-ridden all the obstacles of money, influence and power that the music industry and the media had erected against them and forced their way into the big time through sheer talent and the popularity of their sound. The Shirelles were the first girl group ever to have a number one hit; and the song remained in the chart so long that an earlier track of theirs, 'Dedicated To the One I Love', which had previously been ignored nationally, jumped back in. From then on, the Shirelles could do no wrong: 'Mama Said', 'Baby, It's You', 'Soldier Boy', 'Everybody Loves A Lover' and 'Foolish Little Girl' – the hits just kept coming.

The Shirelles soon became established as the newest sensation in pop. They were fêted by DJs like the eccentric Murray the K; they toured constantly, and met with immense success on the live circuit. Suddenly, every producer and writer in the business was looking for a girl group to hang a hit on. But it wasn't so easy to find another Shirelles; for all their apparent simplicity, they had a unique quality and, unlike many of the girl groups that followed in their wake, they were able to sustain a respect within the industry and an affection amongst the public that remains to this day.

The Shirelles had started out as the Poquellos, a high-school vocal group in Passaic, New Jersey. One of the original members of the Shirelles, Beverly Lee, who today calls herself 'the only one who never left', takes up the story:

We first performed as a group in 1958, at a school show. We sang several songs, like 'Little Darling', and then we did a song that we had all written

The first jewels in Phil Spector's crown: Pat Wright, La La Brooks, Dee Dee Kennibrew and Barbara Alston of the Crystals.

called 'I Met Him On A Sunday'. It was done a cappella, in the style of the day. We were teenagers, so we liked groups such as the Chantels, the Flamingoes and Little Anthony. We used to listen to a radio station called WWRL, which now does gospel, but then it was R&B. Our favourite DJ was Tommy Smalls, known as Doctor Jive. I used to send in dedications because I loved hearing our names on the radio. The other thing that made an impression on me was that I had been to the Apollo in New York with my mother and aunt to see Shep and the Limelights. I never thought I'd be up there too one day!

Well, anyway, the kids loved the song and a classmate of ours, Mary Jane Greenberg, approached us saying her mother had a record label and would like to meet us. We weren't interested; I was a pom-pom girl, I was just living for the matches when I could throw my pom-poms in the air, and that's all I cared about. So we didn't pay her no mind. She kept pestering us until finally we went to meet her mother, Florence.

Florence offered us a contract and, as we were minors, our parents got their lawyers to deal with it. Of course, those lawyers knew nothing about showbusiness. The label, which was then called Tiara, released our first record, 'I Met Him On A Sunday', while we were still at school. It did quite well, because Tiara leased it out to Decca who gave it a big distribution. Then we went out on tour, doing what was called the chitlin' circuit: the Uptown in Philly, the Regal in Chicago, the Royal in Baltimore, the Brooklyn Fox and Paramount, and of course the Apollo. I came from a very strict black Baptist family, and my parents were concerned about these young kids going off on tour ... but they didn't have to worry. I was a good daughter.

The Shirelles' parents insisted on their having chaperones when they were out on the road. On their first tour, these turned out to be those legendary sirens of R&B, Etta James and Ruth Brown, hardly the staid matrons their parents had perhaps imagined. But, says Beverly,

They taught us a lot, broke us in. When we got on to the bus, we were all dressed up in high heels and crinoline skirts. Can you imagine seven hours in a bus in a crinoline skirt? I was seventeen; I thought we looked so grown-up and sophisticated. They were so nice to us, though; they just told us, you can't travel like this. You've got to wear jeans, be comfortable, otherwise you'll get tired. They were great friends and great ladies.

Meanwhile, the girls' recording career was picking up. 'I Met Him On A Sunday' (the tale of a budding romance which begins and ends, in typical teenage style, within a week) had given the girls their initial success, reaching forty-nine on the national charts, but the singles that followed had flopped.

Then Florence Greenberg brought in Luther Dixon as the Shirelles' producer. Dixon had written hits for Perry Como and Pat Boone, and was also known for his song, 'Sixteen Candles', a smash for the Crests in 1958. When Dixon brought the Shirelles a song called 'Will You Love Me Tomorrow' from Aldon music publishers by a couple of young Jewish songwriters, Carole King and Gerry Goffin, the girls were less than thrilled, complaining that it was 'too white'. However, they finally agreed to record it; and when it hit number one, their earlier reservations were, of course, quickly forgotten.

Dixon went on to provide the Shirelles with even more white pop-flavoured material. In 1962, 'Soldier Boy', written by Dixon and Greenberg, became the Shirelles' second number-one hit. It was a sentimental little tribute to the boys in uniform overseas which entirely lacked the charm of 'Will You Love Me Tomorrow?', but the public accepted it, and it proved to be a moneyspinner – which, as was by now beginning to be clear, was fast becoming the teen industry's overriding concern.

Luther Dixon's total artistic control over the Shirelles' output had by now, despite the girls' complaints, brought them tremendous success. It was he, and not they, as Beverly Lee points out, who chose all their material. The group had attracted the cream of the industry's songwriters: besides Goffin and King, there were Bacharach and David, who gave them such classics as 'Baby, It's You'. Bacharach and David were beginning to be recognized as the most accomplished songwriters of their day, craftsmen who could give pop tunes all the subtlety, charm, drama and complexity of a classical concerto; their songs inevitably moved towards a more adult orientation in their work with Dionne Warwick – who had herself started out with the Shirelles as an occasional substitute for whichever member couldn't make a date – but they also, as much as Goffin and King, captured the youthful, innocent quality of the new girl-group sound in their early hits for the Shirelles.

Doubtless, Dixon had a unique talent for choosing the right material for the Shirelles; moreover, claims Beverly, 'He was the only one who could really produce us.' The problem was that the group was now entirely dependent on him. When Dixon suddenly decided to leave Greenberg's label, now called Scepter, the Shirelles were left high and dry. They had one more hit after his departure, 'Foolish Little Girl', and after that their records for the most part deteriorated, as Scepter pursued a cheapskate production policy for them and its other commercial teen groups. The Shirelles began to issue a series of badly made, soundalike records; meanwhile, Florence Greenberg was busy with her more successful act, Dionne Warwick.

The final shock for the Shirelles in their sudden descent from the heights

The Shirelles: voices of a tongue-tied generation.

of chart popularity was to find out that, as the most popular girl group in the US, with worldwide hits to their name, they had made virtually no money. As Alan Betrock points out in his *Girl Groups: The Story of a Sound*, the pathbreaking book in this area, Florence Greenberg had kept the girls' earnings 'in trust' for them until they reached twenty-one; when they did so, they found that the money had been spent; costs such as touring, publicity and recording were cited. The Shirelles also found that they were legally obliged to remain with the label.

Accounts differ as to what happened after that. Beverly Lee, who is still on good terms with Greenberg, refuses to discuss the issue at all. What is certain is that there were major disagreements between the group and the label, and within the group itself. As a result, there are today at least three separate groups, each with one original member, calling themselves the Shirelles. Ironically, Beverly Lee and Florence Greenberg spend much of their time these days trying to stem the tide of all the other completely bogus Shirelles (those without a single original member) who, encouraged by the original group's many incarnations, continue, like ersatz Coasters and Drifters, to proliferate on the 'oldies but goodies' revival circuit.

Beverly still works the revival circuit with her Shirelles, as does Shirley Owens, who previously worked as Shirley and the Shirelles and is now known as Shirley Reeves. There is little contact these days between them or any of the other original members of the group. 'We celebrated our thirtieth anniversary last week,' remarked Beverly when I spoke to her. 'Did you get together with the other Shirelles?' I asked. 'No,' she replied rather wistfully.

As our interview draws to a close, Beverly mentions that she is on the Board of Directors of the Foundation for the Love of Rock 'n' Roll, whose members include Frankie Avalon and Bo Diddley, and whose aim is to 'try to raise funds for facilities for performers, so that they can retire with dignity'. I make one last attempt to draw her out on the related subject of why the Shirelles are not fabulously rich today: 'I'm grateful for what we had,' she says resolutely. 'Some groups didn't even get anything. It's been a fascinating experience and I thank God for it.'

In many ways, the Shirelles had more going for them than many of the girl groups that succeeded them. They had a distinctive lead singer in Shirley Owens, who managed the feat of being constantly on the verge of singing flat and still sounding wonderful; they also had songwriting talents which, in another era, might have been allowed to develop. Their material did not date as quickly as did some of the campy teen-rave records that followed, and after their heyday, they were able to keep up with the times and revert to their soulful origins with Motown-styled stompers like 'Last-Minute Miracle', released in 1967. However, in their quest for contemporaneity after the early sixties, they did suffer the occasional lapse of judgement such as the appalling 'One of the Flower People', a song recorded at the height of psychedelia, which went, 'He's a most unusual guy, he wears plaid shirts, and polka-dot ties' . . . Well, everybody makes mistakes.

Yet even on their tackiest songs, the Shirelles' sterling vocal qualities of natural elegance and honest emotion somehow shone through. In a few short years, they had created an inimitable sound, at once innocent and knowing, serious and flip, that seemed to capture perfectly the moment of a girl's life between childhood and adulthood. It was a sound that made them the blueprint for all the girl groups that followed.

*   *   *

The Shirelles, as the first popular rock 'n' roll girl group, were largely responsible for introducing what we think of as 'pop' music to a wide public. In the fifties, there had been two very separate strands of popular music: on the one hand, rock 'n' roll, and on the other, the showbiz songs written by the professional songwriters of Tin Pan Alley. The mostly Jewish songwriters of Tin Pan Alley traditionally looked to Italian Americans, with their suitably romantic good looks and operatic vocal style, as performers of their songs. The imitation-Elvis, teen-boy pop idols of the late fifties and early sixties were essentially a continuation of this tradition. At the same time, however, the music industry was changing. The songwriters of Tin Pan Alley were no longer all middle-aged men churning out novelty songs; a new breed of young men and women songwriters was coming up who looked to black artists to perform their songs. Pete Waterman explains:

> What happened in the early sixties is that white guys, people like Barry Mann, and white girls like Carole King met, for the first time, black artists. So you had black artists singing doo wop, but you had white songwriters writing white melodies. Suddenly, there was an inter-pollination of black voices with white melodies; and most of the writers at that time were of Jewish descent, so of course you got very different chordal structures. There were these amazing black girls singing Jewish melodies that didn't quite work out; here was a new form of music. Because of the white element, girls like Carole King, arrangers put strings on the records which doo-wop bands could never have afforded. You had major companies like Liberty and Roulette making records with full orchestras! They would pay the money, and they were white; the only black thing about the records was the artists and the management. Suddenly you had this dichotomy of cultures; and it worked, it worked perfectly.

These cultures were being forged together not just by a happy blending

Ellie Greenwich, the great
romantic: pensive between
puffs.

of musical styles, however; the essential element that bound the black artists
and the white songwriters and producers together was that they were young.
They were, however directly or indirectly, part of a teen culture built on
the legacy of fifties' rock 'n' roll whose tendencies towards 'aural mis-
cegenation' – as Gerry Hirshey calls it in her book *Nowhere to Run* – had
so disturbed the establishment both morally and, in the music business,
financially. In a sense, the girl groups who were used to effect the mass
crossover of black music into white pop in the early sixties represented Tin
Pan Alley's attempt to co-opt and control rock 'n' roll; but because the
songwriters and producers involved were so young and so much part of
rock 'n' roll themselves, their very attempt to sweeten up and sanitize the
black sound to appeal to a teenage public brought with it something
genuine: a new, female-centred pop sensibility that was wonderfully fresh.

Carole King entered the music business in New York as a teenage
songwriter at a time when the industry had recognized the huge profits to
be made out of selling pop records to teenagers. She was hired by a music
publisher, Don Kirshner, one of the first to gear his whole output towards

the teenage market. Aldon, as his company was called, was part of the Brill Building on Broadway, where virtually everyone in the music business congregated. There was a frantic atmosphere of wheeling and dealing in the building, almost like that of the stock exchange; songs were written, demos were cut, and tracks were recorded and released, all at a speed which now seems quite incredible; a song could be written in the morning, recorded in the afternoon and released a few days later on one of the many small labels that operated out of the Brill. It was a production line, as Carole King pointed out to writer Paula Taylor in 1976:

> We each had a little cubby hole with just enough room for a piano, a bench, and maybe a chair for the lyricist – if you were lucky. You'd sit there and write, and you could hear someone in the next cubby hole composing some song exactly like yourself.

In the offices of another publisher, Leiber and Stoller, plans were also being made to cash in on the teen boom. Ellie Greenwich was one of the star songwriters the duo hired to give them those teen hits, and she did, coming up with such classics as 'Da Doo Ron Ron', 'Then He Kissed Me', 'Doh Wah Diddy' and 'Chapel of Love'.

Today Ellie lives in a New York apartment not far from Broadway. A big brass musical note adorns her front door, and the theme is continued throughout the apartment, even to treble and bass clefs on the wallpaper in the bathroom and piano-key motifs on the toilet seat. Still working in the music business, and looking a million dollars with a Dusty Springfield hairdo, Ellie beams warmly at me, welcomes me like an old friend and settles back to entertain me with stories of those early days. Chain smoking her way through a heavy cold, which only improves her husky New York tones, she remembers the past with affection:

> I went to Leiber and Stoller's office to wait for my appointment. They thought I was Carole King, so they went, 'Hey, Carole, come on in.' I told them who I was and started playing away, a nervous wreck. They offered me a job writing, $75 a week. I said, no, $100, and they agreed. Wow! I thought. A hundred bucks a week! I'm flying here. And I have my own cubby hole where I can write my stuff to my heart's content, and who knows who I might meet . . .
>
> There were many small labels in the Brill Building that offered you the opportunity to just run up there and say, 'Hey, listen to this song.' There was a spontaneity there, the doors were easy to walk through. If you played a song and they liked it, they'd say, 'Let's think. Do we know anyone who can do this? Do you?' So then you could go out and look for an artist, and a record label would give you a shot to produce a single.

If it did well, great, you started getting a name for yourself. If it didn't, so what, no big deal. Not any more. Now it's album, album ... nobody would hire you just like that.

It was a happy time. Monetarily stupid, maybe, but on a creative level you just weren't bothered with any problems. All you did was come in and hone in on your craft. We were very grateful to be signed to a music publisher and get our weekly little paycheck. We always got our royalties. But we never knew to ask about retaining songs. So I didn't finally make $200,000. I got $25,000. Fine. Who knew those songs would live on?

By 1962, when Ellie joined Leiber and Stoller, Carole King was already making a name for herself as a songwriter after her success with 'Will You Love Me Tomorrow?'. In partnership with lyricist Gerry Goffin, an ex-chemistry student she married at the age of eighteen, Carole was now writing for white teen idols like Bobby Vee. A whole industry was by this time building up around TV shows like American Bandstand, which not only introduced a never-ending stream of wooden boy idols to the nation's teenagers but also created hundreds of dance crazes. When the Goffins came up with 'The Locomotion', a new dance tune, they asked their babysitter – who had inspired the song by her style of dancing – to cut the demo for them. Kirschner liked the demo so much that he released it as it was on his new Dimension label, and in no time, 'The Locomotion' had reached the number-one spot. Little Eva, as she was now called, became an overnight sensation; such a huge success by an unknown artist on a new label was extraordinary. Yet her subsequent records, like 'Let's Turkey Trot' did not match 'The Locomotion'. Her sister Idalia was pulled in to make a record, a track called 'Hula Hoppin'; but by now the label was flogging a dead horse. Having been fêted in Europe and America, in less than two years, Eva's career was over.

The tale of Little Eva showed the industry both at its best and at its worst. In the Brill Building, individuals, often working freelance, could set up a series of loose relationships: songwriters could sell their songs to different publishers or record labels, producers could look for songs amongst the many publishers, and so on. Often, a single individual would perform some or all of these functions; many songwriters set up their own labels, produced and even sang on the records. The speed at which all this happened meant that a trend could be quickly spotted and exploited. The sheer volume of records that such a system produced made it likely that a certain percentage at least would chart.

The advantages of the system were that it allowed for an extraordinary degree of creative flexibility and a fast response to an ever-changing market, so that the small labels could make it. Monolithic recording corporations

Little Eva, the girl who quit babysitting to do the locomotion, but her fame was outlived by her song.

like RCA Victor, although they had all the financial muscle, simply could not keep up with what was going on. But there were clear disadvantages for the artists, as the Shirelles had already seen. Singers were at the very bottom of the hierarchy. Producers could take their pick from the many talented young black singers who were desperate to succeed and sold their skills cheap. For these singers, the world of entertainment was the only way out from a life of poverty, unemployment or hard labour; they would characteristically record songs for nothing, or for a flat fee, in order to get their start.

Also, because the functions of singing and songwriting were completely split at the time, so that singers seldom wrote or recorded their own songs, their voices came to be regarded virtually as sounds only, for the producer to use as he wished. Thus for any singer who wanted to build a career in the music industry, the situation was a disaster.

Little Eva at least had her moment of fame. The other girls that King and Goffin were writing for did not fare so well. The Cookies were a trio who provided backing vocals for many of the releases on Aldon's label, and who also recorded songs written for them by Goffin and King. Some of these did well at the time: 'Chains' and 'Don't Say Nothin' Bad About My Baby' were hits for the Cookies, while Earl-Jean, their lead singer, charted with 'I'm Into Something Good'. The follow-up to 'Don't Say Nothin' Bad', 'Will Power', didn't do so well, but it is interesting as an example of the kind of powerful, contained sexuality that the supposedly over-naive, romantic girl groups actually presented their teenage listeners with:

Dorothy Jones, Earl-Jean McCrae and Margaret Ross: unsung heroines of the sixties, the Cookies were the voices behind many of Goffin and King's greatest tunes.

It's been an hour since we reached my door
I really ought to say goodnight
It's been an hour since you said
won't you give me five minutes more
don't you see that I hardly even know you yet
I should be playing hard to get
oh baby what you do
to my will power

The doo-wah, doo-wah choruses and the young, sweet voices of the Cookies disguised the fact that what was being described here were not the joys of coy femininity but its awful restrictions.

As with Little Eva, Aldon was keener to make the most of the Cookies while the going was good than to help the group sustain its popularity over the long term. The group never got the attention they deserved, and soon disappeared from view. Their songs are now best remembered for the cover versions they inspired: the Beatles' 'Chains' and Herman's Hermits' 'I'm Into Something Good'. In the space of two years, the sudden rise of black girl singers, whether singly or in groups, and their equally sudden fall from popularity as they released a string of soundalike records after their initial hit, was fast becoming a time-honoured tradition of Teen Pan Alley.

*   *   *

Over at Leiber and Stoller's, Ellie Greenwich was beginning to rival Carole King as the songwriting queen of teen pop. She had arrived in the business in 1962, later than Carole King, and began by teaming up with several different writers until she settled into a partnership with Jeff Barry. In the early days, she remembers:

Most of the women in the industry were background singers or lyricists. There were very few women that played piano, wrote songs and could produce a session, go into a studio and work those controls.

The studio would be booked from two to five and those singers would go in there and read off the songs; maybe they'd do seventeen songs in three hours. I couldn't do that. I'd write a song and go in and put the background parts on myself; I learnt about overdubbing and laying down tracks, so a different sound started coming out.

Ellie had not set out to be a producer, but she soon found herself becoming one:

Myself and Carole King ... we came into an industry strictly as song-writers. We also sang. So we'd go in and make demos on our songs and they sometimes sounded great. The publishers would take the demo off to a record label who would say, 'OK, let's put this out.' And then they'd ask, 'Who produced this?' Well, Carole King, or Jeff and I ... we didn't think about being producers; it sort of happened to us, we came in through the back door.

Not only was Ellie the songwriter finding herself in the position of producer, she was also effectively becoming an artist too. Since record companies were beginning to release the demos they got from publishers as records, Ellie soon became the voice behind a host of fictitious teen groups:

A case like that was the Raindrops, which was just myself and Jeff doing all the voices. We did this demo for a group called the Sensations; it was a song called 'What A Guy', which we thought would be great for them. We made the demo, and the publishers said, 'This could be a record.' I said, 'What do you mean? There is no group.' But there had to be a group. So we released it as a record by 'The Raindrops'. Back then, a lot of labels put out 'dummy groups'. We'd throw a few people together and have them go out and lip synch the record. There really wasn't a Raindrops.

Naturally Ellie's success as a singer, albeit only in the studio, made her consider the possibility of becoming a performer. Carole King had had a brief recording career as a solo artist on one of Don Kirschner's labels; in 1962 her single, 'It Might As Well Rain Until September' had charted, doing particularly well in Britain, but no more hits followed; clearly, Carole was more valuable to Aldon as a songwriter than as an artist. Ellie Green-wich, for her part, had recorded solo under various pseudonyms, as Ellie Gaye, Ellie Gee, and Kellie Douglas. Her work on the Raindrops' recordings and a later single, 'You Don't Know', were further proof of her vocal talent.

However, by now she was married to her songwriting partner Jeff Barry, and she opted to stay behind the scenes:

> I did want to perform in the sixties but Jeff didn't feel I should; we were very busy writing for all the groups, and producing. I didn't mind saying no, but it always sat there, the thought, 'Gee, what if I had.' And then, as time went on, I got scared …

On a personal level, being married to her work partner was beginning to have its drawbacks:

> When things were working, what could be better? Here's the person you're in love with and you're being creative together, it's the highest high imaginable. However, when there were disagreements it was very hard to leave it at the office, go home and change hats.
>
> Jeff and I were putting in the same hours at the studio. We'd get home after a long day and he'd be hungry. Now you tell me who's going to cook the meal, it wasn't like I was home all day and could say, 'Here's your little dinner dear.' There were some difficulties, because this was the sixties; back then, the man was the breadwinner, he was the husband, and you cooked his meals.

On a professional level, too, Ellie was not altogether happy:

> The Raindrops' records said 'produced by Ellie and Jeff Barry'. Then Jeff said we should split our names so it's more defined. The next group of records that came out read 'produced by Jeff Barry and Ellie Greenwich'. Then Jeff said – and I understand where he was coming from – at some point, we'd have kids, he'd be the sole breadwinner, I'd be at home. Maybe he should start building his name as the producer. My name would be on somewhere as vocal arranger or whatever. I didn't like the idea, but I thought, he has a point. So the next group of records came out with something like 'coffee gotten by Ellie Greenwich, produced by Jeff Barry'. If you look at that run of records, it ends with just Jeff Barry.

Like Goffin and King, the Greenwich-Barry partnership ended in divorce:

> There's a built-in competitiveness. You wish your partner well, God knows, but if one goes ahead and the other doesn't, there's an envy … and where to place that sometimes, I don't know. The only husband-and-wife team from that time who has maintained their relationship is Barry Mann and Cynthia Weil, and I think that's partly because Cynthia just writes lyrics and Barry does all the production.

After the divorce, Ellie had to adjust to being a woman producer on her own in the industry:

In the days when I went into the studio with Jeff, I had a security blanket, a husband, a male with me. But on my own, if I told one of the guitarists, could you please try this, you could see them thinking, yeuch! I'd say, what's the problem? And they admitted they didn't like taking orders from a woman. They liked me, they cared about me, but after I got divorced, the attitudes were flying.

Finally, Ellie Greenwich did have her solo career, but at a time when, she admits, she was really not up to it. Carole King had managed to navigate her way through the mid sixties and emerge in the seventies as an artist in a completely different vein. When her album *Tapestry* was released, it was clear that Carole had made a natural transition from teen anthems of adolescence to more mature songs of womanhood; even the famous song on the album from her early days, 'Will You Love Me Tomorrow?' had an altogether more contemporary, adult emotional drive than the Shirelles' original. The album was a ten-million seller, and established Carole King as one of the great singer-songwriters of her day. Ellie Greenwich was pushed into trying to accomplish the same feat:

All the record companies were calling me. I had no concept, no idea of myself at that time, nothing to say, but I went ahead and released 'Let It Be Written, Let It Be Sung'. I had to tour to promote it. I was absolutely petrified. I had to lip synch everything, I just couldn't sing live in front of all those people. It was awful.

Ellie, the great romantic, had been completely shattered by her divorce and, unlike Carole, could find nothing to say about it. She simply recorded her old songs, reiterating the by now rather battered optimism of her early days; and, not surprisingly, the album met with little success. Fortunately, however, she did eventually claim a personal triumph as a performer in the eighties, in the revue 'Leader of the Pack' at New York's Bottom Line.

Today, she feels, perhaps as a result of the continued interest in and popularity of her songs, that there is still a place for the naive, romantic optimism of the girl-group era in which she played such an important part:

If you look at my personal life and the way it's gone, and then you look at my songs, you'd say, man this lady was dreaming. No, it didn't exactly happen the way I was writing it. However, the point is, I would have liked it to have gone that way. Most of us get little bits of happiness, but we can't sustain it. I think those songs are about wanting it to last. There's nothing wrong with that. It would be nice if birds sang when you fell in love, it would be nice to have a relationship that was meaningful; however much of a feminist you are, I think it's in all of us to want that. Men too.

We were able to write the kind of music that makes people happy. You didn't sit back and say, 'What are they trying to say? What does that mean?' It was a feeling, a sound, to create a memory: I meet you, I like you, I love you, be my baby, uh oh there's a problem but we'll work it out ... there was always that optimism. That's still important to people.

Girl-group music did not so much contradict the reality of difficult, messy, imperfect relationships between men and women as give a voice to very human, youthful aspirations towards something better.

*   *   *

Ellie Greenwich's first major triumphs in the pop industry were the songs that she and Jeff Barry wrote with Phil Spector for the Crystals. 'Da Doo Ron Ron (When He Walked Me Home)' and 'Then He Kissed Me', both released in 1963, are amongst the most spectacularly successful and durable of all the girl-group recordings of the early sixties. Yet before Spector teamed up with Greenwich and Barry he had already scored major hits with the Crystals, including that milestone of girl pop, 'He's A Rebel'.

In 1960, Spector was fast becoming New York's hottest young producer. He had started out in the music business on the West Coast, and had first made a name for himself in 1958 at the age of seventeen, when his group the Teddy Bears scored a number one hit, 'To Know Him Is To Love Him', a phrase which he had allegedly derived from the inscription on his father's tombstone. When the Teddy Bears failed to receive the money owing to them, he walked out of his record company contract, claiming he was a minor and that the contract was therefore invalid. This was the type of smart move that his own later girl groups, who were mostly very young, seemed rarely to think of pulling on him – whether because of their apparently more naive attitude or, perhaps more likely, because of their much lower expectations of themselves. At any rate, Spector's early experience of losing money on a million-selling record meant that when he came to producing his own teenage girl groups, he knew all the clever dodges in advance: for example, he, like most other producers, made very sure he owned all his groups' names in order to prevent them working without him.

When Spector moved to New York in 1960, initially under the aegis of Leiber and Stoller, he began to gain a reputation as an eccentric. He dressed in romantic ruffled shirts and capes, and wore his hair long, to the great amusement of old hands in the studio. More alarmingly, he crammed the recording booths with musicians and, once at the studio controls, began to break all the accepted rules of sound engineering. He created huge, massed sonic edifices and great orchestral extravaganzas, mixing the tracks down on to mono so that each instrument blurred into another instead of being a separate, identifiable sound. He was able to gain a depth and complexity

To know him was to love him? Phil Spector's first group the Teddy Bears also featured high-school pals Marshall Leib (left) and Annette Kleinbard.

of sound on disc that was quite astounding – and quite unheard of outside the world of classical music – using only three or four tracks where today producers might use more than forty. And that was not all. Before Spector, it was always the group or the artist who had a particular, identifiable sound; after Spector, it was the producer. The artist became a mere part of the overall arrangement of a song, as Arlene Smith had complained. Spector's manic musical vision ensured that now it was a sound, not a singer, that the listener recognized on disc.

In 1961, after a successful period in New York, Spector flew back to Los Angeles to produce his first girl group, a white trio called the Paris Sisters who had been recording since the fifties. The group's first single with Spector did not do much, but their second, 'I Love How You Love Me', written by Barry Mann and Larry Kolber from Aldon, was a smash. The success of 'I Love How You Love Me' gave Spector the credibility he needed; it proved that his techniques, however unorthodox – and expensive   worked. Returning to New York, Spector next began to look for a young black girl group to flesh out his musical fantasies, and he soon found one: the Crystals.

Dee Dee Kennibrew, the only original member of the Crystals who has worked continuously under that name for almost thirty years, today tours on the gruelling 'oldies but goodies' circuit that the Chantels and the Shirelles share. I met her backstage after a show in London, in which she and her co-singers had worked hard all evening to crank up an ageing audience and house band (called, ironically enough, Sex Machine) – and succeeded. She was tired but polite, and as she talked about the Crystals' early days, the others in the dressing room stopped to listen:

Our first manager formed the group. His name was Benny Wells, and he just hand-picked us separately. There were five of us at the time. One of the girls was his niece, Barbara Alston, and she brought two girls that she was going to school with. And then he knew my mother from school, and then she knew La La Brooks from school . . . and that's how the five of us got together.

The next step was to find a recording deal for the girls. This was where Spector came in:

We were rehearsing some original material up at a publishing company one night and Phil Spector overheard us. He came in and asked us to sing the song again, so we did; he asked us if we were interested in recording and were we signed with anyone, and we said yes, we were looking for a deal. Then he asked us if we'd want to work with him. Our manager was very happy at the time, because Phil Spector had just had his success with Gene Pitney's 'Every Breath I Take' and with Ben E.

King's 'Spanish Harlem', but we ... well, we didn't know Phil Spector from a hole in the ground!

When Spector began to work with the Crystals, everything seemed to go smoothly. Their first release in 1961 was 'There's No Other Like My Baby':

> We did the record in three hours, musicians and everybody. He recorded us in May, he released the record about September, and by November I was working. My first rock 'n' roll TV show that I ever saw, I was on it. And that was just the beginning from there.

But then the problems started:

> When 'There's No Other' was a big hit for us, because it went up to number twenty, he began to get more meticulous and draw things out more. He had his own company at that point, Philles, and he called all the shots, so I guess he just took his own leisure. We were never allowed any say in what we did at all. We were very young, of course, but we were teenagers making teenage music, and we would have liked, you know, some input. But no way! There was nothing we could do; Phil Spector was our record company, our producer, our everything; I don't think our manager at that time had the experience to keep up with what was going on.

The Crystals were daily losing more and more control over their lives. But at this stage, it was still the original group members, Dee Dee, La La Brooks, Mary Thomas, Barbara Alston and Pat Wright, who were singing on the Crystals records that Spector put out, and not, as later happened, session singers pulled in for the job. The follow-up to 'There's No Other' was a wonderful song called 'Uptown' which went up to number thirteen on the charts, written by Barry Mann and Cynthia Weil of Aldon music. Where Goffin and King wrote upbeat, innocent, optimistic songs, Mann and Weil added an element of social awareness; the song began:

> *He gets up each morning and he goes downtown*
> *where everyone's his boss and he's lost in an angry land*
> *he's a little man*
> *but then he comes uptown each evening to my tenement*
> *uptown, where folks don't have to pay much rent*
> *and when he's there with me he can see that he's everything*
> *then he's tall, he don't crawl, he's a king*

Despite its idealism, the song mirrored the preoccupations of city life. With the mass exodus of the white middle classes out into the suburbs in the fifties, New York and other cities had been left with a resident ethnic population who lived side by side with swarms of commuters coming in daily to work in the big corporations. The girl's lover in the song is evidently a ghetto man who has somehow climbed up into the white corporate world, and who moves between two starkly contrasting worlds, uptown and downtown. Her role, as it is for the suburban housewife, is to give him back the self-respect that he has lost during the day. Thus, although the main romantic theme in 'Uptown' is the classic one of female support for the male, the more forceful message is one of upward mobility for the black and ethnic population living in the city. The other strand in the song is the Latin baion rhythm and Spanish guitar; as in 'Spanish Harlem', Spector fused the black vocal tradition with Spanish instrumental and percussion arrangements, thus creating – like Leiber and Stoller before him – a genuine popular music which reflected the melting-pot of musical culture in the city.

By now, the Crystals were unwittingly becoming involved in Spector's complicated plans to gain the upper hand at Philles. As Alan Betrock recounts, Spector suddenly took a job with the large company Liberty, apparently to scare his partners at Philles, Lester Sill and Harry Finfer, into accepting his sole authority. Whilst at Liberty, he produced a Crystals record for Philles which some felt he knew would be a dud. It was called 'He Hit Me (And It Felt Like A Kiss)':

He hit me and it felt like a kiss
he hit me, but it didn't hurt me
he couldn't stand to hear me say
that I'd been with someone new
And when I told him I had been untrue
He hit me and it felt like a kiss
He hit me and I knew he loved me
If he didn't care for me, I could never have made him mad
But he hit me, and I was glad

This ode to teenage sado-masochism, coupled with a stark, plodding beat which was minimalist to say the least, not surprisingly met with general dismay. The Crystals too thought the record was terrible. Dee Dee:

We hated it! We couldn't understand why Phil wanted us to record it. It just went thump, thump, thump ... and then there were the words! Of course, all the stations and the parents disapproved of it, and it was quickly withdrawn.

The release of 'He Hit Me' may have been part of Spector's master plan to upset his rivals at Philles, by demonstrating that it was his creative talent alone that could make or break the company, but it could equally have been a lapse of taste on his part. Coming from a man who, it was later reported, threatened to put his wife in a glass coffin if she dared leave him, 'He Hit Me' was pretty tame stuff, indeed positively tender and affectionate by comparison. The song had not in fact been written by Spector but by Goffin and King, who were also responsible for such cheerful ditties as 'Please Hurt Me':

If you gotta hurt somebody, please hurt me
and if you gotta break a heart, then
please break mine
I won't cry if you deceive me
I'll take it with a smile
I know someday you will leave me
but at least I'll have you for a while

(Sniff.) Perhaps the truth of the matter was that the writers and producers on the teen scene did not always get the idea of pleasurable, adolescent self-pity quite right. ('Please Hurt Me' was evidently closer to it than 'He Hit Me', with its softer musical arrangement.) The broken-hearted innocent of 'Maybe' had touched a chord with teenagers, and many songs of the early sixties had continued to play on the theme; fortunately, the battered masochist of 'He Hit Me' did not have the same appeal and was rejected – even by the Crystals themselves – as creepy and tasteless.

The next Crystals' record was a landmark. 'He's A Rebel' reached the number-one spot in August 1962 and ushered in a new era of hip sophistication amongst teenage girls. Gone was the innocent sincerity of the Shirelles; in came generational rebellion, eyeliner and going out with the wrong type of guy.

*   *   *

'He's A Rebel', written by Gene Pitney, was simultaneously recorded on Liberty by Vicki Carr (she of the painful sixties' telephone drama 'It Must Be Him') and on Philles by the Crystals, who really brought the song to life. The Crystals' version quickly overtook Vicki's on the charts; here at last was what the girl groups had been waiting for: a pop James Dean.

He's a rebel and he'll never ever be any good
he's a rebel cos he never ever does what he should
And just because he doesn't do what everybody else does
Oh that's no reason why I can't give him all my love
He is always good to me
always treats me tenderly
He's not a rebel, no no no
He's not a rebel no, no, no
to me

This was stirring stuff for 1962. No wonder Florence Greenberg had turned the song down for the Shirelles, for it was clear that, albeit in a rather polite way, 'He's A Rebel' did express a fundamental discontent amongst teenage girls with the future on offer to them: if you fell for the rebel, you were hardly going to end up in a nice house with two nice children, as your parents had planned. For the teenage girl, the rebel hero was undoubtedly a symbol of freedom from the restraints of conventional society, perhaps even from marriage; by identifying herself with him, she was able to proclaim her own rebellious individuality. However, there was an ambiguity in the song; the teenage singer also pointed to the possibility that having her as his girlfriend might be a civilizing influence on our boy hero, causing him not to be a rebel at all, oh no no no. Perhaps, after all, marriage might be on the cards.

The new Mr Right: rebel biker boy with a heart of gold.

The boy on the album sleeve of *He's A Rebel* was pictured astride a motorbike, with leather jacket and shades à la Marlon Brando, but looking a lot less mean than The Wild One himself. Both the picture and the song showed that rock 'n' roll roll was in fact being cleaned up by girl groups like the Crystals. After all, in the fifties it had been pretty wild; there had even been the odd girl out there on a motorbike, as evidenced by Leiber and Stoller's song for the Coasters, 'Ladylike', which told of a tomboy on her 'motorsickle', hanging around the blue light diner 'which ain't no place for a girl or a minor'. Nice girls like the Crystals wouldn't have been seen dead in a place like that. They may have admired the boy biker, but they certainly wouldn't have hopped on a bike themselves, unless in a very daring frame of mind, to ride pillion.

Yet although the Crystals seemed to be trying to tame the rebels of rock 'n' roll – at the same time giving themselves a frisson of excitement by identifying with them – something else was also happening. The rock 'n' roll idol had now become the subject of the girls' songs, rather than the instigator of the music himself. The girls had him swap his guitar for a motorbike, as they took over the centre stage of pop music themselves. They relegated him to the role of the cool guy who does nothing much at all, except remain on show as a status symbol so that his girlfriend can show off to her friends: 'When he holds my hand, I'm so proud.' Now in the pop lyrics, it was the girls who watched the pretty boy walking down the street and nudged each other, instead of the other way round.

'He's A Rebel' was the highest point of the Crystals' career; but it was also one of the lowest. Here, Darlene Love takes up the story. When I visited her, she was living in style at the Royal Shakespeare Company in Stratford on Avon, during the first run of the musical *Carrie*, which later bombed on Broadway. We sat in her dressing room overlooking the river, and she told me:

I first met Phil in Los Angeles through his partner Lester Sill, because I was doing a lot of sessions for Lester singing back-up. I was called in to do 'He's A Rebel'. I went in, he showed me the song, and within three or four days, we had recorded it.

But why did Phil Spector choose Darlene rather than the real Crystals back in New York to do the song?

Something had happened with their friendship at the time. Phil owned the name of the Crystals. During that time, producers owned groups' names so they could record anyone they wanted under any name. Phil gave me my name, in fact; at that time I was called Darlene Wright. He asked me if I liked the name 'Love' – there was a gospel singer called Dorothy Love that he admired – and I said yes . . . so I became Darlene Love.

During the sixties, the scale for 'after' background singers, for three or less, was $22.50 an hour. I told Phil I'd do 'He's A Rebel' for him if he paid me triple scale. So I got about 1,500 dollars.

I was nineteen when I met Phil, and I was a professional singer. That probably gave me the edge on the rest of the girls he was working with, because they were really young, about thirteen up. He always had to pay me because, as professionals, me and the Blossoms went through the union; we always got paid session fees, but not necessarily royalties. The only money I ever made in those days was through sessions.

After 'He's A Rebel', I wanted a contract. I wanted royalties – they were three cents a record in those days, or something ridiculous like that. Well, I never got what I felt was due to me.

Meanwhile, back in New York, the real Crystals were astonished to find themselves with their first number-one hit, a record that they had not even made. There was nothing they could do; indeed, they were helpless without Spector. To this day, Dee Dee Kennibrew of the Crystals, who did finally manage to retrieve the group's name from Spector and work under it, refuses to acknowledge Darlene Love's part in the Crystals' career.

Darlene's story is, however, that Spector, like so many other producers in the business, paid no regard to anyone's names, including her own:

When we went to record with Phil we never knew which record was going to be by who. After 'He's A Rebel', the next thing he wanted was another record for the Crystals. I said, this time you're going to pay me a royalty, not just no $1,500. But I didn't get it. Well, the next record was 'He's Sure the Boy I Love' which was supposed to be my Darlene Love record – I was going to record it under my own name. But no. When I heard it on the radio, they announced that it was by the Crystals.

I asked for a contract again with 'Da Doo Ron Ron'. Phil said OK, but I wasn't convinced and I never gave him a clean finish of the song so he brought La La Brooks in from the Crystals and put her voice on top of what I had already done. We didn't sign contracts in the end until after 'Da Doo Ron Ron'.

Clearly, Spector's by now very powerful role as the Boy Wonder of the pop industry gave him carte blanche to override the inconvenient demands of his young singers. Records were issued by fictitious groups, mere names dreamed up by Spector; polished, experienced session singers like Darlene would be brought in to record, and then they or others who looked the part would pose for publicity shots. To all intents and purposes, groups like the Crystals appeared only to exist now in Spector's imagination as concepts for the next single.

The public did not seem to mind or notice what was going on. The Crystals – whoever they were – scored big hits in 1963 with 'He's Sure the

Preacher's daughter and pop diva, Darlene Love's unmistakable voice graced many a Spector track of the sixties. She recorded under her own name and with her group, the Blossoms, but as a highly professional session singer she also played many other musical parts: as one of Bob B. Soxx's Blue Jeans, for instance. She even, on occasion, stood in as a Crystal.

Boy I Love', 'Da Doo Ron Ron' and 'Then He Kissed Me'. The records were now usually in the confident, romantic boy-meets-girl-they-fall-in-love-and-marry vein that had replaced the plaintive, adolescent uncertainties of the early girl groups, but writers like Barry Mann and Cynthia Weil still held out for a bit of social realism in songs like 'He's Sure the Boy I Love':

> He doesn't hang diamonds round my neck
> all he's got is an unemployment check
> He sure ain't the boy I've been dreaming of, but
> He's sure the boy I love

Besides recording as the Crystals, Darlene also then became – with Bobby Sheen and Fanita James of the Blossoms – Bob B. Soxx and the Blue Jeans:

> Phil had this idea of recording 'Zip-A-Dee-Doo-Dah'. We thought that was the funniest thing we'd ever heard; everybody knew that song, what could he possibly do with it? But it was a huge hit, and we became Bob B. Soxx and the Blue Jeans. After that, I finally recorded as Darlene Love. Nobody knew who I was at all. They were trying to figure out if there was one person doing all the singing on Phil's records. They thought it was Barbara Alston of the Crystals.

Darlene's wonderful voice put her solo recordings, like 'Today I Met the Boy I'm Gonna Marry' and 'Christmas (Baby Please Come Home)', in a class of their own amongst Spector's by now unbelievably successful teen pop discs. Yet she still did not emerge as a solo artist in her own right:

> I didn't really push my career as Darlene Love. I was a very successful back-up singer, and that was important, because I had something to fall back on; it was a job, like being a secretary. I didn't just depend on Phil, I had my own career. Also, I had children and I didn't want to tour. I've had a very full career; in the sixties, I sang with all kinds of people, including Elvis on his comeback special in 1968. From 1972 to 1981 I sang back-up for Dionne Warwick. In the eighties, my career has really taken off; I got a part in 'Lethal Weapon', then there was *Carrie*, and my new album is coming out too.
>
> You know, I started off in 1959, and in 1981 I started a solo career! That's kind of unusual. It helps that no one has ever really seen me. I'm a fresh idea.

Darlene's career has had its ups and downs, like most singers, but on the face of it, trading in the opportunity of touring as a solo artist for a successful and lucrative career as a session singer has had its advantages over the years. Today, Darlene is in a different league from those on the revivals circuit like Dee Dee Kennibrew of the Crystals, who says:

> I started when I was very young; this is the only job I've ever done. What else can I do? I've been out here for years. There were only three years when I didn't work as a Crystal, that was when I was married. But apart from that, I've been working constantly. The other girls left the group because of children, marriage, things that women usually leave the work-force for; husbands that say 'no way'. Because if you have a husband, how are you gonna tour and be away so much? You just can't be away months on end. It doesn't make for a good family life.

So how had Dee Dee managed it? 'Well . . . because I didn't keep a husband very long!'

The Crystals may have been singing about meeting Mr Right (in 'Da Doo Ron Ron'), being there when he came home from a hard day's work (in 'Uptown') and always staying right by his side (in 'Then He Kissed Me'), but the reality was that they themselves were out on tour, singing songs of eternal love and happiness while their marriages broke up. Even if they shared in the idealistic beliefs and sentiments of the songs, which it seems that most of them did, the fact was that they could not live them. And, increasingly, neither could the generation of young women listening to those songs.

*   *   *

Before long, Spector began to tire of his faceless teen acts and started to concentrate all his efforts on a girl group that promised to supply what, up to now, the others had lacked: image. He found his dream girls with the Ronettes. The Ronettes were bad girls, gum-chewing, streetwise teenagers who at night turned into sexbombs with tight skirts and hair piled high. Sisters Veronica and Estelle Bennett hung out with their cousin Nedra Talley in New York's famed Peppermint Lounge, where Tom Wolfe and the wealthy glitterati mixed with ordinary teenage riff-raff in the hopes that some of that adolescent street style would rub off on them. The Ronettes were part of a female underground that still exists today: teenage girl clones who turn up to clubs in groups to devote their whole evening to serious dancing, who know that when all kitted out in exactly the same gear – however seductive or outrageous – they are totally unapproachable.

According to rock 'n' roll legend, the threesome turned up to the Peppermint, all wearing the same outfits and looking a million dollars; they were apparently mistaken for the band, hired, and became the Ronettes from that day. It seems likely, however, that their rise was in fact somewhat less meteoric.

As youngsters, the girls' grandmother had sent them to singing school;

they became known first as the Dolly Sisters, then as Ronnie and the Relatives, and finally as the Ronettes. The Ronettes then began to move in the satellite circles of the New York pop scene. At the Peppermint Lounge, some of the girls who came to the club as clients were employed as regular dancers on stage to go on between the acts. The Ronettes were amongst them. The Ronettes danced to the music of Joey Dee's house band, and also worked with the famous Murray the K, the DJ who had championed the Shirelles; they were also dancers on a touring show, Clay Cole's Twist-A-Rama. Apart from dancing, they did back-up vocals for teen recording stars like Del Shannon and Bobby Rydell and recorded as the Ronettes

The Ronettes: bad girls with beehives.

for the record company Colpix. They seemed likely to continue in this mode, as popular but unremarkable young starlets, until they met Phil Spector.

The story goes that Estelle dialled a wrong number, got Spector on the end of the line, and wound up talking him into meeting the Ronettes. When Spector saw the girls, and heard Ronnie sing, he immediately signed them up. He was particularly struck with Veronica Bennett: she had a unique voice, hard-edged but sweet, not technically anything special but perfect for pop: individual and unmistakable. Ronnie was also spectacularly beautiful, with enough street cool and style to blow any audience away. Spector now got his big chance to play Pygmalion: Ronnie was his creation, and he would make sure that, on disc, everyone fell head over heels in love with her just as he had.

If the Shirelles and the Crystals were all about teenage identification with the newly-felt emotions of young love, proffering the image of a sweet, understanding girl next door, the Ronettes were a much more dangerous proposition: they were about seduction, pure and simple. The Shirelles had in a sense been pop stars, but their role as go-betweens, matchmakers almost, sending messages of love and desire between the sexes had made them almost too friendly and approachable to be regarded as true idols. The Crystals in their turn were such a nebulous concept as a group that they could hardly have been called idols either. Moreover, before the Ronettes came along, black girl groups like the Shirelles and the Crystals had received very little publicity as groups. Their records were popular, but aside from their performances on tour and very occasional TV appearances, nobody really had much idea of what they looked like or who they were. Often, they would not be pictured at all on their record sleeves. As far as the music industry was concerned, white record buyers were simply not interested in a bunch of black girl singers.

The Ronettes proved the industry wrong. They were the first true girl pop stars to induce hysteria on a par with Elvis. In the early days of the so-called British Invasion, when British beat groups like the Beatles and the Stones hit America and threatened to destroy the established US pop business ('Noose on neck, bye bye' is how Ellie Greenwich described the feelings of American pop songwriters at the time), the Ronettes, far from being knocked out of the running by the boy groups, were a perfect female parallel to them. On their first British tour in 1964 with the Rolling Stones, they drew a fantastic response: 'Girls Scream At Stones: Boys At Ronettes!' ran the headlines. Who could blame the boys, what with the reports that the group sounded great, danced wildly, and looked incredible, performing 'contortions in diamanté-encrusted pale orange sheath dresses' as one newspaper report put it. *Pop Weekly*, the sober British magazine for the schoolboy muso, wrote in 1964:

> Watching them on TV is exciting but nothing like as exciting as seeing them on a one-nighter. Then, with their tight slit skirts and their swaying figures literally making the audience sway they leap into their fantastic songs ranging from their latest 'Baby I Love You' and 'Be My Baby' to the sensational R&B number which I heard them sing but couldn't get the title because of the amount of screaming and clapping from the audience, who were obviously enjoying themselves in a way that they wouldn't normally have done on most package shows ... the girls are an absolute knock-out – and have proved that their sound off-disc can be just as good!!!

On tour with the Rolling Stones in the UK, the Ronettes stole the show.

The Ronettes' first hit, 'Be My Baby', which took the charts by storm in October 1963 was a huge, symphonic rhapsody of love. This time, Spector had surpassed himself; Brian Wilson of the Beach Boys called 'Be My Baby' 'the most perfect pop record of all time'. Next was 'Baby I Love You' in early 1964 which did not chart so high, but was still a big hit. 'The Best Part of Breakin' Up' and 'Do I Love You' followed; then there was 'Walking in the Rain', which probably crams more cloudbursts, thunderclaps and torrential downpours on to the grooves than any other single in the vastly popular rain-and-romance pop tradition.

The records were marvels of teenage passion, but except for 'Be My Baby', they did not reach the top ten, remaining in the twenties and thirties. Evidently, the Ronettes' singles were not selling as they should have done. There seem to have been many reasons, but certainly, the fact that Spector's empire was beginning to crumble had something to do with it. By now, he had made many enemies in the music business, often those jealous of his earlier success. His behaviour as well as his records were often bizarre, and he refused to make friends in the right places. His acts like the Crystals and Darlene Love were leaving him; and he was becoming more and more possessive about Ronnie; finally, he married her in 1966.

After that, the Ronettes' career came to an abrupt end. Spector did not want his wife to appear on stage; he kept her away from the public eye, refusing to do more than issue the odd single for her. He tried hard to smooth her rough edges, locking her in his mansion away from her friends and from the sociable night life she knew and loved, calling her 'Veronica' and playing her nothing but classical music. However, eventually, she managed to launch herself on a solo career. In 1970 she cajoled Spector into producing a single for her, 'Try Some, Buy Some', which was released on the Beatles' Apple label; but it did not chart. Ronnie fared no better after the break-up of her relationship with Spector, whom she accused of trying to sabotage her career. Neither her 1977 single, 'Say Goodbye to

Hollywood', written by Billy Joel, or her 1979 LP, *Siren*, brought her success. With *Siren*, Ronnie tried to revamp her image updating it to a punk, Blondie-meets-heavy-metal, sex bomb mode – which was somewhat ironic given that Debbie Harry had styled herself so much on the look and sound of the early sixties' groups. The attempt at a comeback failed, however; and a further LP on CBS in 1988 confirmed that by now, Ronnie's career as rock 'n' roll's first female heartthrob was well and truly over.

The Ronettes' songs represented a shift from those that Greenwich and Barry had come up with before, like 'Da Doo Ron Ron' and 'Then He Kissed Me'. Traditionally, the lead singer in the girl group told her friends about her latest boyfriend, in classic teenage girl-talk style; but Ronnie sang directly to the boy himself, and this was what made the Ronettes' male fans flip. Here, for the first time, were unequivocal expressions of adoration addressed by girls to boys; this was seductive, but unnerving stuff. Since when had it been the girl's prerogative to implore 'Be My Baby' to the boy who took her fancy? If the Ronettes were the first female sex goddesses of pop, the models for the industry's favourite way of selling young girls to audiences today – on the basis of their sex appeal alone – they also had a kind of dignity which is now often lacking. Far from merely cooing and simpering in an effort to flatter the male ego, the Ronettes demanded total adoration and submission from the boy of their dreams; in their songs, they asked for nothing short of everlasting love. A passing fling with a no-good runaround, a chance to ride pillion with the boy rebel hero, was simply not enough; now they, the girls, were the stars, and the boys looked on. Suddenly, the rock 'n' roll guitar heroes, the good-looking pin-up boys of pop, the wild motorbike rebels and the boys-next-door were no longer the idols that the girl groups and their fans worshipped in song. The new idols were themselves.

*　　*　　*

Surprisingly enough, the Ronettes' shortlived success was not followed by any other group of teenage girls with that same highly stylized, seductive image, even though there were hundreds of dance-crazed, fashion-obsessed teenage girls like them around who might have taken on the mantle. Perhaps it was because now there were no Phil Spectors to produce the music; or perhaps the idea of overtly sexual female pop idols on a par with the wild men of rock 'n' roll was too much at odds with the fans' expectations and ambitions about women to take hold in their imagination at this time. The narcissism inherent in the world of teen pop had, for girls, to take a different route; and the image of the female pop star came to be modelled after a more traditional female icon: that of the bride.

Shelley Fabares, a teen girl star who had a hit in 1962 with the breathless

'Johnny Angel', summed up the narcissism of the concept when she wrote an article that same year in *16* magazine, entitled 'When I Get Married':

> I used to look at the pictures of brides in the Sunday paper. I'd sigh wistfully over them and wonder if I could ever possibly look like that . . . Sometimes I'd practise my stance in front of the mirror in my room – always carefully closing the door first, because if anyone caught me I'd feel like a real idiot! I'd hold one of the pictures and try to copy the girl – leaning back ever so slightly, head tilted to one side and with just the faintest trace of a smile . . . Rather vaguely, I pictured my groom as a tall dark handsome Prince Charming – the kind who always got the girl in fairy tales. But he wasn't the number one figure in my daydream – I was.

Shelley had taken the female icon of the bride and transformed it into the female equivalent of that male icon, the pop star. All eyes were on her; this was her special moment. If she fantasized about marriage, it was not because she wanted to be a wife and play second fiddle to the male; on the contrary, she wanted to be the centre of attention.

By 1964, the theme of marriage had become absolutely central to girl-group music; songs of suffocating sweetness and cloying schmaltz about The Big Day were everywhere. And the couple on top of the wedding cake in the pop music industry were, besides Phil and Ronnie, songwriters Ellie Greenwich and Jeff Barry.

The success of the new girl groups had prompted songwriters Leiber and Stoller and entrepreneur George Goldner to set up their own label, Red Bird, for the teen market, using the talents of the Greenwich-Barry team. Leiber and Stoller themselves professed to loathe teen pop, but they could see how lucrative it was. Jerry Leiber in a *Melody Maker* interview recounted how the new label found one of its biggest hit records:

> Goldner was in early next morning, his eyeballs hanging out of his head, and he was very excited and enthusiastic. He held up this one acetate and said, 'This is it – I'll bet my life on it.' And it was 'Chapel of Love' by the Dixie Cups, a record I really hated with a passion . . . This whole level and category of songs and recording was out of my ken. I didn't dig it. It was the forerunner of bubblegum music – teenage ballads. Jeff and Ellie wrote most of it. They were like super-aces at making this type of material.

It was obvious why Leiber and Stoller heartily disliked this new trend in pop. Their own work, especially with the Coasters, had always concentrated on the seamy side of ghetto life: the prisons, the bars, the hustling, the one-night stands. They did write teen songs, but these were always humorous not romantic, like 'Yakety Yak', 'Poison Ivy' and 'Charlie Brown'. Theirs was a male world, and whether their subject matter was high-school pranks or street life, they wrote with an exuberance, confidence and flamboyance far removed from the world of fragile introspection, innocent optimism and romantic yearnings that the girl-group writers did their best to communicate. Leiber and Stoller's songs were hard-hitting and realist; if they wrote about the middle classes at all, it was with a sense of humour. To them it must have seemed that the new girl-group popsters expressed nothing but twee sentiments and middle-class values.

Yet the clash between the two styles was not so simple. The songs of Leiber and Stoller did show a social awareness, but they also consistently portrayed black people in the most negative light imaginable – at worst, as stupid and ignorant buffoons, at best as crafty, untrustworthy spivs. The new generation of Tin Pan Alley songwriters like Ellie Greenwich did not continue in this pattern; by now, black music had thoroughly crossed over into white pop. In a sense, this new form of black music – pop – absorbed white values, in particular, the emphasis on desexualized romance and marriage; this made the music respectable and acceptable to the white market at a time when many black R&B songs – and even some of the cleaned-up rock 'n' roll versions of them – were still frowned on because of their overt sexual content. But in a different sense, the new young songwriters like Greenwich and her generation, were, in focusing so much on marriage, giving voice to the demands of upward mobility amongst young people, particularly girls. There were, moreover, usually no identifiably black or white people in their songs; the overriding concept was youth.

The emphasis on marriage was especially important to black teenage girls – who after all were making the music and therefore would to some extent be identified with it – because it showed that they were no longer outside the mores of white society. Marriage for them, and for many white working-class girls, represented a step up, a bit of social climbing for those traditionally left on their own to raise their children. Respectability may have been repressive, but it also allowed women to make demands on their men. Also, marrying into a higher class could quite literally be a step into a better, or at least more moneyed world.

Thus, the fantasy of marriage in girl-group music expressed firstly, the teenage girl's ambition to be a star, to be somebody; and secondly, for many, the desire to move up into the middle class instead of remaining at the bottom of the heap.

Perhaps such aims were merely fantasies, but they were powerful ones. The Dixie Cups' ode to the day it would all happen, 'Chapel of Love', proved a winner, as George Goldner had hoped. In May 1964 it reached number one in the US and stayed in the charts for fourteen weeks, selling two million copies. The song was very simple; it began with an a cappella chorus of girls' voices that had all the solemnity and innocence of the Chantels back in the convent school choir, and then swung into an uptempo, happy little melody. Simple words, simple tune, a simple emotion, but finally, 'Chapel of Love' said it all:

Spring is here, the sky is blue
birds all sing as if they knew
today's the day we'll say 'I do'
and we'll never be lonely any more

*   *   *

Throughout 1964, Red Bird continued to have tremendous success with its girl groups. The Dixie Cups, Barbara and Rosa Hawkins and Joan Johnson from New Orleans, introduced an element of naive sincerity into girl-group music that seemed even more youthfully disingenuous than the Shirelles. 'People Say' and 'You Should Have Seen the Way He Looked At Me', both chart hits, were followed up with their classic recording, 'Iko Iko', which reached number twenty. 'Iko Iko' was a New Orleans folk chant which the girls had just happened to start singing during a break in the studio; Greenwich and Barry liked it, recorded it in a matter of minutes with minimal percussion – consisting mostly of banging bottles and sticks on any available surface – and, after a little editing, released the result. With its sing-song tune and simple backing, 'Iko Iko' had the genuine feel of a group of young girls, children almost, playing games in the school yard; and, as in the Jaynettes' 'Sally Go Round the Roses', there were slightly sinister nursery-rhyme images in the lyrics, although this time in the atmospheric setting of the cajun south as the singers' chant picked out the mythical characters of Mardi Gras: 'See that man all dressed in green, he's not a man he's a lovin' machine; see that man all dressed in red, bet you five dollars he'll shoot you dead ...'

Today, it would be hard to imagine how a song recorded in such a spontaneous, casual way could get straight into the US charts; currently, the vast sums of money spent on the publicity machines behind stars mean that there is absolutely no possibility of adopting such an experimental hit-or-miss style of doing things, on the major labels at least. But in the early sixties, small independent labels like Red Bird represented a bigger slice of chart action with the result that, although personal fortunes were made and lost, the fate of huge corporations and millions of dollars did not hang in the balance when records were released; therefore, people could afford to be much less cautious. Even on the big labels like Roulette and Liberty, teen pop records were seen to some extent as a get-rich-quick option; singles were not, as they are today, carefully analysed as to their hit potential months before their release. This situation had its bad side and its good: on the one hand, hundreds of appallingly badly made records were pushed out on to a very volatile market in an effort to make money with the least input possible; on the other, simple, direct and unusual tracks like 'Iko Iko', as well as the more ambitious, adventurous sounds of someone like Phil Spector, could get through, catch on, and make the charts in a matter of weeks after their release. What made the girl-group music of the time so appealing was precisely this quality of natural, throwaway verve and flair, so genuinely close to the style of the ordinary teenage girl. However, the fly-by-night approach of the record companies also had its downside as far as the artists themselves were concerned.

Many of the groups on Red Bird, for instance, just had one hit and were quickly forgotten by their record company. The Jelly Beans were a group of four girls and a guy from New Jersey who hit with 'I Wanna Love Him So Bad' in June 1964. Their follow-up, 'Baby Be Mine', was a gorgeous, breathy song of gentle passion which, however, proved less commercially successful for the company, so the group were quickly dropped. Another Red Bird combo, the Butterflys, had an even more transient career: their first release, 'Goodnight Baby', was a minor success, but their next, 'I Wonder', saw no chart action ... and that was more or less the end of the Butterflys, along with Red Bird's other girl groups like the Bouquets and the Goodees.

Perhaps groups like the Jelly Beans and the Butterflys had a limited teen appeal and could not have lasted long at the best of times, but the fact that record companies of the day issued material by their black artists, particularly their young teen girl groups, in a less than thoughtful manner hardly helped matters. By now, there were scores of girl groups in New York alone and it was difficult for any of them to establish an identity.

Over at Laurie, another independent company, a talented group called the Chiffons struggled to create a recognizable profile for themselves by following up their first smash hit, 'He's So Fine', with others that used the same word in the title: there was Carole King's 'One Fine Day' and then 'A Love So Fine', after which the Chiffons ceased to mine that particular territory. What really characterized the Chiffons, however, was not just the 'fine' motif but the confident, breezy air of their songs, which seemed to typify the attitude of the modern, self-possessed teenage girl at her best. 'He's So Fine' had the heroine coolly sizing up her dreamboat and wondering how best to catch him:

He's so fine
sure wish he were mine

The final hit for the Doo-Lang girls in 1966.

that handsome boy over there
the one with the wavy hair
I don't know how I'm gonna do it
but I'm gonna make him mine
be the envy of all the girls
it's just a matter of time

There was not much doubt in her mind that she would succeed; and loverboy himself didn't have much say in the matter either:

He's a soft-spoken guy
kinda sweet, kinda shy
makes me wonder if I
should even give him a try

So much for simpering, coy young girls suffering the attentions of over-eager young men; as far as the Chiffons were concerned the boot was firmly on the other foot. In 'One Fine Day', our heroine once again was to be found plotting her next conquest:

One fine day
you'll look at me
and you will know our love was
meant to be
one fine day
you're gonna want me for your girl

No question about it; if she wanted him she could get him, if only through pure nerve and conceit, never mind the fact that at present he might not see reason. With Carole King's raucous piano crashing along in the background, the track was bursting with high spirits and it betrayed a determined optimism that was poignant in its total rejection of adult pain and the possibility of future disappointment. Anything and everything was possible . . . one fine day.

The Chiffons, Patricia Bennett, Barbara Lee, Sylvia Peterson and lead singer Judy Craig from the South Bronx, had started their career with 'Tonight's The Night', only to be pipped at the post with the same song by the Shirelles. Then, as with so many girl groups, they had been picked up by an enterprising manager, Ronnie Mack, who worked hard on their behalf to get them a deal. It was Ronnie who wrote the Chiffons' first hit, 'He's So Fine', a song that introduced the irresistibly meaningless chant 'doo-lang, doo-lang, doo-lang' into girl-group vocabulary. 'He's So Fine' burst into the charts in 1963, remaining in the top ten for over two months, and the Chiffons subsequently enjoyed a sizeable run of chart hits, including 'I Have A Boyfriend' in 1964, which proclaimed, in typical Chiffons' style, the simplicity of the love-and-marriage scenario: 'I have a boyfriend, met him a week ago; he's mine for ever, last night he told me so.' It's that easy, folks. The Chiffons also recorded for Laurie under the name of the Four Pennies, producing a minor classic, 'My Block', with Latin arrangements in the style of the Crystals' 'Uptown'. At the same time, they continued to have hits under their own name. In 1965 there was an attempt to cash in on the West Coast psychedelia of the period when the group recorded 'Nobody Knows What's Going On In My Mind But Me', fusing traditional girl talk with the solipsistic, 'man, the colours!' meanderings of the flower people. The Chiffons' psychedelic outing was slightly more credible than the Shirelles' 'One of the Flower People', but it did not quite do the trick; the group's big hit came the following year with the Motown-styled 'Sweet-Talkin' Guy'.

Not a bad run by girl-group standards; but like the Shirelles and the Crystals, it was the Chiffons' distinctive sound and lyric style that pulled them through, in spite of the decidedly low-profile, low-rent image that their record company foisted on them.

Whilst New York epitomized the girl-group sound of the early sixties, there was also a thriving teen pop recording scene in Philadelphia centred

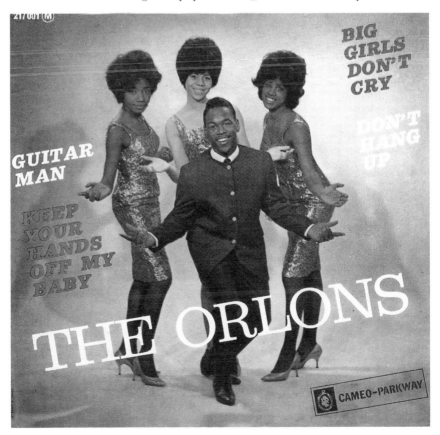

Philadelphia's Orlons, so named after the latest wonder fabric, watusied their way up the charts in 1962.

around, and almost entirely sustained by, the TV show American Bandstand. Pop labels in Philadelphia like Cameo-Parkway and Chancellor issued vast numbers of teen records, especially dance tunes which sold because of the dances viewers saw on the programme : the hully gully, the froog, the pony, the fly, the popeye, the watusi, the Bristol stomp, the South Street, the Madison, the mashed potato and, of course, the twist. Dee Dee Sharp, a young black girl from Philadelphia, had a huge hit in 1962 with 'Mashed Potato Time'; she was immediately and conveniently paired off in the teen magazines with Chubby Checker, America's other black teen star. Unlike Chubby, who had an amazingly long lifespan considering the limitations imposed on him by having to make endless twist records, Dee Dee did not sustain her success. Like Little Eva, she made a few follow-ups to her hit such as 'Gravy (For My Mashed Potato)', and then disappeared from view. Later, however, Dee Dee married producer Kenny Gamble and attempted a solo career as a serious singer; but she was unable to shake off her former image as the Mashed Potato Girl. As author Tony Cummings put it, the mashed potato had stuck.

The best-known girl group to emerge from the Philly teen scene were the Orlons. Time had moved on since the days of the Cadillacs; now it was wonder fabrics, not cars, that inspired the young American. The Orlons were pictured popping up amongst yards of what was presumably orlon; and looking just as cute as the girls amongst the fancy wrapping was the male member of the group, Steve Caldwell. Despite Steve's presence, there was never any doubt that the Orlons were a girl group; the chorus behind the girl lead singer was predominantly female, with Steve's voice adding a bit of spicey bass to the sound. The group's first hit was a dance tune, 'Wah Watusi', followed by 'Don't Hang Up' and 'South Street', after which there were a couple more hits until 1963, when the group left the chart scene.

There were several other girl groups in the early sixties who, like the Orlons, featured male singers. In New York, the Exciters had a big hit in 1962 with 'Tell Him', written by Bert Berns of 'Twist and Shout' fame. Produced by Leiber and Stoller, the Exciters were far more polished and versatile than most of the teen acts of the day, and lead singer Brenda Reid had a powerful voice; however, after 'Tell Him', strong subsequent singles like 'He's Got the Power' were not the resounding success that was expected. Ironically, the Exciters' biggest claim to fame once the British Invasion hit America in 1964 was that one of the new beat groups from England, Manfred Mann, took their unsuccessful 1963 Greenwich-Barry release 'Do Wah Diddy' to number one in the US charts.

The Essex were another group who had a girlie sound, even though the female lead was backed entirely by a male chorus. They had two hit singles in 1963, 'Easier Said Than Done' and 'Walkin' Miracle' . The boys-in-the-chorus tradition of girl groups continued up until 1965 with a group called the Ad Libs (produced, like the Exciters, by Leiber and Stoller) who came up with 'The Boy from New York City', a single with terrific verve. Promotional pictures of the group showed various different line-ups, but the Ad Libs were essentially a female lead, Mary Ann Thomas, with a male back-up. Despite the male voices, the song's gossipy girl-talk lyrics, albeit a little more hardheaded and realistic than most, put it in the girl-group category:

> *Ooh wah, ooh wah, cool cool Kitty*
> *tell us about the boy from New York City*
> *'Well, he's really cute, in his mohair suit*
> *and he keeps his pockets full of spending loot'*

Evidently, the exclusion of male voices was not what defined a girl group; there had only to be a girl lead singer with a story of romance to tell, and a group of mates, perhaps including a boy, to tell it to. The token male of the girl groups was a confidant, part of a closeted female society who shared the lead singer's emotional ups and downs with her, rather than a symbol of love's young dream in his own right; and so in the early days of girl-group music, he did not seem in the least out of place lurking amongst the petticoats of the chorus line.

*   *   *

By the mid sixties, there were countless girl groups fighting for their place in the charts against the onslaught of the British Invasion. Most of them had arisen from the black teen milieu of doo wop. But the groups who really took the genre to the max were the white punkettes of rock 'n' roll: the Angels, Reparata and the Delrons, and the Shangri-las.

❸ I can never go home any more

Jiggs Allbut of the Angels sits in the lobby of the Gramercy Park Hotel in New York with her husband Stan – who, as I later find out, is an Angel himself these days – and their small daughter. Jiggs is a slight, pretty woman in her early forties who is easily recognizable from her early pictures and who talks in a quiet but animated voice about the ups and downs of her career since the sixties. Unlike many of her contemporaries, she seems to have emerged unscathed from those traumas of success and failure and reveals a remarkably balanced outlook as she discusses what has happened to her and the other Angels over the years.

Back in 1963, the Angels were the first white girl group to hit it big with a rock 'n' roll record in the New York girl teen style. The song was called 'My Boyfriend's Back', and it tore up the charts immediately after its release, selling over a million copies. Jiggs describes what had led up to that moment:

> We grew up in a middle-class family in Orange, New Jersey. My sister Barbara played the piano; she taught me some harmony parts and as little kids, we would entertain the family. We liked the Everly Brothers, and since there were two of us, we sang their songs.
>
> We were both born on the same day, two years apart. One birthday, we had gotten some money, so we found a little recording studio in town and went in to record some songs Barbara had written. I don't know what we thought we were going to do with them! But we met a songwriter there who asked us to sing some of his stuff, and from there we just kept meeting people. We started singing at local teenage dances; the music we liked was early rock 'n' roll, basically R&B, but I think somewhere at the back of our minds we had an idea that if we did have a rock 'n' roll hit, it would give us the break to do something serious like the McGuire

The Shangri-las: angels of angst, queens of carnage, myrmidons of melodrama.

Sisters, something that would really show we could sing. Because back then, rock 'n' roll was not totally legitimate.

For the next few years, the girls wavered between rock 'n' roll, which, as teenagers, they loved, and the more old-fashioned sedate ballad style of earlier white girl groups like the Chordettes:

Before we were the Angels we called ourselves the Starlets; there was my sister, myself and two other girls. We did a version of an old song, 'P.S. I Love You', originally by the Hilltoppers I think, and then we found a little record label, Astro records, to release it. It got a little play from a DJ in New York and we became very excited, but then he was thrown off the air and arrested for taking payola, so that ended our first record! But the company who had distributed the record for Astro, Caprice, was still interested in us.

Dire warning: the Angels model 1963's precursor to the puffball skirt.

The group, now called the Angels, put out another old standard as their first release for Caprice. After seven months of hard work on the part of the label's publicity team, the record, a Tony Bennett number called "Till', charted at number fourteen. The Angels' new success gave them a wide choice of material to record, and they picked up a good song for their next release. 'Cry, Baby, Cry' only reached the national top forty, but it was a big hit on the R&B charts. The girls themselves loved the song and performed it with verve; and in no time, they found themselves in the strange situation of playing Harlem's Apollo Theatre:

We were living in New Jersey, so every day we would come in in the morning and meet at the Port Authority and take the subway up to Harlem. The bars were all jumping at nine o'clock in the morning, the music was blasting out of them. It was wonderful, it was really like another world to us. We'd go up to the theatre and do four or five shows a day, and then our manager would pick us up and take us home at night. It was a great experience. We were the only white act on the show. Bobby 'Blue' Bland was headlining, there was Erma Franklin, Aretha's sister, and a group called the Corsairs; then one night Ben E. King came up from the audience and sang. It was fantastic.

After this excitement, however, came a period when the girls once more reverted to old-fashioned ballads. The Angels evidently had mixed feelings about the type of image they wanted to present. Rock 'n' roll was still not respectable; for the most part it was a fly-by-night affair, both in terms of record sales and the way the business was organized. For three white girls, it did not seem to offer the best job prospects, and whilst Jiggs was fairly easygoing and in it for the fun, Barbara was very serious about a long-term career in music. Popular singers still had to look to the world of middle-of-the-road, light entertainment to provide them with any real chance of a proper long-term career; thus for the Angels, as a white group with more than fleeting ambitions, there was a strong pressure to go in the direction of the mainstream. Moreover, for white girls entering the world of rock 'n' roll, there was a certain amount of parental disapproval to contend with:

> My parents didn't try to stop us, I must say, but inwardly I know my mother was cringing. She was not happy about our career at all. Actually, I think she was afraid that we weren't going to do well, and that we'd embarrass ourselves. She didn't like to talk about what we were doing to other people. But my father was proud of us on the sly. If he'd see our record on the jukebox he'd play it and tell all his friends, 'That's my daughters!'

Fortunately, as it turned out, the Angels' attempts at a more upmarket respectability than teen pop could give them failed entirely:

> Our more pop, legitimate type records didn't sell; we were doing plenty of work, though, singing background. That's how we met the guys who did 'My Boyfriend's Back', Richard Gottehrer and Bob Feldman. They came to us and said, 'We have this song', and the minute I heard it, I said, 'Yes, that's the one.' After we recorded it, we would go to our sessions and tell everyone, 'We've done this song, and it's going to be a hit; we're not going to be singing background any more pretty soon . . .' I really felt sure, and everyone else did too.

The record was pure teen coquettishness, a variation on the popular female brush-off theme of 'I've got a big hunk of a boyfriend, so get lost quick or he'll thump you one.' As a statement of feminine independence, this left something to be desired, but there was a camp, tongue-in-cheek humour to the song that appealed to adults and teenagers alike. Or perhaps it was that the adult TV shows like Ed Sullivan's found it easier to stomach these white girls, who almost parodied the capriciousness of the teenage miss, than black singers like the Shirelles or the Crystals. At any rate, with their bouffant hairdos, floral gowns, big smiles and wagging forefingers, the Angels bore a reassuring visual resemblance to the familiar white girl groups of the fifties, even if the music was a bit close to rock 'n' roll for comfort.

As for the Angels themselves, they were in heaven:

> We had a great time, visiting DJs in different cities and doing record hops; in those days, groups always did a lot of record promotion. We were very popular because of the song; it was such a lot of fun to do, and we loved having something fast to sing, something a little less pretty and 'swing and sway' than our usual material.

The success proved shortlived, however:

> It was real difficult to figure out what to put out after that. Our second record was terrible, it was called 'I Adore Him'. I hated it. We left Smash, the company that put out 'My Boyfriend's Back', and got a lot of deals, from RCA, Polydor ... but nothing hit. Then we completely changed our act and stopped doing our hits, because in those days nobody wanted to hear an oldie. For years we worked out on the road as a regular supper-club act like any other. It wasn't until the revival started in about 1972 that we started singing our own songs again.

Today, it is ironically enough Barbara who has left the Angels, disappointed with what had happened to the group. Jiggs continues with Peggy Santiglia and a new member, Stan Sirico, who follows in the great tradition of girl-group boys; he sings harmony with the girls, plays the guitar and looks after the band. Currently, like virtually every girl group I spoke to, the Angels are involved in litigation regarding royalties for their songs. But for Jiggs, life looks good again:

> Sure it's tough. There is always a difference between the way the male and female artists get treated. The men get paid more on bookings, that's a fact. And there's a stigma attached to being an older woman; they always want the token young, single girl singer. But nowadays, we basically do things on our own terms. We've come off the road after years of nearly going crazy – it was down in Puerto Rico that we finally all went to pieces and realized we were cracking up being out there for so long! – and these days, we just do what we want: one-nighters and weekends at big arenas and fairs, not those little clubs that can't pay properly where you have to come on so late. There's a lot of work and it's getting better every year. We've come to see it as a business. It's not all fun and wah hoo, you know.

*   *   *

The Angels were part of a wave of white girl singers who followed the success of the black New York girl groups, and who brought to the music the minxy, spoilt-brat attitudes of the white suburban teenage girl. Many of these singers were actually solo artists whose records sounded like girl-group productions; even in those days of simple studio equipment, it was easy to create the illusion of a whole chorus of singers by double tracking one voice, as Ellie Greenwich had done. Because of the popularity of the girl-group sound, girl solo acts who had started out as the female equivalents of teen boy pin-ups like Frankie Avalon and Bobby Rydell were pushed into the girl-group mould. For most of the solo girls, this was not a good career move; they wanted to be like Connie Francis, who had had a very long stint in the charts, and who appealed as much to the adult market as to teenagers. The girl-group end of teen music was particularly unpromising, basing itself more on a sound than on the appeal of identifiable stars and specializing in one-off hits by transient groups virtually unknown to the public except as names on discs. But there was not much these would-be solo stars could do; record companies more or less forced them into adopting the most saleable style of the moment: teen songs with a girl-group feel.

Amongst the many budding white starlets, there was Linda Scott, who hit the charts with 'I Told Every Little Star' in 1961; 1962 saw Marcie Blane's 'Bobby's Girl' and 'Johnny Angel' by Shelley Fabares; then Peggy March scored with 'I Will Follow Him' in 1963; and Diane Renay had a hit with 'Navy Blue' in 1964. Few of these singers managed to follow up their initial success; and others, like Tracey Dey and Linda Laurie, never had a lot of success in the first place. The white singers got more media attention than the black girl groups received, but they seldom had such big hits, fundamentally because their records weren't as strong; at the same time, they could not rely on the big publicity drives that record companies mounted behind the equally weak songs of their male counterparts, the Paul Ankas and Fabians. There was one singer, however, who managed to overcome these problems with a tremendously successful run of hits: Lesley Gore.

In April 1963, 'It's My Party' blared out over the nation's radio waves. Produced by Quincy Jones (who now produces Michael Jackson's records),

Lesley Gore: proto-feminist Jewish American princess belts out a number in the movie *The Girls on the Beach*.

it reached number one in less than four weeks. Here was another teenage heartbreak story but it introduced a new element into the standard format, that of the teenage temper tantrums. Now, instead of the singer sounding tearful and vulnerable, as was so often the case, she sounded furious. 'Judy's Turn to Cry', Lesley's follow-up disc, continued in this mood, this time turning to the theme of revenge on Judy, the girl who had the nerve to run off with Johnny at our heroine's party. Lesley sounded like a beastly little girl pouting and stamping her foot, but at the same time, she displayed a spirited attitude that was more amusing and appealing than the passive, treacly cooings of a Shelley Fabares or a Linda Scott. Her big hit in 1964, 'You Don't Own Me', again presented this aspect of the teenage girl's personality as independent and wilful rather than sentimental, in what is surely the most direct feminist statement in the whole of girl-group music:

> *You don't own me*
> *I'm not just one of your precious toys*
> *You don't own me*
> *Don't say I can't go with other boys*
> *Don't tell me what to do*
> *Don't tell me what to say*
> *And when I go out with you*
> *Don't look the other way, cos*
> *You don't own me*

Lesley's later hits, written by Jeff Barry and Ellie Greenwich, returned to more familiar territory of female passivity; the bouncy 'Maybe I Know' contains the reflection: 'Maybe I know that he's been cheating, maybe I know that he's been untrue; but what can I do?' Yet the way she sings it, you get the impression that Lesley isn't particularly upset about the situation, and might just as well have said 'so what?', if it had happened to rhyme, instead of 'what can I do?'. The appeal of Lesley Gore's records was that, although Lesley sang of tough emotional situations, she also conveyed a strong-minded, youthfully simplistic attitude in dealing with them. She did not agonize; she just got on with the job, whether it was wreaking revenge on a rival or giving her boyfriend an earful.

Lesley Gore was one of the few teen girl singers to carve out a public persona for herself, although it was one she didn't particularly relish in the long term. Unlike the black girl groups, whose very existence appeared to be an embarrassment to the media, Lesley had a high profile; her tastes and lifestyle as an all-American white teenager, a sixteen-year-old who lived in a nice New Jersey home with her family, were carefully reported. She stayed in school at the height of her success, continuing her education whilst becoming the nation's best known teen pop girl; all this was highly approved of. At the same time, the media's patronizing attitude towards her prevented her from gaining serious recognition as an artist. As far as Lesley was concerned, her music was honest, well-produced and respected by her peers. She felt she had the same kind of genuine rapport with her teenage listeners as did Frank Sinatra and Dean Martin with their adult following, and that her songs were no more 'dumb' than theirs. However, her early success had cast her in the mould of teen trash artist, and she was eventually unable to break through into an adult market as she had hoped. This was not such a big leap as one might think now; in the early sixties, middle-of-the-road singers like Frank Sinatra had become big in the pop charts, along with the girl groups, after the initial big wave of rock 'n' roll had died down.

*   *   *

By 1963, the hard, nasal New Jersey tones of singers like the Angels and Lesley Gore typified the girl-group sound. The style of the white girls, with their self-centred, mock-serious attitude seemed a million miles away from the earnest yearnings and feverish sincerity of early black groups like the Chantels. But in fact, the links between the black and the white singers were in some cases very close, as I found out when I talked to Mary O'Leary from Brooklyn, alias Reparata. Reparata and the Delrons are a white girl group who in the sixties had two major hits: 'Whenever A Teenager Cries' and 'Captain of Your Ship' (the latter charting in the UK only). As we laid into the gin and tonics at eleven a.m. one crisp Manhattan morning, Mary told me her story, one that in some ways surprisingly mirrored the career of Arlene Smith:

The sound of teenage Catholic angst: Reparata (right) and her Delrons, spiritual successors to the Chantels of the fifties.

> I started out in the choir in the Good Shepherd Catholic elementary school. That was my first training. We sang a lot of Gregorian chant, and the different masses. The songs, the harmonies, the Latin ... it was just beautiful. Then I went to St Bernard's high school in Brooklyn and formed the group. We met up with a fellow named Steve Jerome that a friend at school had told us about; he auditioned us and liked what he heard, and we were in the studio a couple of months after that.
>
> We had to find a name for the group, so I chose the name Reparata because the nun who headed up the choir in my elementary school was called Sister Mary Reparata. At confirmation, you take the name of a saint, or some religious event; and I was that fond of this nun that I took her name.
>
> The very first song we recorded was 'Your Big Mistake' by Ernie Maresca on Laurie. We weren't that crazy about it and it didn't do anything, but it was our first record and that was a thrill at seventeen years old.

Next we went to World Artist records, still with Steve Jerome, and released 'Whenever A Teenager Cries'. The company only had two groups, us and Chad and Jeremy, but they had a lot of money to spend on promotion. They took us out for outfits, wigs and the whole bit. Nationally, the record went top twenty and it was an even bigger hit here on the east coast, on local stations like WINS, WABC and WMCA. So we went out on two lengthy Dick Clark tours. They were tough times workwise but there were good memories. We worked with Little Anthony and the Imperials, Herman's Hermits and the Rolling Stones.

My parents were very supportive. I had to take a leave of absence from school to got out on tour, but they didn't balk at all. They thought it was a good life experience, whether it amounted to anything or not. But they insisted I went back to school afterwards, and I'm glad I did; I've been teaching for seventeen years now.

The next song was 'Tommy' which was a mild hit, and that kept us working. And then it all died down. We were doing local clubs, and it wasn't feasible to carry on, let alone make money at. A few years later, though, we had a hit in England, 'Captain of Your Ship', so we went over to do a tour there.

We were greenhorns, I'd say. There was a reception for us, the Beatles were there, and David Niven, and Lulu; then we went off and played just about every city in England. We went over to Germany too. There were interviews and parties and we were travelling constantly. We would get up at seven in the morning and go to bed at three or four in the morning. We were exhausted, mentally and physically; the situation was mindboggling, but you never got a chance to put your foot down and say, 'Hey, wait a minute.' I think we made some big mistakes as a result; we weren't prepared for the tour, we didn't rehearse long enough, we weren't aware of the English audiences. I really wish the English public could see the group as we are now; our audiences come away from our shows now a lot happier than they did in the sixties.

Coming back to the US was a let-down. It was such a strange feeling to come back to New York and be nobodies again. And to make matters worse, we hadn't made any money out of either of our records. World Artist here in the States had conveniently gone bankrupt when it came time to pay royalties. If you canvassed all the groups to see who had been ripped off the most, you're looking at them! My mother is still crying the blues over it.

The problem at the time, though, was that I was so anxious to be part of the business. Even if I had known upfront what the situation was, I would still have gone ahead and done it. And in their hearts, my parents knew that. You felt at the time that if you got too smart, if you got too demanding, they'd find somebody else to do it ... and that usually was the case.

After we came back from England, that was it; nobody wanted to know, so it was back to work and business as usual. It wasn't until the revivals started in the seventies that we could get going again.

Mary goes on to talk about the professionalism of the 1989 version of the group, which she now manages herself. But, I ask her, isn't there something a little incongruous about a forty-year-old Reparata singing songs of teenage romance today?

There is a perfect balance where you can recall those years authentically – we don't goof on any of that material – and retain your dignity as a woman in her forties. Those songs are near and dear to us. They were our teenage years. I will always want to hear them done properly, with love and care, and that's how we do them.

There are a lot of big venues now, more than in the sixties: the Nassau Coliseum, Madison Square Garden, Radio City ... all the places that are selling expensive tickets have to cater to their clientele, and the clientele are people in their thirties and forties who want to hear the music of their youth. It's the same for our fans as it is for us. It's the music we know and love.

Isn't there a big gap, though, between the attitudes of the sixties' teenage girl and those of women today? Hasn't the women's movement made those songs sound ridiculously dated? Mary thinks hard, and then replies with characteristic honesty and intelligence:

The very fact that we're performing says to me that we are feminists. Most of the time, we're the only women on an all-male bill. We share the hardships with the men, the travel, the rotten dressing rooms and no sleep the night before, but we do our job and we hold our own with them. And they don't have the responsibilities at home that we do: a sick child they left behind, or who's going to be at the PTA meeting, or your daughter wants you to be at her concert and you've got your own concert to do. It's difficult juggling two careers – three careers – and doing all three fairly well. So we're feminists. I believe truly in the feminist movement. I think for many years girl groups were seen as empty-headed: look pretty, smile, wear your wig. Now, as in every other area, we are taking control of our business, our material, our producers. And if we knew then what we know now, things would have been a lot different with Reparata and the Delrons.

The Angels and Reparata and the Delrons had their brief moment of fame,

The Shangri-las: purveyors of soap opera on wax to an era's teenagers. A rare shot of all four girls.

The Jaynettes transformed a playground rhyme into a metaphysical experience with 'Sally Go Round the Roses', later a cult hit. Andy Warhol claimed that it was his favourite pop single.

but the white girl group who made the biggest mark in the early years of the decade and who eclipsed all the others were four girls from Queens, the Shangri-las.

The Shangri-las blasted into the US charts in 1964 with a record that squeezed more torrid narrative drama on to a three-minute teen single than had ever been done before. 'Remember (Walking in the Sand)' was idiosyncratic to a point of absurdity, but it also had a strong teenage emotional credibility. The record managed to pack every detail of a particular romantic tragedy into the song, whilst interspersing the story with the heroine's agonized cries of anguish as she recalled it. In 'Remember', the girl receives a letter from her boyfriend telling her it's all over; 'Oh no!' (Crash) she exclaims, 'Oh no! (Crash!) Oh no, no, no no!'; and then, to the accompaniment of hordes of seagulls, she remembers the happy days of her first love. The whole effect was ridiculously overblown, but there was no denying the absolute sincerity of the singers, nor the strange, atmospheric mood created by the crashing drums and seaside sounds.

'Remember' seemed at first to be a one-off, one of those surprisingly emotive records that come out of nowhere, capture a transient mood in pop, and then disappear. A similarly atmospheric track had been recorded by the Jaynettes in 1963, 'Sally Go Round the Roses'; the Jaynettes never again had a hit, but 'Sally Go Round the Roses' remained a classic, with its mysterious, eerie feel. Artie Butler, the arranger on the Jaynettes' hit, was in fact responsible for the arrangements on 'Remember'; but the unique vocal style of the Shangri-las, together with the bizarre material that their producer, George 'Shadow' Morton, wrote for them, made them more than ephemeral. Far from being one-hit wonders, the Shangri-las went on to make a string of the most memorable mini-dramas on disc to come out of the sixties.

The Shangri-las were Betty and Mary Weiss, and twins Marge and Mary Ann Ganser, two sets of sisters from Jackson High School in Queens who, after a short and unsuccessful attempt at recording on a small local label, formed what seemed to be another no-hope alliance with an eccentric aspiring record producer, George Morton. The girls, at that time performing regularly at local dances and record hops, were called in to make a demo for Morton, who had a contact at Red Bird in Ellie Greenwich. In the usual way, 'Remember' was hastily recorded; Morton then went to Red Bird with his demo and, realizing the track's potential – or at least its quirky originality – the company released it. The single promptly tore up the charts, eventually hitting number five. This was a triumph for Morton; he had no experience in the business, was unable even to play an instrument, and (he claims) had written the song in twenty minutes. Amazed at the single's success, Red Bird took some care with the follow-up; Morton was teamed with hitmakers Greenwich and Barry, and together they came up with the Shangri-las' next outing, a teen anthem to out-schlock all others, 'Leader of the Pack', which began with this conversation:

> *'Is she really going out with him?'*
> *'Well there she is, let's ask her.'*
> *'Betty, is that Jimmy's ring you're wearing?'*
> *'Mmm hmmm'*
> *'Gee, it must be great riding with him'*
> *'Is he picking you up after school today?'*
> *'Nnn hmmm'*
> *'By the way, where'd you meet him?'*
> *'I MET HIM AT THE CANDY STORE,*
> *HE TURNED AROUND AND SMILED AT ME,*
> *you get the picture?'*
> *'Yes we see'*
> *'THAT'S WHEN I FELL FOR THE LEADER OF THE PACK'*
> *(Vroooooom, vroom, vroom, vroooooom)*

Even the opening lines of the song were an absolute marvel of ingenuity; the heroine hums smugly to herself while her friends question her and then, finally unable to contain herself, bursts out with the whole story. This was classic radio-drama stuff, all gossipy dialogue, tearful reminiscences and studio sound effects. This time, instead of massed seagulls, there was the roar of the motorcycle; and instead of remorse over a broken romance, the story went one step further and had our hero actually die, crashing his motorbike in a fit of misery after our heroine had told him she didn't want to go out with him any more, forced into doing so by her father . . . Yet this was a pop single, not a radio play. The writers had grafted the concentrated dialogue of the radio drama on to the standard patterns of girl-talk records in pop; the old call-and-response of the lead and the chorus in the black girl groups was now completely transformed through the conventions of different, white media forms.

George Morton was probably no more aware than were pop fans that he was marrying up such odd but familiar cultural strands; as for the Shangri-las, they were steeped in the traditions of black teen pop around them, and were trying their best to emulate the exuberant sincerity of vocal groups they admired, like Little Anthony and the Imperials and the Four Seasons. Morton's weird playlets and the Shangri-las' style of doing them was, however, something completely new; but it did have a link with black teen pop: there was a certain crazy genuineness about the Shangri-las' records that calls to mind the manic emotionalism of fifties' doo wop.

Ellie Greenwich recalls how the team came up with the song:

'Leader of the Pack' was, believe it or not, one hundred per cent serious. There was always that bad guy that every girl wanted to go out with, but no, mum and dad would never allow it. Then there was the motorbike. Back in the sixties, when you started making money, you'd buy a motorcycle. So we figured, ooh, we'll take a trend that's happening, the motorbikes, and we'll make it a boy-girl romance – must have that – and let's give it a little bit of a sick element. Let's have the guy die. So it was a small soap opera we wrote there.

The Shangri-las arrive in Britain for a 1965 promotional tour.

The Morton-Greenwich-Barry team were evidently bang on target with their new formula, for 'Leader of the Pack' hit number one shortly after its release and caused a major stir both in the record industry and outside it. The reasons for the record's popularity were many. First, there were the girls themselves. The Shangri-las exuded an air of tough independence that spoke to a whole new generation of hip, white working-class city girls. By now, they wore street clothes on stage, dressed to kill in shiny boots and tight pants; they chewed gum; they sang love songs to leather-clad layabouts; in short, they were a Bad Example. But it was also clear, to teenagers at least, that the Shangri-las were at heart nice, ordinary girls. Ellie explains:

Girl groups overall had a very sweet image, except maybe for the Ronettes and the Shangri-las. By today's standards they were as innocent as the day is long! But back then, they had a real street toughness ... though with a lot of vulnerability attached. Look at Mary Weiss, who sang lead. Sweet. This long, straight hair, this angelic little face. Then that nasal voice comes out and that little attitude.

The Shangri-las were kind of rebellious, but not anything drastic. The most they'd ever do with us was refuse to sing something; they'd cross their arms and say 'We're *not* going to do it.' Then ten minutes later they were doing it. That's about as bad as it got!

As well as the way the girls looked, there was their live performance. Instead of the usual girl-group dance routines, the Shangri-las went in for highly choreographed gestures, acting out each story as they sang. This whole pantomime approach could have been ridiculous, but it managed not to be. The Shangri-las, like the Ronettes, were tough girls with a total commitment to their music as a way of life; what they did was no more ridiculous and no more serious than the teenage habits they sang about: falling in love and fighting with parents.

The teenage fantasy conjured up by 'The Leader of the Pack' also had a major impact at the time. Here was the return of the Crystals' rebel hero, but now it was clear from the words of the song that he actually owned a motorbike; equipped with this new means of transport, he would be able to whisk his heroine away from the boredom of conventional domestic life to a more dangerous, exciting world of romantic bliss ... if only her parents had not ruined everything by intervening. But the story made the teenage girl's parents pay for their authoritarian behaviour by giving them a crushing burden of guilt for the death of the hero, and for destroying their daughter's chance of happiness.

The leader of the pack's demise also had the added advantage of sustaining true romance indefinitely. For the teenage girl, the resolution of love was still marriage; and yet this was unlikely to work out if you fell in love with the bad boy. How much better to have him dead and maintain everlasting adoration for him that way.

'Leader of the Pack' prompted a spate of death records. In the US, there was 'Nightmare' by the Whyte Boots, in which a girl by mistake kills a rival for her boyfriend's affections: 'Well, I thought I'd like to scare her,' the lead singer soliloquizes remorsefully after the event, adding rather unconvincingly, 'but I never meant to hurt her or anything.' In England, a girl called Twinkle brought out another motorbike tragedy hit, 'Terry', which told of the hero's fate and then begged: 'Please wait at the gate of heaven for me, Te-e-rry.' Even the British magazine *Pop Weekly* commented that it wasn't sure how to take Twinkle's offering; surely it was meant as a spoof?

A certain amount of furore was created by this new teenage preoccupation with death. In Britain, which has always had a habit of protecting the public from anything remotely disturbing in the arts, thereby of course intensifying everyone's interest, 'Leader of the Pack' was banned. Yet in reality this wallowing in death and disaster in pop records conspicuously lacked the sinister overtones that the guardians of public morals were looking for; in the death records, morbid sentimentality and fantasies of the 'If I die, you'll all be sorry' variety ruled the day, rather than anything more seriously destructive or psychopathic.

The Shangri-las too may have given adults cause for alarm, but like Elvis they were in many ways model Americans. Despite their hip clothes, they did not come on as ultra-sexy and slinky like the Ronettes. They were fresh-faced and natural, especially Mary Weiss, who looked more like a Swiss milkmaid than a New York doll. And their songs were mostly very innocent. Their third release, for example, was 'Give Him A Great Big Kiss', an exuberant single which continued the girl talk with:

'What colour are his eyes?'
'I don't know, he's always wearing shades'
'Is he tall?'
'Well, I gotta look up'

'Yeah? Well, I hear he's bad'
'Hmm, he's good bad, but he's not evil'
'Tell me more, tell me more' . . .

Here was the rebel again, this time marginally more threatening; where the Crystals had sung 'He's not a rebel to me,' Mary Weiss of the Shangri-las made the more ambiguous remark, 'He's good bad, but he's not evil.' Yet the song was essentially fairly harmless, all high spirits and gossip in the best girl-group tradition. The Shangri-las might look tough, they might fancy cool street guys, but their hearts were in the right place; they were just excitable teenagers, who liked to act mean but whose sentiments seemed pretty much those of the all-American girl.

The group's next big hit, 'I Can Never Go Home Any More', revealed other such exemplary feelings, this time towards the family. The song was a plea to adolescent girls not to leave home for the sake of teenage romance. It told the story of a girl who fights with her mother over a boy, packs her bags and says goodbye, only to fall out of love immediately. She bitterly regrets what she has done and ends with this advice on how to treat your mother:

Do you ever get the feeling you want to kiss and hug her?
Do it right now, tell her you love her
Don't do to your mom what I did to mine
She grew so lonely in the end, the angels picked her for a friend

Thus did the Shangri-las mete out the same fate to poor old mom as had befallen the leader of the pack. In an earlier single, 'Give Us Your Blessing', it had been the romantic couple themselves who were bumped off for purposes of poetic justice; they had eloped against their parents' wishes, and were immediately killed in a car crash, such was the emotional state they had been reduced to. It seemed that the teenage girl, forever trapped between parental and romantic love, was destined to cause misery and pain all round, whatever she did.

'I Can Never Go Home Any More' was, in true Shangri-las' style, a steamy episode of the true-life drama in which young girls struggle to become adults; in the most heartrending terms, our heroine, now in the arms of her lover, fantasized in the song about being tucked up in bed at home by mom. The whole effect was highly sentimental to say the least; but as usual, the Shangri-las had in their naive way touched a very raw nerve in the teenage girl's psyche.

'I Can Never Go Home Any More' was the Shangri-las' final hit, despite their later attempts to preach reconciliation between the generations and the importance of the American way of life. The girls' next outing, 'Long Live Our Love', capitalized on the wave of patriotism that accompanied the first forays of American soldiers into Vietnam; to the sounds of a brass band, pipes, drums and a refrain of 'When Johnny Comes Marching Home Again', the girls chorused their approval of their boy's departure to war:

> *Something's come between us, and it's not a girl,*
> *Other people need you, there's trouble in this world*

The awfulness of this record defied description and it was quite understandably not a hit; without the tension of adolescent psychodrama which by now characterized a Shangri-las song, the whole effort seemed unutterably tacky. A subsequent release, 'Past, Present and Future', returned to more solid Shangri-las territory, that of broken romance; but despite the inspired Mortonesque idea of backing the whole track with the Moonlight Sonata, the record failed to put the group back on top.

Detroit writers were drafted in to produce this stab at the Motown sound, but the single did not meet with commercial success.

For most of their career, the Shangri-las had been touring the country, often without a manager or any proper support from their record company. Betty had left the group early on, and the three remaining girls stayed out on the road almost continuously, sometimes with new girls standing in for one or other of them. The arrangements made for them were typically chaotic. Inevitably the hard work, the long hours of travelling, the lack of financial or emotional support from adults who should have been responsible for them, and the severing of any contact with normal home life while they were growing up took their toll, and the group finally fell apart. The Shangri-las had by now developed a reputation for being wild; there were even rumours that they had been involved in gunrunning and kidnapping. The group did make an attempt to come back during the seventies, but after that the girls disappeared into obscurity. Then, sadly, came the news of the death of Mary Ann Ganser, variously reported as being due to a serious illness or to a drug overdose. Today, the Shangri-las are conspicuously absent from the oldies' revival scene, and Mary Weiss is said to be running a furniture store with her husband. Perhaps their graceful retirement from the scene is just as well; as the most outrageously and essentially teenage of all the sixties' girl groups, how could they possibly sustain such an image today? As Reparata of the Delrons remarks, 'What would they wear now? Would it be leather jackets or sequinned gowns?'

In 1965, the Shangri-las recorded 'Out in the Streets', one of their best singles which, however, did not do particularly well for them. The lyrics of the song wistfully conveyed an idea that was to run through a great deal of subsequent girl-group music until the eighties; that being female was not very cool at all; that this lack of cool rubbed off on the male, making him as conventional and dull as his partner; and that, unfair as all this was, the most one could do as a member of the boring female sex was to try to be magnanimous:

He don't hang around with the gang no more
He don't do the wild things that he did before
He used to act bad, used to but he quit
It makes me so sad, cos I know that he did it for me
And I can see
His heart is out in the street

Evidently, the cheerful confidence of the early girl groups that they were the coolest creatures imaginable had suddenly taken a very big knock.

*　　*　　*

By 1964, the British boy beat groups were threatening to push all the American girl groups right out of the charts. Reparata remembers:

> At that time, I think the record-buying public and the people who bought tickets to the concerts were your teenage girls. The boys were more involved in sport. So that meant the male British groups had an edge; all the girls loved them of course, and they weren't interested in us. It sure was a tough time for us.

Teenage girls wanted to see the boys on stage, fantasy lovers that they could adore from a distance, not ordinary girls like themselves. Moreover, the new boy heroes were exotically foreign, from unknown parts of the world like Liverpool. They looked different too, almost feminine with their long hair; and this had an odd effect, as one early American Beatles fan pointed out to me:

> A girl could kind of identify with the Beatles; you could imagine yourself up there playing guitar like them. That was new. I mean there was no way a girl would have been able to identify with the American boy groups before that, like the Crew Cuts or the Four Freshmen, was there?

Thus the new boy groups were both love objects and people that girl fans could somehow see themselves as emulating. The combination was a winner.

For the girl groups, it was becoming more and more difficult to compete with the new British lover boys of pop, particularly on live tours, which were for most of the girl groups the mainstay of their careers. Jiggs Allbut of the Angels remembers what it was like:

> We were out on tour with Gerry and the Pacemakers and our bus was always being mobbed. Of course the girls really hated us, because we were in the bus with their idols. They tried to rip us apart, they really did. I have never been so terrified in my life!

There is no doubt that the British groups were a major source of the girl groups' decline in popularity. They appealed so much to teenage girls, who formed the biggest slice of the market, that the girl groups had to take a back seat. After all, the girl groups could only sing about their dreamboats; John, Paul, George and Ringo were the real thing. But received wisdom usually exaggerates the situation, presenting the British Invasion in 1964 as dealing a sudden death-blow to all the girl groups, who were immediately discarded as hopelessly old-fashioned with their naive songs of romance, their stiff wigs and their party dresses. In fact, the situation was not quite so simple.

The year 1964 was in fact a very good one for the girl groups, which saw for example the emergence of the Shangri-las. Although there was competition from the British boys, the girl groups were not initially seen as passé; rather the opposite. The Beatles themselves made no secret of their admiration for the girl groups and modelled their musical style on them. In fact, the Beatles' first album featured several girl-group covers, including 'Chains' by the Cookies and two Shirelles' songs, 'Boys' and 'Baby, It's You'. The Beatles' early image, too, as evidenced by their TV film appearances, was every bit as upbeat and fun as that of the American girl groups. As for the new bad boys of pop, the Rolling Stones, they met their match with the wildly seductive Ronettes. No, style and image were not initially the problems.

What really lay behind the gradual decline of the girl groups after 1964 was the collapse of the Brill Building system, upon which the girls were utterly dependent. The great strength of the boy beat groups was that they wrote their own material – or so it was perceived: many of the British groups in fact had their biggest hits with covers of little-known American songs, some by girl groups. But when the British arrived, the Brill Building songwriters took fright, ran for cover and gave up before they had really had a chance to take a closer look at the enemy. All of a sudden, the singer-songwriter became the only credible type of artist; now groups had to write their own material. The girl groups, who had traditionally been seen as incapable of singing anything other than what producers and songwriters put before them, were left stranded.

There were also movements afoot within other areas of American music that put pressure on the girl groups. Bob Dylan had been working in the folk genre since 1962, but by 1965 he burst right out of it with a series of albums that revolutionized popular music. As a result of his introducing notions of art, politics and the intellect into pop, a huge split began to develop in the music industry between commercial teen pop, put out on singles, and 'progressive' adult rock which relied on album sales. The girl groups, of course, were very firmly in the teen pop bracket; albums for them had always just consisted of a group's hits plus a few quick covers to fill in the gaps. Now, all the rules of the game were changed; suddenly, only albums sold, and the music was supposed to be about such things as the state of the world and heavy relationships. Meanwhile, the Beatles had begun to ponder the mysteries of the East, and the Stones to transform the blues into white music of a crass sexism and humourless arrogance seldom before witnessed in pop. How could the girl groups compete? Not only were they teenagers, not only were their songs the opposite of intellectually profound, but worst of all they were female. Here were the new male intellectual heavyweights of popular music, then, Bob Dylan, the Beatles and the Stones, fast being accredited the status of visionaries and seers, whilst the New York girl groups quietly slunk off the stage leaving pop to the new clever dicks.

To be fair, the American element of the pop revolution as represented by Bob Dylan did have a genuine political drive behind it. His music came out of a folk tradition of union activism which was still alive and kicking even after the McCarthy years of the fifties. Dylan himself came to embody the rebellion of a new generation with different political preoccupations. Since 1960, the civil rights movement had been sweeping over the South, involving not only blacks but whites too. The first soldiers were being drafted to Vietnam; and with this issue becoming paramount amongst young people, they, along with the civil rights activists, began to oppose the establishment. Dylan gave a voice to this generation of middle-class young Americans who now began to feel the brunt of the racist and imperialistic values of their society themselves. But very gradually, Dylan and the new folk rock bands began to emerge as politically empty. Their early promise of radicalism died as they got richer and more important, until finally most of them had little more to say on the subject of politics than the Shangri-las. Like the Shangri-las, the rock bands were part of a youth culture of generational rebellion and not, in the end, instigators of a political revolution. They were just an awful lot more pretentious.

One of the reasons that rock blanded out so quickly was that, in the mid sixties, there was a sudden move from New York to California. The early folkies had hung round Greenwich Village, where their styles of dress and image – if nothing else – were copied by girls like the Shangri-las, who took to sporting sandals and looking intense. But once youth culture switched into the laid-back West Coast mode, the slick New York girl groups began to look and sound all wrong, as records like the Shirelles' 'One of the Flower People' showed. There was an element of tongue-in-cheek about teen girl music, a sly humour that was completely out of place in the West Coast wonderland. The flower people may have had fun, but they took their fun pretty seriously, investing it with all sorts of mystic justifications; the girl groups, used as they were to celebrating youth, romance and having a good time for its own sake, could not really adjust to this paradoxical hippy mixture of puritanism and hedonism.

Thus, it was not simply that the boy beat groups had come along and stolen the girls' thunder. The Beatles and their cohorts had, at the beginning, shared a great deal in common with the girl groups' lighthearted approach; yet once the boys changed and were co-opted into the male-dominated, pseudo-intellectual Californian folk-rock camp, the girl groups were left behind and began to look desperately unfashionable.

*   *   *

The Orchids: Coventry schoolgirls whose sound most closely resembled that of America's Crystals.

The Vernons Girls were a TV singing troupe of the fifties; by 1962, they'd slimmed down to a hit-making trio.

The beat boom that rocked America in the mid sixties had begun on the other side of the Atlantic on 15 December 1962 precisely, when a record called 'Love Me Do' by an unknown Liverpool group called the Beatles hit the UK charts. As a result of the Beatles' ensuing impact during the sixties, Britain quickly became the creative centre of the pop world, exporting its best acts to the huge American market where the real money in the music industry lay.

Amongst the hordes of groups from the north of England and from London that arose in the wake of the Beatles, there were a few girl groups: for instance, the Vernons, the Orchids and the Caravelles. However, although these groups had the trendiness of being British on their side, not to mention access to the indigenous Merseyside sound, they none of them achieved any major success. One of the problems was that they did not look like proper groups. The Beatles had effectively knocked the tradition of vocal harmony groups on the head, and now every outfit was expected to play its own instruments. Three girls standing there singing on their own did not look right. But then neither did it seem appropriate for girls to play electric guitars or to bang drums; those who did, like drummer Honey Langtree, or the few now-obscure 'garage' girl groups modelled on the Beatles – the Liver Birds, for example – were seen at best as a bit of an aberration. It did not occur to the majority of girls to play rock instruments; they did not have the confidence to make mistakes in public like the boys. So, for girls, forming a group on the model of the Beatles was not an obvious step to take as they grew up, in the same way as it was for thousands of would-be boy stars who picked up guitars at school and formed their first bands.

This did not mean, however, that girls made no contribution to the beat explosion. On the contrary, in Britain a new image of young women arose which was much more sophisticated than that of the American girl teenagers who had squealed on Bandstand. For a start, the archetypal sixties' British dolly bird was older than the American teenage miss, probably in her early twenties; she was assumed to have a job of some kind, and to have left her childhood girlfriends behind. She was portrayed as more interested in going out with men than in girl talk, and as having a fairly blasé attitude towards sex; none of that 'wearing his ring' nonsense for her. Whether such a swinging Samantha really existed was beside the point; for young girls growing up outside the capital, the image of what was in store as a single girl in the big city was a powerful one.

The new young women of British pop reflected this image to perfection. Not surprisingly, given their more mature status, they were single girls rather than groups of schoolchums. But musically, artists like Lulu, Cilla Black, Sandie Shaw and Dusty Springfield were close to the American girl groups, though often, with the exception of Dusty, they were a lot less skilled as singers than their US counterparts; however they more than made up for their vocal faults in terms of style. In Britain, the sixties had ushered in a new breed of home-grown pop stars who were, on the whole, far more impressive than those of the decade before.

*　　*　　*

During the fifties, the state of white mainstream popular music in Britain had been very similar to that of the United States ... only worse. The British charts were full of American crooners like Frankie Laine and Rosemary Clooney; the Chordettes had a string of hits in the UK, ending with 'Lollipop' in 1958, and the Fontaine Sisters scored an early hit with 'Seventeen'. The British contingent did little more than imitate these American singers (who, more often than not, were themselves imitations, pumping out whitewashed versions of black songs). British singers like Ruby Murray, Dickie Valentine and Jimmy Young were all middle-of-the road chart regulars; only Alma Cogan exhibited a little more verve than most with her cover of Frankie Lymon's 'Why Do Fools Fall in Love' in 1956. The normal procedure in the British music industry seemed to be that American artists would hit the UK charts, at which point a British artist would rush out a cover; the two versions would then chase each other up the chart, until one or other won out – usually the American version, although sometimes a sense of decency and loyalty to the home-grown product would prevail.

Thus, the British charts in the fifties were full of American records and indigenous soundalikes. There was very little in the way of black music and rock 'n' roll on the radio. Unlike the US, there was no network of independent local stations across the country; only the light programme on the BBC catered to popular taste in music, and the likes of Elvis Presley were most definitely beyond the pale there, despite the fact that by 1956, American rock 'n' roll records had begun to infiltrate the British charts.

Amongst the stalwarts of the BBC's light entertainment programme was a girl group called the Beverley Sisters. Although the Beverley Sisters were comparable to American girl groups like the Chordettes or singers like Patti

Page, whose 'Doggie in the Window' the group covered in 1953, they in fact represented something rather different which was, in its own way, quite innovative. In Britain, the media was almost as inaccessible to white working-class people as it was to black people in the US; the Beverley Sisters were amongst the first to break down the barriers of class and become big radio and TV stars.

Today, meeting twins Babs and Teddy of the Beverley Sisters is quite an experience. The pair arrive dressed identically in yellow jumpsuits and straw hats, looking the picture of health and talking nineteen to the dozen, often almost in unison. Daughters of variety theatre performers who had fallen on hard times during the war, Babs, Teddy and their sister Joy broke into showbusiness as children, when they got a job advertising Rowntrees' cocoa:

> The company sent Fox photos up from London to set the session up. We couldn't do the session indoors because we were in digs, we'd been evacuated from London to the Midlands. So the photographer took us to the park. He asked us what is your hobby, do you play tennis?
> . . . I mean, tennis, that was a joke, kids as poor as us . . .
> . . . So we said no, we sing a bit, and . . .
> . . . We started to sing and he put the camera down and said, 'That is so

Babs, Joy and Teddy: there were never such devoted sisters.

good. I've got a friend at the BBC ...'

... A week later we got a letter from the BBC but we couldn't go down there because of the war. But when the war ended and we left school, our mother said, 'Now what are you going to do?' So we got the letter out and said, 'We're going to the BBC.'

... We walked up to the front desk, but they said the man we wanted to see was out. We thought, that's it, the elbow. But then he wrote to us asking us to come and see him. Well, he put us on radio immediately he heard us, and the moment television started, we were on that too.

Unlike America in the fifties, which was beginning a consumer boom, the bulk of the population in Britain was still suffering intense poverty as a result of the Second World War:

Television was the big thing. Can you imagine how exciting it was? It was totally unbelievable after the austerity of the war. Twenty families would come to watch the only set in the street. They used to walk up and down looking for an aerial and then knock at the door ...

... There was only two hours' TV a night, and only one light entertainment show in the week, and that was the Beverley Sisters.

Glamour and fashion sense were scarce commodities in fifties' Britain and the Beverley Sisters supplied them on screen:

You had to wear a long evening dress if you sang, and we wouldn't do that. We wore short evening dresses, and that was shocking at the time. We were the first ever to wear trousers. We wore see-through things and that was banned. You could show a cleavage, but we weren't interested in that old-fashioned cleavage business ...

... But we never shocked our audiences. We shocked the BBC. And then we became so big we could do what we wanted. We had our own TV show seven years in a row.

The Beverley Sisters provoked many a scandal in the fifties, as when they dared show their midriffs to the world, wearing short white dresses that anticipated the sixties' look. Not only their appearance but much of their material was considered extremely risqué, extraordinary as that might seem today. Songs such as their cover of the calypso tune, 'He Like It, She Like It', were banned. Coming from a music-hall background, double entendre was meat and drink to the girls, but they saw themselves as doing something more modern than that:

Television killed off the variety theatre. Our parents were variety theatre, not us. At the BBC, you could be funny if you were like Gert and Daisy, or Frankie Howerd. But if you were three natural, sexy, high-spirited, working-class girls, no. You couldn't be suggestive and we were suggestive, because we loved getting a laugh . . .

. . . For example, we did a song called 'I Hate Men' and when that Lord got done for the young boys, we wrote a lyric that went:

We like to choose our boyfriends from a class that's known as upper
We do our best to charm them but our plans they always scupper
If only we were three boy scouts they'd take us out to supper,
Oh I hate men!

. . . Yes, we were always a bit feminist.

With their daring clothes and humour, but above all with their stubborn confidence in their own working-class taste and style, the Beverley Sisters helped to challenge the snobbery of the British upper classes at a time when it was well entrenched in British broadcasting:

. . . You had to get posh to be on the BBC. One of our early songs was called 'I'm a Big Girl Now'. You couldn't say 'Ahm' though, it had to be 'Iym'. But we refused to do that . . .

. . . We *were* discriminated against. We were working class, we were girls, we had the wrong accent. But the BBC had to give in to us because the public loved us. We were three little cockney kids who could sing in harmony, that's all, and everyone went bonkers.

Eventually, the Beverley Sisters left show business to bring up their children, returning to stage a comeback in 1985 at Stringfellow's disco. Since then a disco version of their fifties' hit 'Sisters' has appeared, and the Beverley Sisters look set to continue working in their own time-honoured tradition for a long time in the future.

By the end of the fifties, things were beginning to look up for the average British teenager, who now, as in the US, was beginning to command a more powerful role as a consumer of all things pop. Rock 'n' roll had, despite the BBC's strictures, made its mark in Britain, via such avenues as the sale of imported records and Radio Luxembourg's broadcasts, as well as through occasional visits by American stars like Johnnie Ray, Little Richard, Bill Haley, Eddie Cochran and Jerry Lee Lewis. Gene Vincent had taken up residence in Britain for some years and was doing his best to teach a generation of Teds how to play rock 'n' roll.

British television made more attempt than did radio to cater to the new music with its first pop programme on the BBC, Six Five Special, produced by Jack Good. Several programmes followed, like Oh Boy!, Boy Meets Girl and Wham!, also produced by Good, who later went on to greater things with his American TV show Shindig. Gene Vincent as the genuine rock 'n' roll article was of course the star of these shows, along with more homegrown rock 'n' rollers like Marty Wilde and Cliff Richard; and the wild boys of British rock were always backed on television by a huge troupe of British girls known as the Vernons.

The Vernons girls originally came from Liverpool, where they had all worked as clerical staff at Vernon's football pools. Jack Good used them in twos or threes or all together as backing vocalists and dancers throughout his run of programmes on the BBC and on ITV in the late fifties and early sixties. In 1962, three of the Vernons girls had a hit in their own right with 'Lover Please', while three more became well known on TV during the sixties as the Breakaways. Yet two more, Maggie Stredder – better known as 'the one with the glasses' – and Gloria George formed the Ladybirds, who for many years sang back-ups on Top of the Pops. One of the Vernons later married Marty Wilde and produced offspring Kim, whilst another wed cockney rocker Joe Brown. Yet although the Vernons in their various incarnations remained part of British pop throughout the sixties, backing all the major singers who came to town, they remained pretty much a footnote to history as girl groups in their own right.

The same was true of later sixties' girl groups in Britain, most of whom jumped on the bandwagon of the Merseyside sound. There were amongst others the Orchids, three youngsters who were presented to the world in their school jumpers sucking ice lollies, an unsophisticated image that actually came very close to that of the early American girl groups; the Caravelles, a breathy, folksy duo who were described by one commentator as making 'a not exactly pleasant sound' and 'appearing to sing in French'; the McKinleys, Scottish beat girls dressed in tartan caps and kinky boots; and the Three Bells, who looked like an updated version of the Beverley Sisters. But none of these now obscure groups was a match for the new solo girls of pop, the queen bees around whom the drone beat groups revolved.

Cathy McGowan, presenter of ITV's Ready Steady Go, was the first 'life is fabulous' girl to hit the screen in the sixties: blinking big eyes through her long fringe and smiling benignly at the camera, she introduced the acts just as an enthusiastic pop fan would. She was hailed as 'natural' and 'ordinary', though she was neither; what commentators meant was that she was part of the scene that Ready Steady Go showcased, and not outside it like most TV presenters.

The subculture behind Ready Steady Go was essentially that of the mods. Whereas in the US, pop music was part of the white, middle-class college student's life, in Britain it had always been very much a working-class taste. Working-class teenagers had jobs, money and free time, whilst the offspring of the middle classes had educations, tight budgets as students, and more

The Ladybirds making a spectacle of themselves; the face furniture was mandatory.

parental restrictions as a result of their financial dependence. However, towards the mid sixties, an element of social mobility began to become possible, whereby young working-class people were sometimes able to enrol in colleges and universities, particularly art colleges, out of which many of the beat groups were born. While the rockers remained defiantly working class, the mods aspired to better themselves, and were dedicated to seeking out the best in everything, be it black American soul music or Italian suits.

As far as young women were concerned, this was quite a healthy development. Mod culture may have created an atmosphere of repressive cool and stultifying elitism but it was an environment in which style, rather than money or class, counted. What job you had was not of interest; a job was simply a means to buying clothes and records. For girls, this was ideal;

suddenly, looking good was more important than anything else; being, rather than doing, had become the main occupation in life; and luckily, this just happened to be women's traditional forte.

The dolly bird was the creation of the mods. Despite her appearance of complete passivity and feminine quiescence, she was a complex being who in some ways defied accepted notions of how women should look and behave. If she was blank, she was also inscrutable; if she was the epitome of delicate femininity, she was also curiously masculine – the skinny, waif-like female personified by Twiggy was much berated in the British tabloids for committing the sins of having no breasts and wearing her hair short like a boy's. In the days before the emaciated look became a tyranny for women, it was quite clearly a radical statement against a previous ideal of beauty, one that in the fifties emphasized the voluptuousness of the female form almost to the point of parody.

The image of Twiggy's anorexic frame was something new: it was as much the strange product of an unhealthy and, to most people, incomprehensible mod culture based around fashion, music and amphetamines, as it was an expression of the teenage girl's refusal to grow up into a woman. Moreover, Twiggy embodied a new ideal in Britain of the working class as fashionable; along with David Bailey and Michael Caine, she was a cockney, street smart and arrogant in a way that the educated middle classes could never be.

It was not long, however, before the middle classes got in on the mod act, transforming what was still largely an underground subculture into Britain's biggest selling product of the time: Swinging London. The Chelsea Set moved in on the mods, and in no time had created a more upper-class version of the whole thing, with expensive discotheques and boutiques in the King's Road and London's West End. This in turn became a crass commercialism in which anything from Carnaby Street signs in Tudoresque lettering to pictures of the Queen were sold in their millions to tourists. Yet despite the obviously commercial and bogus nature of the whole enterprise, an extraordinary idealism was attached to this apparent renaissance of Britain. No longer was the country perceived as a boring little set of islands steeped in colonial prejudice; it was now the hub of a groovy universe, peopled by classless youth and an avuncular older generation of policemen and politicians. And at the centre of this universe were the Chelsea girls, the dolly birds turned breezy jetsetters, whom Mary Quant in 1965 described like this:

These girls may have their faults. Often they may be too opinionated and extravagant. But the important thing is that they are alive ... looking, listening, ready to try anything new.

It is their questioning attitude which makes them important and different. They conform to their own set of values but not to the values and standards laid down by a past generation. But they don't sneer at other points of view. If they don't wish to campaign against the Bomb they don't sneer at those who do. They are not silly or flirtatious or militant. Being militant and aggressive is as ridiculous to them as being coy and deliberately seductive. They make no pretensions.

Sex is taken for granted. They talk candidly about everything from puberty to homosexuality. The girls are curiously feminine but their femininity lies in their attitude rather than in their appearance. They may be dukes' daughters, doctors' daughters or dockers' daughters. They are not interested in status symbols. They don't worry about accents or class; they are neither determinedly county or working class . . . Snobbery has gone out of fashion, and in our shops you will find duchesses jostling with typists to buy the same dresses.

. . . They think for themselves. They are committed and involved. Prejudices no longer exist. They represent the whole new spirit that is present-day Britain, a classless spirit that has grown out of the Second World War.

They will not accept truisms or propaganda. They are superbly international. The same clothes are worn in Britain, Europe and America. The same sort of food is eaten too. I think there may be a chance that you can't swing a war on a generation which does not think in terms of 'us' against the foreigners.

So much for the mini skirt. But not only had the new, pioneering Chelsea girl out on a shopping spree inadvertently become the harbinger of a social revolution, she had also become indestructible, according to Quant:

I've seen the girls give the cold shoulder in a way that must be devastating to the male. I don't really believe that it is possible for an American man to rape an amusing and intelligent English girl . . . except by brute force, of course. She is far too witty and amusing. She'd simply laugh the whole thing off.

The 'life is fabulous' philosophy evinced by Mary Quant flatly denied the glaring realities of racism, sexism and class prejudice inherent in British life; in her book, even rape had become impossible (except by brute force, of course). Yet despite the absurd naivety and covert snobbery of her views – the Chelsea girl appears to be entirely modelled on the debs who, in their classless way, whiled away their time by working as her shop assistants – there was an element of truth in Quant's assessment of the aspirations, if not the reality, of the sixties' generation in Britain. And whilst it was difficult

Marianne Faithfull: posh,
pretty and prone to disaster.

to point to exactly what the new young woman actually did besides being
so tremendously stylish and egalitarian, there was no doubt that her image
was central to the swinging British sixties.

The ideal young woman of the sixties was a vague combination of fan,
model, pop star's girlfriend, and pop star – in that order. There was, as we
have seen, the ineffable Cathy McGowan, fan extraordinaire. There was
Twiggy, the cockney model who made a few records. There was Marianne
Faithfull, the pop star's girlfriend who also made a few records, and whose
upper-class ancestry included the man who first popularized sado-
masochism, Count Leopold Von Sacher Masoch himself. Marianne's
quavery voice and fey songs such as 'This Little Bird' and 'As Tears Go By'
would probably have been dismissed as too pathetic for words had it not
been for the intriguing contrast between these and her other activities, such
as her alleged antics with Mick Jagger, Mars Bars and heroin. Then there
were Cilla and Lulu, the pop stars, but they were never all that trendy and
soon became co-opted into the very same British tradition of cheerful,
cheeky lasses loved by the lower orders that the Beverley Sisters had been
trying to escape in the fifties. But best of all, there was the girl that every
reader of *Rave*, *Teenscene* or *Petticoat* wanted to be: Sandra Goodrich, the
ugly duckling from Dagenham, who had turned into Sandie Shaw, the
swan.

True to the mod code, Sandie didn't actually do much. But she looked
great. She was the epitome of the singing fashion plate, all big eyes, shiny
hair and long, bony legs. In a gesture that preceded hippiedom, she went
barefoot; so fascinated were people by this development in the whacky
world of pop that whenever she appeared on TV, the camera seemed to be
permanently on her feet. Sandie shot to number one in 1964 with '(There's)
Always Something There to Remind Me', following this up with lesser hits

until she won the Eurovision song contest in 1967. 'Puppet on a String' was not as bad as Lulu's offering to the contest two years later, but it marked the beginning of a decline in Sandie's credibility as Britain's female answer to the swarms of post-Beatles boy groups who were invading the charts both in the UK and the US. This credibility was only regained in the eighties, when British pop star Morrissey recorded his boyhood heroine.

It was not the extraordinary skill and talent of pop girls like Cathy McGowan and Sandie Shaw that fascinated the public; quite the opposite. Cathy sometimes gave the impression of being remarkably thick as a presenter, and Sandie often sang out of tune. It was the fact that the British pop girls epitomized the arrogant cool of ordinary young, single women who no longer knew their place. Cathy and Sandie had no reason to think themselves special, and yet they obviously did. As such, they were quite extraordinary.

This youthful confidence was very much in keeping with the ethos of the American girl groups, but musically the British girls came out of a rather different tradition. British songwriters tended to be at the light entertainment or showbiz end of pop, and often saddled the girls with staid string arrangements and razamatazz horns that made the songs sound more than a little old-fashioned. The artist who managed to break out of this mould, and combine the deadpan cool of the British dolly bird with an ability to sing like the black American girl groups was Dusty Springfield.

In her role as fashion heroine, Dusty Springfield outdid all the other British girl stars of the sixties. Not for her the understated good looks and taste of a Françoise Hardy; Dusty went for glamour with a capital 'G'. Other girls might wear mascara, but Dusty wore more; other girls might backcomb their hair, but Dusty wore it higher and with more lacquer than anybody else. Amongst schoolgirls, it was rumoured that Dusty never took her make up off or brushed out her hair, *even when she went to bed*! For the teenage girl, Dusty was the height of decadence; she was grown up, but not in the boring way most adults were; Dusty's adulthood suggested all sorts of unknown indulgences and pleasures, including the intensely contradictory, confusing experience of sex and romance. But more than being a blonde pop queen, Dusty could actually sing. She was of Irish and Scottish descent, her real name being Mary Isabel Catherine Bernadette O'Brien, and had grown up in London's Irish stronghold of West Hampstead. Her career had begun in a girl group, the Lana Sisters, who were akin to other British girl groups in the fifties like the Beverley Sisters and the Kaye Sisters. By 1960, there was still a good deal of life left in this genre, as evidenced by the Kaye Sisters' 'Paper Roses', a hit in the group's own right after many years of backing Frankie Vaughan. The Lana Sisters, however, did not fare so well; they worked as a live group but had no chart hits, and by 1960 had stopped recording. Dusty went on to join her brother's folk outfit the Springfields, where she met with her first real success. In 1961, the Springfields won the *New Musical Express* poll as the top English vocal group. The following year, the group had their first US hit, 'Silver Threads and Golden Needles', which reached number twenty. In Britain, 'Silver Threads' did not chart; but subsequent releases like 'Bambino', 'Island of Dreams' and 'Say I Won't Be There' all found their way into the British hit parade. By October 1963, however, the Springfields had split up; but Dusty continued to record for their label, Philips, as a solo artist.

Her first solo release, 'I Only Want To Be With You', was an immediate success; it was an exuberant, uptempo number very much in the American girl-group style. There followed a wonderful run of hits which proved her to be a singer that could hold her own with the best of the black 'uptown' R&B artists like Dionne Warwick. Apart from two spirited, fast singles, 'In the Middle of Nowhere' and 'Little By Little', and a midtempo song, 'Stay Awhile', that sounded like the Shirelles, the Ronettes and the Chiffons all rolled into one, Dusty's hit releases tended to be 'big, ballady things' as she called them, sung with a sensitivity that more than made up for the rather slushy, unimaginative musical arrangements favoured by her producers. In 1964, there was a gorgeous ballad, 'I Just Don't Know What To Do With Myself', a cover of Tommy Hunt's American hit, written by Bacharach and David. Dusty was very influenced by Dionne Warwick, and traces of Shirley Owens of the Shirelles could also be heard in her poignant, understated vocal style. 'Losing You' and 'Some of Your Lovin'' followed, both reaching the British top ten, but it was not until 1966 that Dusty made number one.

'You Don't Have To Say You Love Me' was a dramatic Italian pop ballad of a type that has always had a following in Britain, a great opera of a song in the grand style, all crashing drums and massed violins. The words were banal in the extreme, giving the whole thing a sort of Shangri-las-meets-Las-Vegas feel, but it worked; somehow Dusty's voice made the song totally convincing. Dusty's friend Vicki Wickham, producer of Ready Steady Go, had co-written the English lyrics to the song, which had first appeared in the original Italian version as 'Lo Che No Vivo Senza Te'. Vicki, who now lives and works in New York, told me the story of how she came to compose the English version:

Dusty had this great song, but no words for it, so she asked me to come up with something. I was having supper with Simon Napier-Bell and I asked him to help me out. We were completely drunk, but we wrote the thing. The next day, I gave it to Dusty, and she said, 'This is awful!' I said, 'I know.' But her producer Johnny Franz said 'Oh, it'll be all right once you sing it', so they went ahead and used the words.

Despite the way the lyrics came about, they did seem to sum up a certain quality in Dusty that was new to girl pop. This was a kind of masochism that was more than mere teen melodrama; it was a genuine, if rather overblown, expression of real female vulnerability. Most of Dusty's ballads elaborated one theme: that of a young woman whose identification with a freedom-loving, cavalier male hero is so strong that she lets herself be used and abused, in a defiant but ultimately self-defeating gesture against conventional commitment, responsibility and marriage. 'You Don't Have To Say You Love Me' was just one among many ballads that explored this scenario; another, 'Some of Your Lovin'', pleaded bitterly, 'I know you've got a lot of wild oats to sow, but darling, when I see you, don't you tell me no . . .' Dusty was all about the predicament of the unconventional girl who refuses to tie her man down, and in the mid to late sixties this was beginning to be of central importance to the young woman battling to find her place in an era of sexual liberation. On the one hand, she rejected the confines of an orthodox relationship – or could, perhaps, no longer make such a demand; on the other, she experienced a loss of social status and emotional security by involving herself in an affair with no strings attached. If the girl groups had explored the frustrations of leaving their lover at the garden gate, Dusty now expressed the confusions and regrets that arose once he had stayed the night and departed the morning after.

By 1968, after three more hit ballads, 'Goin' Back', 'All I See Is You' and 'Give Me Time', Dusty was delving further into what was obviously her real love: black music. She recorded an album in Memphis which produced, among other great tracks, 'Son of a Preacher Man'. Here at last was grown-up soul, and from then on, Dusty moved right away from the schmaltzy pop ballads she was known for into R&B and soul, at which point the mainstream pop world ceased to take very much notice of her. More recently, she surfaced in the charts on singles with the Pet Shop Boys, during a phase when male stars took to hauling out pop divas like Shirley Bassey and Sandie Shaw to grace their efforts. Vicki Wickham, who now manages Dusty, says today that she is planning a comeback; but as Vicki herself admits, 'Where does she fit in now? She has the voice, and I think people will always want to hear that voice; but apart from Las Vegas, it's difficult to know where to place her these days.'

*   *   *

Back in the halcyon days of Ready Steady Go, however, Dusty Springfield's feel for black music had put her at the forefront of British pop. Her position as the British ambassador of American black music led her in 1965 to host a special music TV show introducing a British audience to the stars of a young black record label whose music she loved: Motown.

❹ you can't hurry love

In the early sixties, Motown was a tiny independent record company based in an ordinary house at 2648 West Grand Boulevard, Detroit. The only feature that distinguished the house from others in the street was the sign above its door: Hitsville USA. For a new company, this was a laughably optimistic title but, miraculously, Motown did eventually become the 'sound of young America' as it always boasted itself to be; and by the mid sixties it had produced the only new strand of US pop that could compete with the beat groups of the British Invasion. Even more miraculously, the company was able to succeed in the face of a music industry run entirely by whites. Motown was unique in the commercial world as a company staffed from top to bottom by blacks; it thus challenged the traditional hierarchy of the pop industry, so evident in New York's Brill Building, which was that the businessmen and songwriters were white, often Jewish, while the artists and sometimes the managers were black. At Motown, the whole team of businessmen and women, managers, producers, songwriters, publicists and artists was black; and it was headed by the redoubtable Berry Gordy Jnr, ex-boxer turned songwriter and entrepreneur.

Berry Gordy had had a successful songwriting career in the late fifties which had included hits like 'Reet Petite' for Jackie Wilson, 'Money' recorded by Barrett Strong, Marv Johnson's 'Come To Me' and the Miracles' first hit single, 'Got A Job'. However, despite Gordy's growing reputation as a songwriter, by the age of thirty-one he was still making very little money out of his work, so together with William 'Smokey' Robinson of the Miracles, he decided that the only solution to the problem was to set up his own company, Motown Record Corporation. From the beginning, the ground rules were clear; he and he alone would have strict financial and artistic control over every aspect of the company, from auditing the

The Supremes in 1963: fresh from charm school.

books to deciding which records to release to hiring and firing staff. In the ensuing years, Gordy's resolutely autocratic style of working caused many of his artists and employees to resent him bitterly, but none could deny that he had an impressive business sense and an unerring instinct for creating hits in the world of pop music.

Berry Gordy's first attempt to create a solo star at Motown was with Mary Wells. Mary had everything going for her to become America's premier black teen idol: she had a sweet way of singing, but her voice also had a cool adult quality to it; she was pretty and plump, in the style fashionable before the waiflike dolly-bird look became popular; and, although she was not a mesmerizing performer – instead of dancing, she tended to stand stock still on stage – she had very strong songs, written for her by Smokey Robinson, who was also her producer. In 1964 she became Motown's biggest solo success story when 'My Guy' hit number one.

'My Guy' was a girl's song of devotion and loyalty to her unremarkable and by all accounts unprepossessing boyfriend: 'No handsome face could ever take the place of my guy' boasted Mary. The song caught the public imagination in a big way. Perhaps it was that the boys could take comfort from the thought that it didn't matter if they weren't up to much, while the girls could feel better about going out with someone who wasn't very flash – which, after all, was bound to be the reality for most of them; as Mary pointed out, 'He may not be a movie star, but when it comes to being happy – we are.' Smokey, the arch-romantic, had once again pulled off the trick of idealizing a relationship while at the same time touching on an emotional reality for his listeners.

Mary Wells was Motown's brightest early star. 'Your Old Standby' was a top forty hit in 1963, but a year later she had left the company.

Mary looked as though she would continue to be Motown's biggest-selling artist; yet her sights were set on even higher things. She wanted to become a film star rather than a mere singer. In the hope of furthering this ambition she left Motown and signed to Twentieth Century Fox Records – where, sadly, her career as a recording artist bombed, even before she had the chance to investigate what turned out to be the rather remote possibility of going into the movies. Her departure from Motown had proved too hasty, and was in retrospect unwise; and the message of her downfall was clear: if anybody was going to make black stars, it had to be Motown. Motown may have had its faults, but Motown was all there was; no other major company in the music business had the slightest interest in building careers for black artists in the first place.

Despite Mary's shortlived career at Motown, her records had helped to establish the new sound of black pop: it was young, it was intensely romantic and for the most part it expressed emotions that were highly respectable. Smokey Robinson, who wrote many songs for other Motown artists as well for his own group the Miracles, had created a male hero who emerged as the 'new man' of sixties pop. Nothing could have been further from the love 'em and leave 'em image of the freewheeling male immortalized in traditional black toasts, rhymes and stories, in the blues, and in much R&B, than Smokey Robinson's image of the sweet, devoted lover. Gone was the reprobate Jody, the guy who sneaked off with other men's women while their husbands and lovers were away at war or in prison; gone was the bragging sixty-minute man; in came the lovestruck suitor with his heart on his sleeve, humbly offering himself as faithful husband. Smokey's songs were in the doo-wop vein, all extravagant romantic claims; at the same time, his songs were clever; he played with language, always giving the narratives, metaphors and proverbs he loved to use in his verses a certain twist to them that made his protestations of love completely irresistible. Smokey's lover was every girl's dream come true: suave, intelligent, worldly and sophisticated – yet totally, naively almost, dedicated to lifelong worship of her and her alone.

'The One Who Really Loves You', 'You Beat Me To The Punch' and 'Two Lovers', all successfully released by Mary Wells prior to 'My Guy', were characteristic of Smokey Robinson's output. In 'Two Lovers', Mary Wells tells us, 'I got two lovers, and I ain't ashamed, two lovers and I love them both the same', but it is only later, towards the end of the song, that she explains this rather indiscreet revelation: 'You're a split personality and in reality – both of them are you.' Corny stuff, perhaps, but in 1962 the song had a wit, skill and insight that was totally original.

The tender love songs of Smokey Robinson betrayed a strong feminine, if not exactly feminist, perspective in the new 'sound of young America'. Smokey was talking the same language as the New York girl groups: true-love teen romance leading to marriage, white suburban style. Yet if Smokey's songs were not macho, neither were they by now considered particularly girlish. The girl-group ethos had successfully penetrated the male world of popular music to such a degree that men as well as women could now sing innocent, idealistic songs of love and romance. The new generation of artists at Motown seemed to be leaving behind the emotional world that their mothers and fathers had inhabited: the men no longer wanted to celebrate the brief joys of sexual independence nor the women bemoan the loneliness of loving an absent man; a happy courtship and ensuing wedded bliss seemed a better prospect. And such a prospect was becoming real; escape from the poverty, insecurity and painful separations of much black family life into the ranks of the respectable middle classes no longer seemed a mere fantasy. Thus black music now needed to be an expression of hope, excitement and youthful idealism rather than of endurance and comfort in sorrow.

In the same way that the New York girl groups were helping black music to cross over to the mainstream, sanitizing it to some degree and making it respectable, so Motown was creating a sound based in black music but acceptable to a white audience. Motown's tight, driving Detroit rhythm section gave its music an appeal to black record buyers that the New York girl groups had sometimes lacked, but its airy, light melodies and romantic sentiments also made it very attractive to an expanding white pop market. Gordy had a clear idea of a new, youthful sound that did not differentiate in terms of colour and which for blacks seemed to promise the safety and lighthearted pleasures of a suburban paradise in place of the danger and tensions of ghetto life. Not until the late sixties when the black experience of Vietnam, the assassination of Martin Luther King and the emergence of the black power movement began to show how hollow, or at least fragile, that dream was did Motown, through its stars like Stevie Wonder and Marvin Gaye, become briefly identified with a vision more radical than that of upward mobility and true love in a house with its own front lawn – by which time Gordy himself was planning, in the wake of the Detroit riots of 1967, to move to a nicer area – Tinseltown.

Like every other independent record company in the early sixties, Motown had its quota of girl groups. The first of these to be successful was the Marvelettes. Today, Gladys Horton of the Marvelettes tells a fairly damning story of the group's treatment at the hands of Motown, but without much bitterness. She is an extraordinarily resilient woman who has had more than her fair share of knocks in life, so that the ups and downs of her career at Motown seem to her relatively insignificant in comparison with the personal sorrows she has had to contend with. Talking about her life, Gladys conveys a spiritual generosity and optimism that is both impressive and touching. She begins:

The Marvelettes came from a little town nobody had ever heard of called Inkster, Michigan. It was literally a place at the end of a dirt track. In fact, it was us, the Marvelettes who put Inkster on the map! Inkster was a small community, very quiet. Nothing, but nothing had ever happened there. I was living there with my foster parents, because I was a government baby. I had been born in Florida and at nine months old, my parents had given me to an adopting agency. I can remember once when I was a very little girl, my parents came and took me home for a weekend. But I never knew them at all really. I was on the move all the time, from foster home to foster home; that's the way my life has been. But I consider myself lucky. I have been free all my life; I never had a mother or father telling me what to do. It really was a blessing. And when I came to Motown, it was easy for me to get used to all that touring, 'cos I had been moving around since I could remember.

I was attending high school at Inkster, and there used to be these talent shows. I thought it would be fun to enter one , so I said, 'I'll get me some girls together and we'll sing a couple of songs', and that's what I did. The prize was that the winners got an audition at Motown records in Detroit, but that didn't mean much to me at the time. Anyway, we won first prize but, until we got to Motown, it still hadn't reached my mind how important this was. We met Berry Gordy and the Miracles, and it was then I realized the potential of this meeting. We began to picture ourselves like the Supremes, who were the company's girl group, and we told ourselves, we've got to do our best. We sang for them, and they told us to go off and write some original material; they said that was the only way we'd get a hit.

At that time, the members of the group were Georgia Dobbins, Georgeanna Tillman, Katherine Anderson, Juanita Cowart, Wanda Young and myself. We called ourselves the Marvels, but later at Motown we became the Marvelettes. Well, Georgia told us she knew a guy who was a songwriter, William Garrett was his name. William came over and we picked out some songs to record. Georgia saw this one song, 'Please Mr Postman' and she said, 'That one has a cute title.' William sang it, and it was a blues song. It was not in a young type of frame at all. So Georgia said, 'We like the title but we'll do a different tune on it and make up some new words, if you don't mind.' William said, 'Yes, you can do anything, but I want a credit for the title.' So Georgia reconstructed the song and taught it to us. She prepared us for going back to Motown with it, because she had decided that she wasn't going to go out with the group. Her mother had a bad back, and she had to stay home with her. That's how I got to do lead on the song.

On the girls' return to Motown, the company decided to record their new song, assembling a variety of their best musicians and producers for the session, including Marvin Gaye and Brian Holland. 'Please Mr Postman' turned out sounding a little like the teenage New York girl groups, but the track had a thumping backbeat and a tough drive that was pure Detroit; and in November 1961, the Marvelettes suddenly found themselves with a number one hit.

This unexpected success took its toll on the group however, as Gladys relates:

That first number one came too easy for us. We weren't pretty city girls from the projects like Motown's other girl group, the Supremes, with nice clothes and make up on and long nails. We had no experience of life at all. We were just naive little country girls, and we didn't know how to handle the situation. We had no idea how to behave, we didn't know what to wear, we didn't even know how to put on make up! We learnt as we went along, of course, but at first it was very hard.

On top of that, we weren't getting support from the company. In fact, they hated us. They laughed at us, made fun of us; we were some kind of joke to them. They really looked down on country people like us, because we didn't have their slick city ways. Also, we couldn't sing as good as the Supremes; they had been practising their harmonies for three or four years and we had only just started. But the real reason they were so mad at us, I guess, was that we got a hit before the Supremes. We got Motown their first straight hit with a girl group, and it was with a song we'd written ourselves. Can you imagine? Motown had been grooming the Supremes for years, and the Supremes had done nothing. They had writers there like Smokey Robinson, and each one of them had been trying to get a hit on the Supremes. But all of a sudden there were these little girls from nowhere, these little nobodies, with their own song that they wrote at number one in the charts!

There was so much pressure on us at that time that some of the girls in the group started cracking up. Juanita had a nervous breakdown and left the group. She had made some silly remark on Dick Clark's show, and everyone in the company was constantly teasing her about it. She really took it to heart and became very depressed. She was very young, she was only about sixteen. Then Georgeanna had to leave due to ill health. She was always very tired; there was something wrong with her, and the doctor advised her to get off the road. Berry gave her a job at Motown. She married Billy Gordon of the Contours and later she died, I think it was sickle cell anaemia.

I was OK at that time, I was enjoying myself; I didn't mind what people said. I was always a free person, and all my energy was going into the group. We were really good. Wanda was having fun too, she was taking over more of the leads because Smokey liked to use her voice. She married one of the Miracles and joined the Motown 'in crowd' but after that she had a lot of problems. I guess the people at Motown figured, if we can disunite the Marvelettes, we can fight them.

Despite the problems, the Marvelettes continued to have hits, and were amongst Motown's most popular live acts on tour. Their second release 'Twisting Postman' was a blatant attempt to cash in both on their first single and on the twist craze; it only managed to get into the top forty, but their following single, 'Playboy', written by Gladys Horton and others at Motown, reached the top ten. The group's next outing, 'Beechwood 4-5789' was also a big hit. But after that, there followed a disappointing hiatus; between 1962 and 1964, the Marvelettes dropped right out of the charts.

One of the reasons seemed to be that Berry Gordy had lost interest in the group.

After the Marvelettes' early success, it became clear that Berry Gordy had no special long-term plans for the group. He was offering them only the minimum of what every Motown artist needed in order to do their job for the company properly. The girls were groomed, but not for stardom; they only had to reach a certain level of acceptability which would keep them on a par with other Motown acts. Their records were publicized, but only in the same way that all Motown records were. Their first album contained no pictures of the group, and after their first run of hits, the company paid little attention to them. The group were shunted between different producers and songwriters, releasing a string of singles that made the lower reaches of the charts. In 1964, however, one of the Marvelettes' releases finally took off; 'Too Many Fish in the Sea' hit number twenty-five, but by this time they had lost their position as the company's premier girl group. The Supremes had become Gordy's new stars. It was also around this time that the Marvelettes made a big mistake: they rejected a song called 'Baby Love' written by Brian and Eddie Holland and Lamont Dozier, which went on to become an all-time smash for the Supremes.

Out of all the writers and producers who attempted to get the Marvelettes back on top after 1963, only Smokey Robinson met with any great success. 'Don't Mess With Bill' and 'The Hunter Gets Captured By the Game', a quintessential Smokey song full of clever turns of phrase, proved the Marvelettes' appeal once again. In 1968, the Marvelettes had their final chart hit, 'My Baby Must Be A Magician'. Gladys Horton had, by that time, left the group. She remembers:

Despite providing Motown's first ever number one and nine other top forty hits, the Marvelettes spent the latter half of their career in the shadow of Berry Gordy's pet group, the Supremes.

There were a lot of money fights starting in the company. The songwriters and artists were complaining about their contracts, some were graded higher than others. Each group started leaving, one by one. I couldn't stand to see that happening because back then, it took a long time to make money out of records. A single cost about forty-five cents and albums were three dollars. As I saw it, we all should have stuck together.

I left not because of what was going on at Motown, but because I wanted to get married. I was going through one of my spells! I made a big mistake, though. I was an independent young black woman with money and a career, and my husband took it all away from me. As it turned out, he was just after my money. At first I got him a job playing trumpet with the Marvelettes – and we didn't really need a trumpeter anyway! – but eventually he took me away from Detroit altogether, to California. I guess I went along with it because I felt I was entitled to a proper home and family life after all those years as a foster child. In the back of my mind, I wanted a perfect home life. But it didn't work out that way. He played a lot of tricks on me and robbed me of my money. Then my first child, Sammy, was born with cerebral palsy. And my husband left me.

With Gladys gone from the Marvelettes and caught up in the troubles of her personal life, the prospects did not look good for the remaining members of the group, Katherine and Wanda. Wanda, the lead singer, finally elected to stay in Detroit when Motown moved to Los Angeles, thus severing the final link between the group and the company. Since then, the Marvelettes have reappeared in many guises, featuring, at the most, one original member in the line-up, and putting out various re-releases and compilations of their hits. There are also several bogus versions of the group as I found out when I arranged to interview some women billed as the Marvelettes in New York. As my conversation with their manager progressed, it slowly transpired that no one in the group had ... well, exactly been a *member* of the original Marvelettes ... but anyway, he assured me, his girls were really terrific. I felt quite churlish in politely refusing his offer to meet them.

The Marvelettes had shot to fame with their first disc and had also been a good live act; so why had Berry Gordy hung back in promoting them? In retrospect, it seems that Gordy had found the Marvelettes a little too rough and ready, a little too ordinary, to really push their career beyond that of a touring group with the occasional chart hit. Perhaps, like Gladys, Gordy could not quite picture the Marvelettes cooing and simpering their way through songs like 'Baby Love'. The Marvelettes had an earthy, mature way of singing which, mixed with their youthful romanticism, gave the group a unique appeal. Yet although the group's appeal has proved more real and durable than that of many of their contemporaries, one can see why for the upwardly mobile Berry Gordy in the sixties, the Marvelettes were not quite 'uptown' enough. The mixture was still not quite right: there was too much Detroit R&B in there, and not enough New York pop.

For Gladys, a single woman today living in Los Angeles and continuing to care for her handicapped son as well as her other children, it is still unclear just why Motown has always been, as she sees it, so loath to recognize the Marvelettes as part of the company's history; she says:

They never really respected us. Berry Gordy lost the Marvelettes' name in a gambling game once, that's how much he cared about us. We were just nothing to them. Even today, they don't invite us to perform when they have a get-together at Motown. I really don't know why. We're still good, we could still easily get up there and sing. Wanda calls me and asks, 'What did we do wrong? I don't understand.' It hurts her, it tears her up inside. It's been close to killing her in the past. But it doesn't bother me. You see, I wouldn't take my life for them, or anybody else. They ain't worth it. So I just say, 'Hey Wanda, you know what? I have something else to do that day anyway.'

*   *   *

If the Marvelettes were overlooked at Motown in favour of the Supremes, the same could have been said of the Velvelettes, another of Motown's early girl groups, now best remembered for their two hits, 'Needle in a Haystack' and 'He Was Really Saying Something'. Carolyn Gill of the Velvelettes has managed to keep the group going over the years, and she performs with four of the original five members around their home towns of Kalamazoo and Flint, Michigan. She told me:

> The Velvelettes got involved with Motown after being discovered by Robert Bullock, Berry Gordy's nephew, at Western Michigan University where the group was performing for a fraternity dance. Robert and two Velvelettes, Milly Gill and Bertha Barbee, were students there at the time. Robert encouraged us to make the trip to Detroit, 135 miles away, to audition for Motown records, a fairly new company that was owned by Berry Gordy. My parents drove us there; normally it would have taken around three hours to drive, but we ran into a snowstorm!

The group did finally make it to Detroit, however, and managed to impress Berry Gordy with their performance. Besides Carolyn, Milly and Bertha, the group members included Betty Kelley, who later left to join Martha Reeves' Vandellas, and Bertha's sister Norma. The Velvelettes' first release, 'There He Goes', received little attention, but the next, 'Needle in a Haystack', reached number forty-five on the charts. Carolyn remembers:

> The group did not like the tune at first because it just sounded kind of corny to us. Our writer and producer Norman Whitfield had great confidence in us though and his perception that it would be a hit was accurate. I think that the proverbial message was well received more than anything. Even today 'Needle in a Haystack' would be a hit, especially when you look at the state of marriages and relationships in America and how it directly relates to the message of the song.

The lyrics of 'Needle in a Haystack' made everybody sit up and take notice. If the girl groups had been seen as naive, coy and over-romantic, this song set the record straight with some downhome advice that might have come from the mouth of the most hardened feminist:

I once believed all fellers were nice
but girls listen to me and take my advice
you better get yourself on the right track

cos finding a good man is like finding a
needle in a haystack

Girls, those fellers are sly, slick and shy
so don't you ever let them catch you looking starry-eyed
they'll tell you that their love is true
then they'll walk right over you
now girls, you should know these things right off the back
cos finding a good man is like finding a
needle in a haystack

But the Velvelettes were not altogether immune to the attractions of the opposite sex as it turned out. Their next hit, 'He Was Really Sayin' Something', which this time only reached the top seventy, told this story:

I was walking down the street
when this boy started following me
though I ignored everything he'd say
he moved me in every way
with his collar unbuttoned, by my side he was struttin'
girls, he was really sayin' something

He flirted every step of the way
I could feel every word he'd say
my resistance was getting low
and my feelings started to show
my heart started thumping, blood pressure jumping
girls, he was really sayin' something

As he walked me to my door
I agreed to see him once more
ladylike it may not be
but he moved me tremendously
although he was bold, my heart he stole
hey, he was really sayin' something

Whether warning their girlfriends about male ploys or telling the story of their latest romance, the Velvelettes displayed a spirited, independent attitude in their songs that was very much the style of the sassy teenager rather than the ladylike young woman. Carolyn comments:

The song had a cute story and melody. Norman Whitfield was more excited about it than anyone else, but we did have fun working on this tune, because the ages we were at the time related to the message of the song. And since we were assigned to Whitfield we did not have to compete with the Supremes and the Vandellas for our songs. But as time went on we did have to compete for some of the more commercial tunes other producers and writers were working on. Naturally the better sounding tunes were given to the artists with greater seniority at Motown.

Although the Velvelettes released three more singles, after 'He Was Really Sayin' Something' their hitmaking days were over. Carolyn puts the problem down partly to Motown's management policy:

I do feel that the songs were promoted more than the groups initially. Motown was product oriented and primarily interested in results rather than the vehicle used to accomplish the results. It wasn't until the public became curious about the artist, and colour was no longer an issue, that Motown got behind the artists themselves. They started pushing the artist more once the colour barriers were broken down as a result of young America demanding to see the actual artists perform the tunes.

But she also admits:

The Velvelettes: a latter-day line-up with lead singer Carolyn at centre. Motown never released their album.

The Velvelettes were not as hungry for stardom as the other girl groups. We came from reasonably secure backgrounds and our parents were considered middle-class blacks. So our appetite to be 'stars' and make a lot of money was not as intense as other girl groups at Motown.

Eventually, the Velvelettes left Motown after their contract expired. Not long afterwards, the company moved its headquarters from Detroit to Los Angeles. Although the girls were no longer part of Motown, they like many others in the city's black community felt the loss sharply:

> Motown's departure from Detroit was quite devastating as a matter of fact. We felt as if a limb had been severed from our bodies. Motown was such an integral part of Detroit and Michigan, and it just seemed unfair that they should abandon Detroit for the West Coast. With the recent sale of Motown to MCA that leaves yet another bad taste in our mouths. After all, Motown was the first black-owned music business that received national recognition.

Despite the disappointments over the years, however, Carolyn concludes on an optimistic note:

> Like many artists of the sixties and the Motown reign, the Velvelettes are now taking advantage of the current trend towards nostalgia; it is something we can comfortably relate to. Because however unfortunate it may seem, we are still proud and excited about being a part of the sixties' musical rage. And we're especially proud of having been a part of Motown during that era.

Much more successful than the Velvelettes were another of Motown's girl groups, Martha and the Vandellas. If Carolyn Gill and her friends had lacked the requisite hunger for stardom, there was no shortage of it where Martha Reeves, a secretary working in the company's A&R department, was concerned. Martha had been singing since her childhood; she had learned religious music at her father's methodist church and had received some classical training at her school, Northeastern High. Then, having been scorned by her brothers who would not let her sing with them, she had formed her own girl vocal group, the Del-Phis, with friends Annette Sterling, Rosalind Ashford and Gloria Williams. Martha had initially approached Motown for an audition, but was offered a secretarial job instead; so she took it, deciding to bide her time and wait for her break. To begin with, she did not get it; the Del-Phis were occasionally able to help out at Motown by doing handclaps or singing background for sessions, but the company already had its own regular back-up singers, the Andantes; thus Martha's activities with the Del-Phis became largely restricted to weekend gigs.

Despite these constraints, the Del-Phis managed to sign to a small record label, Check-Mate, a subsidiary of Chess; and they even released an unsuccessful single there. Then the group began to get more work at Motown, singing back-up for Marvin Gaye. Finally, the break came; Mary Wells failed to turn up for a recording session and so the Del-Phis took her place, with Gloria Williams singing lead. The resulting track was released as by the Vells, because the Del-Phis were still under contract to Chess, but it failed to make an impression on the charts, and Gloria quit the group. Martha took her place, and it was not long before she got a chance to record as lead. The girls were now called the Vandellas, a name that Martha concocted from various sources – from Van Dyke Street where her grandma lived, from one of her favourite singers Della Reese whom she had seen perform at the New Liberty Baptist church, and from the group's original name the Del-Phis. The new Vandellas were teamed with producers Eddie and Brian Holland and after another single, 'I'll Have To Let Him Go', they finally hit the charts in 1963 with 'Come and Get These Memories'.

From then on Martha and the Vandellas launched a spate of singles that earned them a reputation as the most soulful of Motown's girl groups. Martha's gospel-influenced vocals had a fiery, exuberant quality that was well matched with the music produced for her by the team of the Holland brothers and Lamont Dozier: biting horns and hot, churchy tambourines, the whole lot tautly anchored down to Motown's rock-solid bass and drum sound.

In July 1963, the next single 'Heat Wave' became a smash, reaching number four on the charts. It was closely followed by a soundalike release, 'Quicksand', which did surprisingly well on the back of the initial single. In 1964 the international million-seller 'Dancing in the Street' hit number one – although this time the similar sounding follow-up 'Wild One' did not do quite so well; and then came 'Nowhere to Run' in 1965 and 'I'm Ready for Love' in 1966, both of them continuing in the powerful Reeves tradition.

But despite Martha's success, there were major problems for her at Motown. By 1964, Martha's group was having huge hits, but for no apparent reason, Berry Gordy was paying far more attention to another girl group at Motown, the Supremes, known in the company at that time as the 'no-hit Supremes' because after several highly publicized releases they had seen no chart success at all. Martha was understandably jealous of her rivals. Her group seemed so much stronger than theirs, as her hits had proved. Moreover, the public loved to see the Vandellas live; they were far more funky than all the other girl groups put together, let alone the Supremes, both in their stage presence and in their sound. Where the other girls executed prim dance movements on stage, Martha and her crew injected a bit of life into those still very constrained dance routines and really got down, exhorting the crowd to party. They were hardly wild – Motown with its charm classes would never have permitted any really raunchy behaviour from its young ladies – but there was a contained sexuality in Martha's way of singing that could not be ignored.

The Vandellas' songs were much more adult than those of the average

The girl group grows up: the fiercely independent spirit of Martha Reeves (centre) was reflected in the gritty, soulful quality of the Vandellas' recordings.

girl group and they had an intense, obsessive quality that sometimes made them a little too close to lowdown R&B for comfort. In 'Nowhere to Run', for instance, Martha sang boldly:

How can I fight a love that shouldn't be
When it's so deep, so deep, deep inside of me?
Nowhere to run baby, nowhere to hide . . .

This was not the excitement of teenage romance, nor even the knowing narrative of the sophisticated, independent young woman; it was the more primitive cry of a human being lost and hurt and in the grip of a sexual obsession. And that condition was the last thing Berry Gordy wanted his girls at Motown to be singing about.

Martha's victory with 'Dancing In the Street' in 1964 coincided with her moral defeat as the Supremes began their staggering run of chart hits that same year and Gordy ceased to take any real interest in the Vandellas. Soon, Martha was steadfastly holding the fort as a succession of Vandellas came and went. There were more hits, 'I'm Ready for Love' in 1966 and the Supremes'-styled 'Jimmy Mack' in 1967. Then, following Diana Ross's example in the Supremes, Martha changed the group's name to Martha Reeves and the Vandellas. The new-look Vandellas had two fairly successful releases, 'Love Bug Leave My Heart Alone' and 'Honey Chile', before Martha finally packed her bags and left Motown in 1972. A series of record deals followed, but to no avail; and today, with her voice reputedly sounding better than ever, Martha Reeves is a stalwart on the oldies' circuit, along with the Chantels, the Shirelles, the Crystals, the Angels, Reparata and the Delrons, Mary Wells and all the rest of them.

Undoubtedly, Martha Reeves's career was hampered by the fact that she did not fit into the sometimes rather insipid mould expected of girl groups in the sixties. At the same time, however, the powerful, aggressive nature that came through so clearly in Martha's voice could also make life difficult for her offstage, and some found her a temperamental person to work with – in particular, there were big personality clashes with Berry Gordy and Diana Ross. Martha's reputation as rather unpredictable was borne out when I spoke to her; at first, she was adamant that she did not want to be interviewed for this book, but she then went on to talk in some detail about the Legendary Ladies bill that she had recently performed on with others like Mary Wells and the Crystals. She then described with some enthusiasm her many fundraising activities for education projects, for children's organizations and for Vietnam veterans. However, after a while she stopped abruptly and said angrily, 'You're getting your interview, aren't you?' Then she added curtly, 'I have done lots of interviews. I am not interested in interviews. My views have been misrepresented. I'm going to write my own book.' And that was the end of our conversation.

*   *   *

Despite all the criticism that Gordy was attracting at Motown for his championing of the Supremes, as it turned out his instinct for choosing the right artists and the right sound had never been sharper. The Supremes had started out as just another girl group who seemed destined like all the others to have a few hits if they were lucky and then drop out of the running. Yet of all Motown's acts, which included all-time greats like Marvin Gaye, Stevie Wonder, Smokey Robinson and the Miracles, and the Temptations, the Supremes eventually became the most successful. Between 1964 and 1969 they had a staggering run of twelve number one hits in the US, the only vocal group to come anywhere near the Beatles' total of eighteen in the same period. Far from dying out, the girl-group sound in the late sixties achieved greater popularity than ever before; the Supremes, along with the Beatles and the Stones, became one of the top few supergroups of the sixties and seventies. Moreover, the Supremes were not just a sound, as all too many girl groups had been before; they were not simply nameless voices used to make real a producer's dream, but became stars in their own right – or, at least, one of them did.

Florence Ballard, Mary Wilson and Diane Ross – who later changed her name to the more middle-class 'Diana' – were three excitable teenage girls from Detroit whose prospects may have been low but whose aspirations were high. They were part of the first generation to grow up in the new housing projects that were being built in the fifties to accommodate families from slum areas. In the days before US housing policy helped turn the projects into ghettos by declaring a limit on residents' earnings, thereby forcing any reasonably successful well-to-do family out of the community, the projects seemed a brave new world to the children of black workers who had moved from the South to the Motor City. Mary Wilson, in her autobiography *Dreamgirl*, remembers:

> Moving to the Brewster projects in 1956 was a turning point in my life. It was a new complex of government-owned apartment buildings and older row houses on the east side of Detroit, within walking distance of downtown. There were about eight fourteen-storey buildings grouped all together, each surrounded by patches of grass, and a brightly painted playground.
>
> Many people would have considered a move into the projects to be a step down ... I felt like I'd just moved into a Park Avenue skyscraper.

In Camden, New Jersey, another young girl was moving into a project building with her family. Cindy Birdsong, who later joined the Supremes, shared the same feeling of hope at going up in the world as the Detroit girls did, as she told me when I met her in the offices of her London record company, Hi Hat:

> We were one of the first families to move into the new project, which was low-income housing, but it was very nice in those days. Not like today, when they call the projects the ghettos. We weren't poor, at least I never looked at it that way. I think I had what every other kid had, even though I came from a large family; I'm the oldest of eight. There were times when I had to do without, but that was because I was the oldest and I never looked at it negatively. If the baby in the family needed something more than me, it seemed fair to give it to the baby. Looking back, I think I had a glorious childhood. I suppose we weren't rich, but we seemed to have everything that mattered.

Besides being like Park Avenue skyscrapers, the project buildings had other advantages: there were acres of corridor and walkway where teenagers could hang out and echoing stairwells with perfect acoustics for singing vocal harmony, the teen craze of the day. Detroit was the home of a harsh, bluesy R&B played by the likes of John Lee Hooker; now, black teenagers were rejecting this downhome style and singing doo wop. This new generation in Detroit were looking for a way up, out of the car factories that their parents had come north to work in and which seemed to be the only employment on offer to them in the future. And not only the young men, but also the young women wanted new alternatives.

For most girls, music was not an obvious choice; there were no very famous black female pop idols to emulate. Mary Wilson's favourite singers of the day were white stars like the McGuire Sisters, Doris Day and Patti Page, idols who could hardly give encouragement to a young black girl hoping to find success in the world of entertainment. Cindy Birdsong remembers her own early ambitions:

> I didn't really want to sing. I wanted to be in showbusiness as an actress. I was studying voice, because I felt that if you were black and you wanted to make it as an actress you had to be multi-talented. Lena Horne and Dorothy Dandridge were the only screen idols that the black girl had to emulate. You knew that they had to sing, dance and do ten times as much and be ten times as pretty as the average white starlet.
>
> My dad used to take me to the movies a lot. Mostly, he took me to westerns, but we also saw Doris Day's movies, and I was a big fan of Doris Day's. For a long time I wanted to be Doris Day! You see, we didn't have the black stars on film to idolize or look up to.

Once Cindy realized the impossibility of becoming Doris Day, however, she turned to something more realistic and joined her first group, the Bluebelles:

It just happened to be the opportunity that arose first. The door opened there and I figured once I get a foot in the door, I can be an actress, so I auditioned and won the part as a singer. I never knew that once I got into the Bluebelles and the Supremes we'd make such a huge career. I thought we'd have a few years out there like most people and then I could get on with my acting.

Like Cindy Birdsong and Mary Wells, who had both set their sights high, Florence Ballard, Mary Wilson and Diana Ross wanted more than just a short career in a fly-by-night girl group. Florence and Mary had met at a talent show where Mary had brought the house down by miming to Frankie Lymon's 'I'm Not a Juvenile Delinquent' – like Frankie, doing her best to create an impression to the contrary – and Florence had impressed the audience with a beautiful rendition of 'Ave Maria'. When Florence was approached by the manager of a local doo-wop group, the Primes, to form a 'sister group', she thought of Mary; another local girl, Diana Ross (then known as Diane), was also roped in, together with Betty McGlowan, a girlfriend of one of the Primes. Under the management of Milton Jenkins, a sharp-dressing entrepreneur, the Primettes as they now called themselves performed at record hops, covering popular hit tunes of the day. One of their showstoppers was the Ray Charles classic, 'Night Time Is the Right Time', on which Flo took Ray Charles's 'call' part while the rest of the group took the 'response' part of the Racletts. There was no doubt that Florence had the best voice in the group; but Mary too was a pleasant singer, while Diane had a thin, nasal vocal style that was unusual but not to everyone's taste.

The Primettes decided to approach Motown through Smokey Robinson who had once been a neighbour of Diana's, and were able to secure an audition with the Miracles. Unfortunately, the only outcome of this was that Smokey stole the girls' guitarist away from them and took him off on tour with his own group. But the girls finally did get to see the boss, Berry Gordy, who at first did not seem over-impressed; he told them to come back when they had finished school. Undeterred, the Primettes decided to meet each day after school and hang out at Motown until something happened. Part of the attraction of spending time there was in meeting the local stars, particularly their hearthrobs like Smokey and Marvin Gaye. So, every day, they took up their position on the bench in the company's reception office and were more or less ignored. They pestered anybody and everybody to record them, until eventually a producer decided to help them out. He arranged bookings for the group and finally recorded them, releasing a single on the LuPine label; but 'Tears of Sorrow', a melodramatic number in classic girl doo-wop mode, got nowhere, partly because the label's distribution company was being investigated for payola. By this time, Betty had left to get married; she was replaced by Barbara Martin, who stayed with the group until 1961, when she became pregnant and also left.

Gordy continued to refuse to sign the Primettes, although they did get a little work at Motown. More often than not all the girls had to do was to perform handclaps, but even this was a start. The Primettes were in growing demand at gigs around town, but still there seemed no sign of interest from Motown. Then, in January 1961, Gordy relented and signed the group, with the proviso that they change their name. It was Florence who came up with the idea of the Supremes, which Gordy accepted; it sounded more sophisticated and adult than the cutesy, childish names favoured by so many of the girls' contemporaries.

Mary Wilson recounts in *Dreamgirl* that under the contract Motown offered the Supremes, no advance and no salaries were to be paid; all expenses were to be recouped from royalties; and Motown proposed that the artists would get a three-per-cent royalty, divided by four for each member, on a percentage only of the retail price of each record sold. Today Mary Wilson claims that, over the years, the provisions in her contract with Motown hardly changed and that she was not allowed full access to her accounts; also that, even after the Supremes' first million-selling hit, the girls were told that they had not actually made any money: expenses had outweighed profits.

But in 1961, none of the group members was bothered about the small print; they had got a deal with Motown, and that was all that mattered. The Supremes were impressed with the trappings of wealth they saw around them at Motown: girls like the Marvelettes were being supplied with diamond rings, the men with Cadillacs, and everybody with champagne. The Supremes wanted the same treatment; but first, they had to get a hit.

The Supremes' first release on the Tamla label was 'I Want A Guy', an unremarkable song in typically cutesy girl-group style which was quickly forgotten. The group's next release, however, was felt by all at Motown to have the makings of a hit – all, that is, except Berry Gordy. 'Buttered Popcorn', on which Florence took the lead, was a funky dance track with plenty of gospel-styled 'whoa whoas' and a hot R&B feel; Mary Wilson describes it as 'the most raucous thing we ever released'. Yet despite the fact that Gordy had written the song, together with the sales manager at Motown, Barney Ales, he seemed unwilling to put a lot of effort into publicizing the Supremes' record once it was released. At the time, this seemed mystifying, especially as Gordy did not seem clear about exactly what he did want from the girls. For the next two years, despite the fact that Gordy assigned all the best talents at Motown to write and produce for the Supremes, the group suffered the indignity of being the company's most spectacular flop, while the Marvelettes and Martha and the Vandellas stormed up the charts.

The Supremes were recording a series of tracks that barely scraped into the hot hundred; only one, 'When the Lovelight Starts Shining Through His Eyes' reached the top forty, but right after this, the group were back down into the nineties again. Only when the Supremes recorded a track called 'Where Did Our Love Go?', written and produced by Brian and Eddie Holland and Lamont Dozier, did the unique sound Gordy had obviously been waiting and looking for begin to materialize.

At last the big break for the 'no-hit' Supremes.

Initially, the Supremes were less than thrilled with the material presented to them by their new producers. Mary in particular found the melody and lyrics of the first two songs, 'Where Did Our Love Go?' and 'Baby Love', simplistic and childish. Certainly, the Holland-Dozier-Holland team were no Smokey Robinsons, and one can hardly blame Mary for failing to see the potential of lines like 'Ooh, ooh baby love, my baby love, ooh ooh I need your love.' Mary and Florence were also taken aback to find that only Diana was to sing lead on the new tracks. Previously, Diana and Florence, who had such different voices, had alternated the leads depending on the song; Mary had usually sung the ballads. Not only this, but the arrangements and production on the songs were such that Diana's voice came to dominate the whole sound; the three-part harmonies were gone, and in their place was Diana's high lead voice with a couple of back-up vocalists chirruping almost inaudible 'oohs' and 'aahs' in the background.

Cindy Birdsong comments:

Florence had a very strong gospel voice and she was the original lead singer. When the Supremes came to Motown, it was Flo's group, she had formed and named it. It was Berry's choice to put Diana as lead. I think Diana's voice appealed to Berry because it had a young, crisp, commercial sound; maybe Flo's voice was a little too strong for that time. I don't think Berry chose Diana because he particularly liked her more than the other girls. They were just highschool kids to him.

But, as Carolyn Gill points out, this situation did not last long:

Over a period of time, favouritism surfaced, which I believe had something to do with the romantic link between Berry Gordy and Diana Ross. It was common knowledge at Motown that there was romantic interest between them. But admittedly, Diana did have a unique vocal quality that proved to be quite commercial.

No wonder Mary and Florence felt that the balance of the Supremes was changing, and not to their advantage.

Their doubts were temporarily dispelled, however, with the release of 'Where Did Our Love Go?'. Mary Wilson recounts in *Dreamgirl* that the Supremes were on tour with Dick Clark when the record hit. They were not a major draw, to say the least, and were halfheartedly received while other more famous acts attracted all the attention. Yet, some way into the tour, they suddenly found that their number 'Where Did Our Love Go?' inexplicably met with rapturous applause. The reason, as they later found out, was that the single, released while they were out on tour, had shot to the number one position in the charts.

'The girls' had finally made it, and any reservations as to how that had come about were quietly cast aside; from now on, the Holland-Dozier-Holland pop format with the Supremes was established as a winner. 'Where Did Our Love Go?' was followed by an extraordinary run of hits, all the more impressive because the rise of the Supremes coincided with the enormous success of the Beatles and other all-male British groups at that time in America. The year 1964 alone saw two more number ones from the Supremes; the once reviled 'Baby Love' hit the top, followed by 'Come See About Me'. After that, the hits came thick and fast: there were three number ones the next year, and four the year after.

It was quite clear after 'Where Did Our Love Go?' that the Supremes were in another league altogether from the girl groups of the chitlin' circuit or Dick Clark's tours with their one-off hits on dodgy record labels. Yet not until the group's return from a British tour towards the end of 1964 did the mainstream American TV shows, teen magazines and entertainment establishment begin to take notice of them as an entity, rather than as voices on a record. Such was the racism of American society that it took the Supremes' enormous success abroad, where racial lines were drawn differently, to convince the Americans that these girls could rank alongside the Andrews Sisters as safe, Ed Sullivan-type entertainment, suitable for family viewing on a Sunday night.

The Supremes' English tours in 1964, 1965 and 1967 also established the girls as honorary members of the swinging British scene. They were pictured in the press posing beside London buses, eating fish and chips, wearing bowler hats, shopping for mini skirts, and generally having a wild time in the capital. Diana took to all this like a duck to water; her thin figure was the height of fashion and she looked terrific in every outfit she wore; Mary too seemed at home in short plastic dresses and big earrings, and became known as 'the sexy one' – like the Beatles, the Supremes now had fans who picked their favourites to fall in love with. Only Florence – 'the quiet one' – sometimes seemed out of place in all this. Originally considered to be the best-looking of the group, in the days when they were the Primettes, she was the opposite of the dolly bird. Her figure, which had been admired in

Detroit as 'stacked', was not suited to the British fashion with its short fringed tops and tight little PVC skirts in purple and sunshine yellow.

If Florence had been a fifties' beauty, Diana epitomized the look of the sixties. And although Florence did her best to wear her groovy clothes with a smile, she could not emulate Diana's upbeat persona, which had by now become that of the swinging sixties' chick. On top of everything else, both she and Mary were completely overshadowed by Diana's magnetic physical presence, on stage and off: with her huge eyes, her nodding head and her teeth bared in a macabre facial grimace somewhere between a smile and a warning, Diana was a fascinating performer, and whether or not people found her divinely beautiful, she was the one that everybody watched.

But although the Supremes were being hailed in England as the darlings of the sixties' pop revolution, they were still very much products of Motown's charm school, an archaic institution modelled on those of the Hollywood studios. The girls had been taught how to get into and out of cars, how to carry their handbags, how to walk, how to stand, how to dance, how to smile – and all of these refinements, mostly inculcated by veterans of the showbiz world, were becoming decidedly dated by 1964. The Supremes in their early days had always been careful to wear matching shoes with their tasteful floral dresses; now, in their British incarnation, they veered more towards the socialite, deb style of their fans like the Duchess of Bedford than the more outré fashions paraded by the dolly birds. Cathy McGowan may have been ironing her hair to get that natural look, but the Supremes still clung to their wigs – particularly Diana, who continued to have a penchant for enormous bouffant hairstyles well after they had gone out of fashion. The Supremes' role was to be young and trendy, yet they were blacks in a white world and as such, were conscious of having to be on their best behaviour. And it was Diana who best carried off the starring role as the black Jackie Kennedy of the pop world.

On their return to the States, the Supremes began to move steadily towards the staid mainstream of showbiz entertainment as their success brought them bigger and more prestigious engagements. The contradictions between their role as hip young popsters in England and elegant, adult entertainers in the States began to emerge, and the British music press started to criticize the girls. Mary Wilson describes how in 1965, when the Supremes' tribute to the British Invasion, *A Bit of Liverpool*, and another album, *Country, Western and Pop*, had been released, the group was being accused of 'selling out'. By 1968, there was further reason to criticize the Supremes; now, pop groups were being expected to write serious, 'relevant' material, not perform dance routines to frivolous, frothy little numbers. The Supremes' image as well-groomed, sophisticated young ladies also began to be ridiculed in the pop world, which as Wilson recalls with some disgust, was now moving towards a macho rock ethic in which it was de rigueur for stars – male stars, that is – to be rude, drunk, stoned or incapable of speech on every public appearance as a gesture of defiance to the establishment that so busily publicized them. Moreover, there was an inverted racism abroad, particularly in Britain, which identified black music solely with the sound of an Aretha Franklin or an Otis Redding, both of whom had now been adopted by white fans as the acceptably rootsy, serious face of soul music.

By the Supremes' own standards, most of this criticism was rather unfair. Whilst they had done a better job than most of the girl groups in keeping up with the swinging Brits, they had never seen themselves as part of a pop subculture. That there should be a gap between pop and showbiz was incomprehensible to them. The whole ethos of Motown was upward mobility, its whole goal that of intruding on the hallowed white halls of the Copacabana and Las Vegas, and of competing on equal terms with white record companies in the music industry. Florence and Mary would certainly have been happier if they had had the opportunity to sing lead parts, and it was a pity that the strength and power of Florence's voice only resulted in her having to stand as much as seventeen feet away from the microphone during recording sessions, as Mary Wilson records in her book; but as far as appearing regularly on all the mainstream American TV shows, like the Ed Sullivan Show, The Tonight Show, and The Hollywood Palace, performing show-tune medleys and extravagant choreographed routines, the Supremes, far from being forced into a musical straitjacket, were in their element.

What the Supremes' British critics did not realize was that the group

Detroit glamour hits British TV screens as Florence, Mary and Diana appear on Thank Your Lucky Stars.

came out of a black teenage subculture, doo wop, which revelled in taking hackneyed songs that everybody knew – show tunes, pop novelties, hymns, spirituals – and customizing them. Once on the set of a TV show with a troupe of dancers and a whole orchestra behind them, instead of at a twenty-five cent houseparty, the Supremes naturally took advantage of the situation and pulled out all the stops.

However, the British music press continued to carp; they had failed entirely to notice the American doo-wop craze in the fifties and were convinced that all black music was blues, gospel or R&B. They were completely unaware that for many black teenagers, these forms were the music of their parents' generation. The last thing feisty girls like the Primettes had wanted was to spend their time in church singing gospel. Yet by 1968, they were being solemnly advised to do so by British music journalists. As Mary Wilson comments in *Dreamgirl*:

What was this church business? None of us had ever sung in church. This segment of the press completely disregarded the fact that our roots were in American music – everything from rock to show tunes – and always had been. We weren't recording standards because they were foisted upon us by Motown; we loved doing them and had since we were fourteen years old.

The British attitude led to some interesting cultural misunderstandings between the Supremes and their UK fans. For example, when Mary Wilson dated Hilton Valentine of the Animals whilst in Britain, he tried to impress her with his vast R&B collection. He was, as she records, astonished to find she hadn't heard of any of the black artists he played her. While Mary had been listening to Patti Page and the Contours in Detroit, Hilton had been busily learning John Lee Hooker songs in North Shields. No wonder that by the time they met, their musical tastes differed.

Despite the critics, the Supremes continued to provide an across-the-board appeal to pop and showbiz fans alike. The year 1968 saw the biggest triumph of their career: their first appearance at New York's Copacabana. This was also a gala occasion for Motown and marked the company's entry into the mainstream of showbusiness. The group began to put out albums with titles like *The Supremes Sing Rodgers and Hart* and even recorded – though did not release – a version of the Chordettes' 'Mr Sandman'; yet they also continued to sell contemporary pop singles in vast quantities, at a time when rock albums were beginning to dominate the market.

For girl fans, the Supremes began to take the place of the Beatles as idols. If girls had been able to identify with the Beatles, how much easier was it for them now to make the Supremes their role models, especially once the Beatles had abandoned the pop scene and entered their profound phase.

There was a period when almost every girl, black or white, saw something of her aspirations towards hip sophistication in the Supremes. Yet the group's extraordinary influence on young women, as evidenced by their enormous record sales to this section of the public, has been largely ignored. Admittedly, the sound and fury of Beatlemania initially overshadowed the Supremes' importance, but considering the group's immense popularity amongst women over more than a decade, it is surprising how little attention feminists have paid to them. For example, Barbara Ehrenreich et al., in *Remaking Love*, write, à propos of Janis Joplin: 'There were no other female singers during the sixties who reached her pinnacle of success.' Apart from three black women, that is, who notched up thirty hit singles during the sixties and seventies in comparison to Janis's solitary 'Me and Bobby McGee' in 1971.

Completely unnoticed, the Supremes were building up a mass following amongst young women, building on the legacy of the earlier girl groups and adding to it a more adult level of worldly sophistication. As well as the Supremes' image, their songs reflected the emotions of young women in the throes of real sexual relationships rather than those of passionate but inexperienced teenage girls. 'Stop! In the Name of Love' was a story of sexual infidelity; 'Back In My Arms Again' touched on the same theme, while 'I Hear A Symphony' reverted to a more romantic mood. 'You Can't Hurry Love' took a pragmatic view; the song harked back to the Shirelles' 'Mama Said' and was part of a tradition in which the singer remembers her mother's sound advice on matters romantic. The desperation apparent in 'You Can't Hurry Love', with Diana wailing 'How long must I wait, how much more can I take?' reached a crescendo in the Supremes' next release, 'You Keep Me Hanging On'. There was more than an element of masochism in the song, except at the point when Diana finally lost patience with her lover and yelled at him, 'Get out, get out of my life, and let me sleep at night!'

The Supremes' songs had developed from the sweet cooings on 'Baby Love' to the drama of 'You Keep Me Hanging On' but because of the group's frothy image and Diana's highly stylized way of singing, which seemed to combine high emotional intensity with total detachment, nobody much – except the record buyers – noticed. Despite their safe image, the Supremes had in their songs gone quite a way to charting the long journey towards female independence that was taking place in the sixties.

In 1967, the Supremes' direction changed somewhat. 'The Happening' recounted a girl-group romance using the 'wow, man' hippy vocabulary of altered perception, as the Shirelles and the Chiffons had done, and the Supremes were now cleverly kitted out in sequinned gowns patterned with psychedelic swirls. 'Reflections' continued in this mode, and in 1968 came the message songs, 'Love Child' and 'I'm Livin' in Shame'. Here, the group's songwriters had the sense to incorporate a specifically woman-orientated line into the message songs of social injustice that were appearing in the pop world at the time. 'Love Child' recounts the tale of a woman born poor and illegitimate who now tells her lover that she does not want to risk the same fate for any child of hers, and thus will not have sex with him. Although somewhat melodramatic, the song hit home to the thousands of women whose thoughts ran along these lines, whether or not their experience of poverty and illegitimacy was direct. For all its melodrama, 'Love Child' was a discussion of the dangers women were considering at a time when sexual favours were being expected of them as a matter of loyalty to the cause of social and sexual freedom. And the song's very emotionalism set it at the heart of the girl-group tradition; had it been more circumspect, it would have come over as an embarrassingly didactic piece of sloganeering, as other pop message songs sometimes did. The Supremes' next hit, 'I'm Livin' in Shame', was less successful, its very title being rather outmoded as a concept by 1969; and the song that marked the departure of Diana Ross from the group that year, 'Someday We'll Be Together' also smacked of false sentiment.

The Supremes may have overstepped the boundaries of good taste more than occasionally; they may have been over-commercial, as when they sponsored 'Supremes' White Bread', a move that few commentators could resist ridiculing; at times they may even have been absurd, as their appearance as three nuns in a TV episode of Tarzan bore out. Such was the Supremes' reputation as airheads that when they supported Democrat Hubert Humphrey's campaign, critics wondered if this was good or bad publicity for the candidate. But the fact was that their thousands of women fans, who were finding less and less to identify with in the rock world, didn't care. Throughout the late sixties and the seventies, it was groups like the Supremes and their female fans who kept the pop scene alive with commercial singles while the male fans were off listening to progressive rock albums.

At the peak of the Supremes' popularity, however, there were terrible problems within the group. In 1967, Cindy Birdsong replaced Florence Ballard permanently. Cindy recalls:

Initially there was a phone call – someone from Motown's office asked me to audition as a replacement for one of the Supremes. I didn't know who it was. I actually thought it was a joke. I knew them, and they were so popular at that time; they had left the chitlin' circuit I was still working on with the Bluebelles. It surprised me. But I got on a plane and went straight over to Berry Gordy's house. The Supremes were in a meeting in another room and I was waiting outside. Then Florence came walking through the living room in tears and that's what made me know it was her they wanted me to replace.

I think I was picked because people saw a likeness between me and Florence. People used to tell me, 'You look like that girl in the Supremes.' Sometimes I'd go to see the Supremes and I'd go backstage to say hello. Florence was always the one to welcome me first, she'd say, 'Hey girl, people are still telling me I look like you!' We were the same size dress, I think Florence was one inch taller than me, same size shoe, and we wore the same style of wigs. Florence was fairer skinned than me, but on stage our general look was the same. Once I got way back at a Supremes' gig and watched Florence, and I could see it. Her movements reminded me of myself.

Believe it or not, we were still friendly after I replaced her. She didn't blame me. I don't know if she blamed anybody really. A lot of fans felt bad; the ones who really loved Florence were mad at me. But even years after, Florence never mentioned anything about it to me. We were always friends. She never seemed to have any bitterness or animosity towards the group, but what was worse was that I felt she did have these feelings only she couldn't express them. There was just a deep sadness there that no one could penetrate. I think she turned it all in on herself.

Florence Ballard: tragically, her solo career never took off.

Ever since the early days, the tensions between Diana and Florence had been mounting. Florence could not bear the fact that Diana had stolen the limelight and was Gordy's favourite; she felt cheated out of her group. Diana constantly ran to Gordy to support her every whim, and she also had an ego to match her ambition, which often prompted her to elbow the others out of the spotlight, sometimes quite literally. Yet there was equally no doubt that Diana had a star quality that Florence could not match. Diana's particular type of insecurity led her to be annoyingly extrovert and to demand complete attention all the time, whereas Florence's made her shy and often miserable. Mary Wilson suggests that Florence's problems may have arisen as a result of her being raped when still a teenager; yet there were many other reasons besides the rape, not least her experiences with the Supremes, that caused Florence in late 1966 to begin drinking heavily. In a downward spiral, she was first sacked from the Supremes; then she blew her solo career; next, she lost all her money and became severely depressed. Cindy Birdsong describes how in the seventies, she and Mary Wilson attempted to revive Florence's failing fortunes:

Florence was really down. She was just staying home and looking after her kids. So we asked her to come to Los Angeles. We flew her over and had a big party around Mary's pool with a barbecue. We had made lots of plans for her, called lots of people, we were lining up stuff for her that was career-oriented. But she didn't really want any part of it. She put a good face on things as much as she could, because everyone was so happy to see her, but I knew she was very sad. After a few days she just said, 'I'm going home. I miss my kids.'

Some time after, news came that Florence, now on welfare, had reached the bottom of the spiral: she had died of a heart attack.

In a sense, Florence had had everything against her from the start. She had been in the wrong place at the wrong time. She was from a large family which, Mary Wilson suggests, clung more to the community and family values of the country than to the new upwardly mobile, individualist aspirations of more modern urban families like the Rosses. By the time her earthy, gospel style of singing had become popular with white fans as soul, Florence had been identified as a frivolous, glamorous Supreme and could not escape the image. In the end she seemed unsure of what she wanted herself; her two solo singles, 'It Doesn't Matter How I Say It' and 'Love Ain't Love' revealed a lack of direction and confidence in choosing her own material. But whatever the historical dynamics of Florence's personal life, her death was a dreadful tragedy, one that pointed up the underside of Motown's success. In the same decade that Florence died, Berry Gordy and Diana Ross conquered Hollywood, a far more socially respected world than that of the tacky pop industry. Diana became such a huge star in both the film and pop worlds that she was able to claim in a TV interview in the eighties, 'I am the American Dream.' Left behind, of course, was the American nightmare: Florence Ballard dead after years of failure on welfare; Detroit, the city abandoned by Motown, today an urban wasteland long known as 'murder capital of the USA'.

Shortly after Cindy Birdsong joined the Supremes, major changes began to take place in the group. In 1967, the Supremes became 'Diana Ross and the Supremes', as Cindy remembers:

First there was the name change. Then the situation behind the scenes changed too. Diana was treated differently from us, she was more the star, we were separated away from her. In the beginning, all of us shared a dressing room. But then Diana would be given the star dressing room, and we'd have a small one down the hall. I didn't mind it as much as Mary did; I just looked at it as a bit unfair, mostly to Mary. And at first I didn't blame Diana, but eventually I did hold it against her because I felt she could have changed things and she didn't. She was enjoying it.

Motown were trying to project Diana as the star, she had to be the spokeswoman for everything. We found it hard to change in mid stream; they had primed us to be a group and now we were just 'and the Supremes'.

At press interviews, we couldn't speak out. A lot of the time Mary and I weren't sure what to do with ourselves. 'Is Diana going to be in this picture alone? Or is it for all of us?' That kind of thing. It was very uncomfortable.

Diana grew more and more estranged from us. We even stopped recording together. If we were just in town for one day during a tour, Diana would do all the leads and then the studio group would do the back-up vocals when we'd left. And that really built up an alienation.

Diana Ross was a woman whose career overrode every other consideration in her life. This was a trait that most people found difficult to like in her, but Cindy Birdsong could not help admiring Diana's hard work and determination:

Diana is a big star because she's always given her career top priority. She worked hard. Not that we all didn't but Diana had this hundred-percent attitude of do or die. I honestly believe she could have lost someone she loved in death and gone on stage five minutes later. She has that in her, 'the show must go on' type of thing. She is a real performer who gives her body and soul when she's on stage. Whatever she has to give, she gives it. That's what made her a star.

We saw that quality in her when we worked with her. We all charged each other up. The electricity between us and the audience was so strong sometimes that people would cry and so would we. Before I got into showbiz I went to see Smokey Robinson one time. Smokey was singing 'ooh eeeh baby baby' and a couple of girls fainted. I couldn't believe it! But later I found they did it for us too. Because Diana did have something the public really wanted.

I never found her aloof. She had her on days and her off days like all of us. When you work that closely with two other women, you're bound to have clashes from time to time. But we all loved each other and we still do. Sisters bicker and fight but they still love each other. When we did seventeen one-nighters in a row for instance, all stuck in the same limousine hopping from city to city, we grew very close. We talked about things like girls talk and there was a real warmth and comradeship. But when we got into the glitter and walked under the spotlight, Diana became a different person.

By 1970, Diana was ready to leave the group altogether and launch herself on solo recording and an acting career. Unlike the majority of group singers who decide to go solo – particularly from Motown where similar career moves had proved disastrous – she was highly successful. And what-

The new-look Supremes: Jean Terrell, Mary Wilson and Linda Laurence: into the seventies, and still wondering which wig to wear.

ever her critics say, she has become a symbol for young women in the entertainment industry, not only because of her fame as a performer but because of her skill as a businesswoman. In the eighties, even Roxanne Shanté, a young black rapper from New York, as unladylike as they come and with no apparent aspirations to emulate the Ross glamour, acknowledges the supreme Supreme's influence by proclaiming on 'Have A Nice Day': 'Like Diana Ross, I'm the boss ... !'

Diana Ross's departure from the Supremes did not spell the end of the group by any means, and they continued to have hits for several years. Diana was replaced by Jean Terrell; far from producing inferior soundalikes to previous records, she, Mary Wilson and Cindy Birdsong made some of the best Supremes singles ever, including 'Up the Ladder to the Roof', a song of hope, upward mobility and love in a concrete jungle that called to

Although the line-up of the Supremes changed throughout the seventies, their trademark remained the same: big grins and glamorous gowns.

mind the optimism of Goffin and King's 'Up On the Roof' in the early sixties. 'Stoned Love', also released in 1970, was another Supremes' classic, followed up in 1971 and 1972 by 'Nathan Jones' and 'Floy Joy'. A series of changes in the group's line-up took place from then on, until the Supremes finally disbanded. However, their ability to survive Diana Ross's departure for so long, and to sound as good as ever during that time, reveals just how important the idea of the Supremes as a unit, as a group, was to its fans. Together, the Supremes had seen girl-group music through its teenage years into young adulthood; and when Diana Ross left to become a fully-fledged solo star, the appeal of the Supremes, 'the girls', still remained.

*   *   *

During the reign of the Supremes, the music industry had undergone a transformation. No longer was pop being produced by rickety independent companies or by small, backwater sections of giants like RCA doing their best to keep up with rock 'n' roll. A few small independents like Motown had got big; plenty had gone under; and the big record companies had finally got in on the act. By 1969, the big rock festivals like Monterey, Woodstock and Altamont had shown the large corporations how much money there was to be made out of 'progressive' music, and they were busily signing every rock band they could get their hands on. CBS even adopted the slogan, 'The Revolutionaries are on CBS'. The nature of the new music was such that the market had completely shifted from singles to albums, creating a yawning gap between 'commercial' pop and 'progressive' rock.

The rise of white rock overshadowed many other forms of popular music throughout the seventies. Black musicians, with a few notable exceptions like Jimi Hendrix and Sly Stone, were paid very little attention even though their records continued to sell. Nowhere were the consquences of white rock's cultural imperialism more devastating than for women involved in the music business either as fans or as artists. For the first time, women, particularly black women, were being pushed right out of the picture altogether. Those who were incontrovertibly there, like Diana Ross and the Supremes, became somehow invisible. Their music and their influence, not to mention their popularity amongst the record-buying public, were simply not taken seriously in the music press – not surprisingly, since their records were mainly bought by young women, who were now regarded in the same light as teenyboppers, as consumers of commercial pap. The few female performers who became part of the rock scene were white solo artists; those such as Janis Joplin and Grace Slick adopted a macho pose as hard-living types who had no trouble keeping up with the boys; or, alternatively, there were the fey girl folk singers with their long shiny hair and acoustic guitars.

Ironically, this dramatic excommunication of all but a few women from the centre of youth music came at time when the women's movement was beginning to be visible in the US as a crucial part of the political radicalism of 1968 and of the ensuing counterculture. Massive social advances for women in terms of sexual and economic independence were being made possible via increased access to employment, birth control and abortion. The public reappraisal of women's roles was at the heart of the sexual revolution that the rock scene purported to be part of. Yet there was no evidence within that part of the counterculture of an increased respect for women as independent social and sexual beings, nor any sign that women were being encouraged to take a creative role in it as artists. On the contrary, 'alternative' music was often characterized by an extreme and quite novel type of sexism, in which the electric guitar replaced the female as object of the male's desire, and in which women were encouraged to take part in this mass worship of the phallic symbol, not as musicians and performers themselves, but as admiring groupies.

This development was, over the years, indirectly encouraged by feminists themselves who, in rejecting the constraints women had had to suffer in the preceding decades, turned their back on the achievements that had been made by women operating within those constraints. This was never more true than in the case of female pop artists. The girl-group heroines of the fifties and sixties had shown extraordinary determination to overcome the obstacles set up for them in the music industry and achieve their career ambitions; contained within their songs were genuine expressions of sexual frustration and social aspiration; and they had created images of themselves as pop stars just as potent as those of the male groups. Yet all this was lost on the feminists of the sixties and seventies, who saw in the girl groups only a reflection of society's expectations of women: subservience to a male ideal of female sexuality, intellectual dependence, and a foolish romanticism that hid not the longing for real equality and love between men and women but a pernicious ideology of patriarchy. Of course, there had always been conservative elements in girl-group music, but any redeeming features that the girl-group tradition may have had, if only because of the singers' status qua female, were ignored.

Yet the blow delivered to the girl-group ethos by the white rock scene was not fatal. The tradition continued to flourish very healthily in defiance of its critics. Debarred from the world of 'progressive' music which for a long time only included single women artists if at all – another reflection of the isolated position in which women in the business now found themselves – throughout the seventies, girl groups blithely continued to make records. And female fans continued to buy them.

⑤ when will I see you again?

In 1971, a girl group called Honey Cone burst into the charts with 'Want Ads', hitting the number one spot and selling a million. The song was a lighthearted attack on errant men, but behind the catchy hookline, the lyric packed quite a punch. It told the story of a woman fed up with staying home while her man went out late; she complained that he was always 'playing cards or drinking at the bar' when she needed him, or worse still, cheating on her, coming home at all hours sporting the inevitable 'lipstick on his collar'. But instead of wallowing in misery, she had resolved to find herself a better model immediately, through the simple method of placing an eyecatching ad in the pages of the *Evening News*:

Wanted! Young man, single and free!
Experience in love preferred but will accept a young trainee
Gonna put it in the want ads, I need a love that's true,
Gonna put it in the want ads, my man and I are through

What made 'Want Ads' so different from most girl-group offerings was the pragmatic nature of its cheerful optimism. There was not an ounce of regret in the song, except perhaps for those wasted nights 'crying bitter tears'; nor, really, of disappointment over shattered romantic ideals. The tone of the song was almost triumphant; it reflected that moment in a woman's life when the role of lovelorn tragedy queen suddenly becomes too tedious and absurd to maintain any longer, that moment when she is able at last to dump Mr Wrong and get back down to the business of enjoying life and looking for somebody a bit more promising.

Like the situation it described, the song was a turning point in the romantic narrative that the girl groups had been presenting since the fifties. Honey Cone were the first amongst a spate of girl groups in the seventies

The 3°Degrees: sophisticated ambassadors of smooth Philly soul.

to combine the tough, hardheaded realism that rock had made it so fashionable for women to adopt with the pop girls' more familiar tradition of generous, romantic idealism. And in order to pull this off, Honey Cone returned to the gospel roots of the girl groups.

The lead singer of Honey Cone, Edna Wright, was the daughter of a minister; and her sister was none other than Darlene Love, Phil Spector's favourite pop diva. Like Darlene, Edna had a magnificent voice that combined a gospel intensity with a cool pop sensibility. She, too, had been a seasoned West Coast session singer whose professional training gave her an ability to touch on a very broad spectrum of styles; but with Edna, perhaps more than with Darlene, the gospel sound prevailed.

This was partly because pop music had changed; by the seventies, the rise of soul music as a commercial form had made Edna's strong gospel delivery, with all its power and intensity, acceptable in lightweight pop. But the difference between Darlene and Edna's vocal styles also had something to do with the changing image of girl groups. If the Supremes had been elegant, cool young ladies who had somehow always managed, in their upwardly mobile way, to hold reality at arm's length, Honey Cone were something more real: they were hip, adventurous young women who liked excitement and a touch of danger, but whose heads were firmly screwed on. Because of this new feminine ideal, which chimed with the contemporary notions of non-conventional, 'alternative' lifestyles that young women as well as men wanted to be a part of, Honey Cone needed to emphasize the gutsy, independent and mature side of the girl-group vocal tradition that came from gospel, rather than the sweet, rather detached style of singing that the Supremes had made so popular.

At the same time, there was more than a touch of the Supremes in Honey Cone's sound. The group's producers were in fact the Holland-Dozier-Holland team who had been behind the Supremes' blockbuster series of hits in the sixties. Eddie Holland remembers what his team were looking for when they left Motown after that period:

I had in mind that we had always enjoyed working with female artists at Motown. As a lyricist I noticed that women were more interesting to write for. Women have a broader sensitivity to emotions than men, I think. We were taught coming up that you don't cry; you take it on the chin. We couldn't say we were hurt if we were hurt; we could only deal with those subjects through writing for women. That's why we liked working with girl groups so much. It wasn't because they were easier to direct, in fact the women got away with more in the studio than the men; male groups like the Four Tops and Chairmen of the Board always took much better direction.

We were sure we wanted to go on working with women artists in our new company, and we also knew there was a market there. We knew it was women who bought all our records. Not just the Supremes' records but the ones by male groups like the Four Tops as well, because there again we had showed a sensitive side, and I think women like to see that side of men.

I knew I was able to write in a way that appealed to women. I spend a lot of time listening to women talking about their views, their problems and so on. I find it interesting. Most men don't.

Eddie Holland's reflections reveal another side to the admittedly fairly accurate stereotype of the male songwriter/producer coldly manipulating a bunch of naive female artists and girl fans to make money out of them. Looked at from a different perspective, it seems that the sexual politics of the day were such that in the music industry at least, only through women could men make public their private and shamefully human emotions. If male fans had occasionally huddled behind girl-group music for emotional warmth, treating it as a bit of a joke but secretly living all the ups and downs of its little romances, how much more might the male writers and producers behind the music have quietly revelled in the freedom to have their cake and eat it: to express their most vulnerable feelings publicly, while at the same time adopting the respectable pose of tough guys who were only in it for the money?

When Eddie saw Edna Wright perform, he knew he had found the person he was looking for:

In 1969 I saw Edna on TV with Carolyn Willis and Shellie Clark. I had a talent scout at the time who found out who she was; he told me she was Darlene Love's sister. I knew Darlene had a great voice, so we flew Edna over. And I was right. Edna's voice had a similar quality to Darlene's but it wasn't the same. What I liked was that Edna's voice had a mellow quality and an intensity at the same time.

We put the group together and named them after an ice cream that I had loved as a child. Honey Cone were not a new Supremes, though. Each artist is a new personality to us, and we wrote songs that would fit Edna's voice. The way she sang was sensitive and vulnerable ... and a little tough too.

For some time, however, the Holland-Dozier-Holland team were involved in a complicated lawsuit with their former employers which tied their hands as far as producing other acts was concerned. Honey Cone's early hits were therefore written and produced by others in the Holland-Dozier-Holland stable such as Greg Perry and General Johnson, who were also members of the group Chairmen of the Board. By the time Holland-Dozier-Holland themselves came to write for Edna she was in full flight, capable of wringing every ounce of feeling from songs such as 'Who's It Gonna Be' ('her or me'?) and 'How Does it Feel' ('You always said I was a habit, now let me see you break it'), ballads that had more in common with exhausting soul marathons like Shirley Brown's 'Woman to Woman' than with the Supremes' stylized pop soap operas.

Honey Cone's early output showed that they were part of a new direction in black pop. Towards the end of the sixties, Norman Whitfield, a producer at Motown, had managed to keep the Temptations abreast with the times by fusing the Motown sound with that of psychedelic rock, combining the hippie lingo of acid experience and social awareness in lyrics with the bubbling synths and wailing wah-wah guitars that were the musical language of progressive rock. In doing so, he had managed to create a credible world of the hip black trip which still maintained the thumping dance beat that the public had come to expect from Motown. Honey Cone, under the aegis of Holland-Dozier-Holland's new company, went one step further and came up with a music that expressed a more overt kind of feminism in its lyrics than there had previously been in pop girl groups. This plus a cartload of the musical hooks that H-D-H were so famous for created the impression

Holland-Dozier-Holland's songs for the Honey Cone (left to right: Shellie Clark, Carolyn Willis and Edna Wright) expressed a new spirit of feisty independence for women in the seventies.

of sassy independence and outright joie de vivre from a new generation of women who had left the restraint of the Supremes somewhere along the road behind them.

'While You're Out Looking for Sugar' was Honey Cone's first release in 1969. It was a big hit in the black charts, and had more than a touch of the blueswoman about it in its lyrics. This was the angry blues of a Julia Lee, a Ruth Brown or an Etta James, and its message was rammed home by an upbeat rhythm and blaring horns:

> *You think without your love I can't exist*
> *Don't think for a minute that cos I'm through*
> *That don't nobody want me but you.*
> *While you're out looking for sugar,*
> *somebody's gonna take your honey and be gone*

The theme of the strong woman asserting her rights and proclaiming her independence was to become a staple of Honey Cone's repertoire. After the group's huge national hit, 'Want Ads' in 1971, came 'Stick Up' in which Edna accuses her man of being a thief, a highway robber; he has stolen her heart and committed a felony, not to say a grand larceny. On top of that, she's being emotionally blackmailed; the man is the father of her child and she's got to 'follow him down the aisle'. The next pop hit, in 1972, was 'One Monkey Don't Stop No Show', a big brassy dance track in which our heroine advises, 'If you don't want to be my leading man, get out of my life and let me live again.' 'Don't Count Your Chickens (Before They Hatch)' was another stern warning; but finally, Edna dropped the metaphors and the threats about other guys altogether and got down to some straight talking in one of the group's best ever releases which, undeservedly, flopped. This was 'The Day I Found Myself', which despite what one might think of its title in the new-age eighties, was nothing to do with colour therapy and meditation. It began: 'The day I lost you, that's the day I found myself' and went on:

> *I was in love, but so unhappy*
> *So many nights I was in the cold*
> *When you left you opened up the door*
> *to a world I'd never seen before*

The song ended on a highly cheerful note: 'I'm so glad you're gone,' coos Edna, 'cos you made me strong.' With its lilting, lolloping beat and calm, sweet delivery, 'The Day I Found Myself' is reminiscent of early girl groups like the Shirelles; only this time, the sweetness is not that of innocent youth, but of contented maturity, of bad times remembered from a vantage point of a hard-won emotional security.

137

If 'The Day I Found Myself' was a source of delight and comfort to any woman who had sent a no-good man packing, 'Are You Man Enough, Are You Strong Enough?' got right down to business. Here, Edna took the part of a woman advising a male friend on what to do about a complicated domestic situation. The man has just found out that the child he's been raising is not his own; as if this weren't enough, it then transpires that his woman has upped and off, and he's been left holding the baby. The singer tells him: 'Although he's not your own you must give him all your love and a happy home'; she acknowledges 'You're trapped between a shattered ego and a child that loves you so', but there's no doubt in her mind where his responsibilities lie, and she asks him over and over, 'Are you man enough, are you strong enough, can you take the strain, can you bear the pain?' This was a real case of turning the tables on traditional male machismo and introducing men to the harsh realities of single parenthood usually shouldered by women, but it also expressed sympathy for a friend caught in a 'bad situation'. 'Are You Man Enough?' made the Supremes' 'Love Child' sound coy; for the Supremes' polite, rather roundabout attempt to ask a lover to keep his hands off, it substituted a straightforward piece of feminist social morality.

'Are You Man Enough?' was part of a growing confidence amongst women, and amongst black women in particular, to explore and express their own world for each other in the pop idiom. Now the problems, anxieties and doubts not just of female adolescent sexuality but of adult life were being aired. Of course, there had always been a long and illustrious tradition of women singers doing this in the blues, R&B and gospel; Aretha Franklin's soul was also part of this line and was, moreover, by the late sixties, in the process of 'crossing over' to the mainstream. But none of these singers could be described as pop. Honey Cone were pop incarnate, and yet they drew on that old blues tradition, creating a new woman in the process: young, excitable, frivolous, maybe . . . but with her priorities firmly intact when it came to asserting her independence and making her demands clear to men.

Not only did Honey Cone pursue a hot feminist line, they also tackled a few other issues while they were about it. 'Sunday Morning People' was a blistering attack on the hypocrisy of bourgeois churchgoers, in true '68 style: 'Sunday morning people,' hollered Edna, 'Practise what you preach! You can't go to church on Sunday and hate your neighbour all week!' The whole track was busting with gospel fervour, with an impressive Aretha-styled vocal, a testifying chorus and churchy tambourines. 'When Will It End?' was an extremely groovy number with lyrics about 'chaos and confusion', keeping one's mind free 'in a world of insa-ni-ty' and so on, over a scorching psychedelic funk bass; the track also featured a far-out moog synth intro and ended in a welter of Doctor-Who type bubble noises. 'Deaf, Blind, Paralysed' was along the same lines, but without such a heavy-duty bass riff. It was more about politics than partying; 'the world is lit, the fuse is burning' warns Edna; for 'too long, we had an old song'. She tells us we're 'strangled by a system that denies a decent living', and we 'feel the need for doing something NOW'. Eat your heart out, Bob Dylan.

Naturally, all this went right over the heads of the rock establishment, who, if they noticed girls like Honey Cone at all, saw in them a reflection of old-fashioned, 'straight' morality and commercial pop values. The fact that Edna at one stage sported a curly blonde wig and the whole group tended to beam happily in their promo shots instead of adopting a faraway look couldn't have helped. And if the male rock critics had investigated these poor, duped sex objects of the crass pop world a little further, they would probably have overlooked the girls' obvious statements of female independence and seen only their more traditionally feminine side. 'Girls It Ain't Easy', for example, which hit the R&B charts in 1969, before 'Want Ads' made the group successful, was a classic call to women to extend sympathy and understanding to their menfolk, even if the men did seem 'ungrateful' and 'unfaithful'. In fact, the song was one of comfort and encouragement to all women caught up in the usual round of domestic and emotional hardship, rather than a confirmation of a woman's subservient role. It also expressed a solidarity between women and men which transcended the daily routine of domestic battles; this was of particular resonance to black people living in a racist society, and of course came straight out of the blues. But such subtleties of race and gender were not a part of white radical politics at the time. Moreover, although 'serious' black women singers would have been accorded a place by radical music critics, such were the entrenched segregations in the music of the early seventies – not only between rock and pop, but between white and black forms of these and other traditions – that groups like Honey Cone had virtually no chance of sustaining a credible profile in any field for long. Once Honey Cone had established themselves on the soul charts, they moved over to the pop charts with 'Want Ads' and several follow-ups; and that was it – there was nowhere else for them to go. Their final release with Holland-Dozier-Holland in 1973, 'If I Can't Fly', flopped and the group went under.

A further factor that caused the music establishment to overlook Honey Cone's pioneering role as the protofeminists of the pop world was that they did not write their own songs. All their material was, after all, written by men, as was the case with most girl groups. As Arlene Smith of the Chantels points out, however, this had more to do with the structure of the music industry than with the fact that female artists were incapable of writing and producing themselves. Considering the circumstances, a remarkable number of girl-group artists, as well as female songwriters, managed to penetrate the male enclaves of writing and production. Moreover, as Eddie Holland makes clear, the girl groups were only able to survive because their male writers and producers adopted a female persona, accurately reflecting the preoccupations of the women fans who bought their records. At the beginning of the seventies, the issues raised by the women's movement were starting to become common currency, and the Holland-Dozier-Holland team recognized this, in contrast to many of the singer-songwriters working in the rock idiom. But one senses that even if Honey Cone had written their own songs, or perhaps even if Holland-Dozier-Holland had been churning out feminist tracts for the group, which they came perilously close to doing from time to time, nobody in the rock establishment would have taken a blind bit of notice. As long as black girl groups like Honey Cone remained within the mainstream of commercial pop they would be invisible to all but their female fans.

Honey Cone had been in the wrong place at the wrong time. As Edna Wright told writer Paul Williams in 1984, looking back on her career: 'Let's just say that had we had hits at the beginning of the eighties instead of the seventies we would all be filthy rich right now.'

*   *   *

A discussion of the Three Degrees' music is like a discussion of Raquel Welch's acting: bound to miss the essential point of what the subject is all about. If you think the Three Degrees are purely music to listen to you're probably blind and paralysed and maybe even deaf.

A hearing of the group's first Philadelphia International album won't challenge you intellectually but your temperature is likely to rise if you see these delectable temptresses in the flesh, that is if you're male chauvinist and susceptible to that totally American idea of presenting black female beauty in a superbly tight, sequin-flashing cabaret act. When I was ushered in to see the beautifully smiling ladies I wondered whether they'd be prepared to talk about such trifling things as records when a whole world of beauty hints or who was seen recently on the arm of Engelbert Humperdinck was there for the discussing.

They are like black Barbi dolls, posturing and wriggling in a dewey-lipped, lacquer haired, synchronized dance stepped orgy of visual theatrics. Their singing is shrill and without grace. But their charisma is total. One cannot avert one's gaze. They are a hypnotic tribute to all that is tasteless, the ultimate plastic performers for a plastic world.

Male music critics in the early seventies like those above (writing in *Black Music* and *The Soul Book* respectively), whether they adored or loathed the

Three Degrees, seemed to be agreed on one matter at least: that the group were a bunch of talentless females who relied solely on their sex appeal to sell themselves and their records to the public. The similarity between the sexism and racism of the establishment view and its inverted forms amongst more radical commentators was not clear at the time, however, and neither was the reason for the strong reaction – lecherous or furious – that the Three Degrees provoked. What really caused all the steam was that the Three Degrees not only broached the thorny issue of women's liberation in their songs, but used their image to put themselves slap bang in the middle of the controversy.

By the early seventies, women's liberation had become a widespread public topic of discussion in the US; there were the stupid jokes, the bumptious articles and the downright vicious attacks on the women's movement in the media, but there was also a sense in which the issue was coming to be treated seriously as a genuine subject of debate outside 'alternative' circles, in mainstream newspapers and women's magazines. Notions of sexism were beginning to have some general currency in American society and were being tackled by all and sundry, from *Playboy* columnists to pop sociologists, with a degree, if not of sympathy towards the movement, of awareness that the issues it had raised were important. In Britain, on the other hand, the reaction of the popular media was, as usual, to reduce the debate to a level of a *Carry On* comedy; the tabloids maintained their traditional obsession with women's underwear and ran stories of bra-burning, trivializing and ridiculing the movement by dubbing it 'women's lib', a name by which it is still generally known in Britain today. (The difference between the two countries vis-à-vis feminism became clear to me when I interviewed women singers for this book in the US and in the UK. In Britain, the question 'Are you a feminist?' usually elicits a mystified response; this is followed up with a nervous laugh and then, 'Oh, you mean a women's libber?!' The Americans for their part appear to find the question almost redundant, assuming that any normal person would be.) For whatever reasons, perhaps to do with the genesis of the women's movement in the US civil rights movement, popular understanding of sexual politics was, and continues to be, more advanced amongst American women than amongst their British counterparts.

The Three Degrees played a crucial role in the mid seventies in airing the mass debate over feminism within popular culture, both in the US and in the UK. They had started out in much the same way as did most of the girl groups of the early sixties, with a producer taking on a bunch of youngsters and hustling to jump on to the girl-group bandwagon. The original members of the group were Linda Turner, Shirley Porter and Fayette Pinkney, all from Philadelphia; their producer was Richard Barrett, who had been behind the Chantels' success in the late fifties. Barrett had by now returned from New York to his home town of Philadelphia and was still busy producing numerous groups, notably for the Swan label. Swan boasted a group called the Sapphires, who had hit with 'Who Do You Love?' in 1964; they then released some wonderful singles that ranged from the direct innocence and joyful celebration of 'Thank You For Loving Me' to the eerie 'Let's Break Up For A While' with its muffled organ and echoing horns, but the group only had one more success, 'Gotta Have Your Love' in 1965. Barrett brought in a new girl group, calling them by the gimmicky name of the 3°Degrees and releasing a track for them called 'Gee Baby I'm Sorry', which became a minor local hit. 'Gee Baby' was followed by several more singles, including 'Look In My Eyes', a song that Barrett had originally written for the Chantels. During this time, there were numerous changes in the line-up of the group; Sonia Goring previously of the Chantels, and Helen Scott, who has today come back as a member of the new-look Three Degrees, were both early members of the group. But by 1967 the position had stabilized: there were Sheila Ferguson, a singer who had cut solos for various independent labels like Landa, Jamie and Swan, Fayette Pinkney, and a new member, Valerie Holiday. This line-up remained the same until 1976. Today, Valerie still lives in Philadelphia and tours as a member of the recently revived Three Degrees. I spoke to her just as she was recording the group's new album, their first for several years:

> Before I joined the Three Degrees I had a solo career going. Somebody saw me perform and introduced me to Mr Barrett. I thought the girls were nice people and good performers, so I joined. At that time the group were just starting to go out on tour – before that it had been record hops and little shows – and it seemed a good progression for me into serious showbusiness.
>
> Like most of the singers at that time, my teaching and feeling for singing came from the church. The singers I admired were not the teenage girl groups – I had never heard the Chantels until I joined the Three Degrees – but solo singers like Aretha Franklin, Nancy Wilson and Barbra Streisand. I was exposed to rock 'n' roll and pop music, but I leaned more towards religious music. Aretha Franklin was my heroine.

Whatever the critics later said, the Three Degrees were all strong singers, closer in many ways to the serious solo artists of the time than to the teen girl groups. After all, both Sheila and Valerie had had professional solo careers. As a group, the Three Degrees were more knowledgeable about the art of singing than most. It was precisely their high standard of performance which distinguished them from many of their girl-group contemporaries:

There was nobody else like us. Mr Barrett was a perfectionist. Our harmonies had to be absolutely perfect. Before we went out on tour, he rehearsed us and rehearsed us. Everything had to be just right. Not only our singing, but our dancing. We were the only group who could sing and be in constant motion all together at precisely the same time throughout a whole show. We were the only ones who could really entertain an audience, telling jokes and so on. We were a very polished act. That takes a lot of work you know! So we were quite surprised and offended by the criticism that we were somehow 'too perfect'. What we had been trying to do was to be professional, to have our own unique act, and to make a niche for ourselves.

Ironically enough, it was the Three Degrees' very professionalism rather than their incompetence which gave them the reputation of being dumb brunettes, the 'black Barbi dolls' of the world of showbiz cabaret.

At the beginning of the seventies, the Three Degrees were constantly out on tour and Valerie did not start recording with them until 1969. In 1970, the group had their first big hit. The song was a version of the girl group classic, the Chantels' 'Maybe', no less. Most people would have been at a loss as to how to translate this ode to innocent teenage passion into the sultry siren come-ons of cabaret, but Valerie had the answer:

I wrote this rap at the beginning of the song – well, all of us wrote bits of it and I put them all together. I really enjoyed doing it on stage. It went something like this: 'You know girls, it's hard to find a guy that really blows your mind. And you just dig everything he does ... girls, you know the kind ...'

The rap was about a woman who had the courage to throw caution to the winds and bare her pretty raunchy feelings to the man of her dreams; says Valerie:

Everybody loved it. It came straight from the soul. The women loved it because it had a down-to-earth feeling. Women weren't used to going up to men and asking them for a date. And the men liked it too because it was so direct. Also, I think it was the timing. In those days, women just didn't do raps like that. Anyway, it was the rap that made our version of 'Maybe' and the song went to number one in all the black charts.

After the success of 'Maybe', the Three Degrees signed to the Philadelphia International label and became very much part of what was known throughout the seventies as 'the Philadelphia sound'.

The main actors in the drama of the Philadelphia sound were Kenny Gamble, Leon Huff and Thom Bell. These producers had surrounded themselves with the cream of Philadelphia's musicians and engineers at a studio in the city known as Sigma Sound. From here emanated a steady stream of superior recordings in which widely differing artists were sensitively produced and arranged to showcase their individual styles; but the unique 'Philadelphia sound' was also unmistakable in all the tracks issuing forth from Sigma. This was a blend of light, airy strings with orchestral and jazzy horns, a solid bass and choppy rhythm guitars over a firm, tight drum beat. MFSB – mother, father, sister, brother – as the musicians called their orchestra, were an extraordinarily varied collection of people, ranging from Hungarian and Polish violinists to black horn players to white southern guitar pickers; yet together they somehow worked perfectly. So appreciated were MFSB, both by other artists at Philadelphia International and by the general public – unlike the Motown musicians, who had never been in the limelight – that they finally began to put out their own singles and albums. 'TSOP', 'The Sound of Philadelphia', was a tremendous hit for MFSB in 1974, reaching the number one spot and featuring the Three Degrees on vocals. By the mid seventies, MFSB and Sigma Sound had become legendary; even Dusty Springfield went there to record, later followed by such rock luminaries as David Bowie.

It was at Sigma Sound that the Three Degrees made their most memorable recordings for Philadelphia International. Their best songs were written by Gamble and Huff, who, like the Holland-Dozier-Holland team, seemed to understand what it was that women record buyers of the day wanted to hear. For, contrary to what most commentators in the music press seemed to believe, the Three Degrees appealed as much, if not more, to women as to men. In the midst of the furore over the Three Degrees' image as sycophantic sex objects in an age of women's liberation, the group were actually in their songs conducting a series of reflections on contemporary sexual relationships that were addressed solely and entirely to women.

It had started with 'Maybe'. The businessmen's wives sitting at supperclub tables across America were about the right age to remember 'Maybe' or teen anthems like it as part of their youth. Whether the song brought back memories of street-corner harmony and twenty-five-cent houseparties, or soda parlours and kissing in Cadillacs, for the women listening, this was the sound of their golden years. When the Three Degrees sang the Chantels' 'Maybe', they spoke to a generation of young women who now had their own cultural tradition in pop. With 'Maybe', the Three Degrees were celebrating the beginning of that tradition. And although this song had a particular resonance for young black women, it also appealed to any woman who had spent her teenage years in the fifties and remembered the romance of the Chantels' pop hit.

Gamble and Huff followed up the Three Degrees' start with a number of songs that were aimed fairly and squarely at women. There was 'Dirty Ol' Man', for example, something of a surprise number coming from a group that were supposed to do nothing but pout at and pander to the male ego. The words of 'Dirty Ol' Man' were hardly designed to flatter the male listener, which was perhaps why in England, the BBC decided to ban the song. Says Valerie bemusedly, 'I still can't see what the problem was. I mean I've looked through that song and I can't find a single rude word in it!' It seems that the message itself, however, was enough:

You're a dirty old man
You can't keep your hands to yourself
Dirty old man,
go mess around with somebody else

Who else could this have been addressed to than the young girlfriends – rather than wives – of those tuxedoed businessmen, out for the evening at some swanky cabaret? Indeed, the song spoke to any woman in the audience who had ever found herself in the situation of being pursued by an older man with no serious interest in anything but a quick bout of sex with her at the end of an evening:

Now I done told you
You can look, but please don't touch
Cos you don't understand what I mean
Can't you see I'm not old enough?
You say that age ain't nothing but a number
You're much too experienced for me
All you want to do is take my love
All you want is another victory

As well as being a warning to men to lay off, in the context of the Three Degrees' stage act 'Dirty Ol' Man' confirmed that women had every right to go out dressed up to the nines without having some revolting old man inflict his advances on her: 'You can look, but please don't touch.' The song was also a put-down to married men who run after single women:

Don't run your game down, don't waste it on me
Cos you're a married man, and I'm still free

'All you want to do is use me,' continued the lead singer, sighing, 'All you want to do is take advantage of me,' while the others whispered, 'Dirty! Dirty! Dirty old man.' Perhaps there was an element of titilation for the men in all this, but it could not outweigh the direct message of the song to all the women in the audience: he may have paid for your dinner tonight, he may be going to drive you home, but in the end he's just a dirty old married man, and you're still young and free and single.

Most of the Three Degrees' material was geared to the adult nightclub scene, but they also sold records to a younger market. In 1973, they released their first major LP after years of highly successful cabaret work; in 1974, 'When Will I See You Again?' was released as a pop single, and became the Three Degrees' only big chart hit in the US (other than 'Maybe' which had reached the top thirty in 1970). In the UK 'When Will I See You Again?' was also fantastically popular, and reached the number one spot.

The song, again one of Gamble and Huff's, was very much orientated towards women, and seemed to express female vulnerability at a time when the sexual revolution of the sixties had filtered down to the rest of society, becoming an ordinary part of sexual mores rather than a radical statement of an alternative lifestyle. In a sense, the Three Degrees were once more pushing young women to confront their men with real demands; now, the onus was on the woman to pluck up her courage and ask 'When will I see you again?' as her boyfriend departed with a satisfied air and a casual 'See you around'. 'Are we in love', the girl wanted to know, 'or just friends?'; 'Is this my beginning' she continued rather dramatically, warming to her theme, 'or is this the end?' This would, in normal circumstances, have been a fair enough question to put to a new lover, but in the seventies it was one that young women found difficult to ask; how could such an embarrassingly old-fashioned need for reassurance and the emotional security of monogamy be articulated in an era where sexual radicalism had turned into a suffoc-ating etiquette of cool, so much so that extraordinarily detached and unpossessive attitudes towards sexual relationships were now thought to be the norm?

In 1960, the Shirelles had sung 'Will You Love Me Tomorrow?'; in the early seventies, the Three Degrees asked, 'When Will I See You Again?' Many of the issues for women and the values implied in these questions had changed, and certainly, the sweet, wholesome-but-soulful image of the Shirelles was light years away from the sultry, look-but-don't-touch pos-turings of the Three Degrees; but the girl groups, after over a decade, were continuing to home in on the same emotional dilemmas. This was still serious girl talk, a private discussion amongst women, the sort that takes place in kitchens or bathrooms. Yet it also had a public face; 'Will You Love Me Tomorrow?' and 'When Will I See You Again?' asked the ques-tions young women wanted to ask men but somehow could not. Pop was still functioning as a messenger service between the sexes.

Throughout the seventies, the Three Degrees were immensely popular as performers in America, but only in Britain did they achieve a long run of chart hits. It would be nice to think that the British public – led by

Prince Charles, who proclaimed the Three Degrees as his favourite group – perceived the truly sterling qualities of the Three Degrees more clearly than did the girls' compatriots, but that was not the case. According to Valerie, the reasons behind the Three Degrees' success in Europe rather than America were rather more prosaic:

> In Europe, we were big news, but Stateside, they couldn't be bothered to push us. There were a lot of other acts to compete with. They had other groups on the front burner in the US and we were just put to one side. It can happen so easily. A lot of it was to do with conflicts of interest between the different heads of record companies. But it was so frustrating. Records would be hot in Europe and they wouldn't even release them here! We kept asking why not, but we never got a real answer. They just weren't particularly interested in promoting us in the US, that's all.

Not only were there increasing problems with record companies, but life on the road was becoming more than a little strained, as Valerie recounts:

> We never had a period of growing up. We were always in a hotel somewhere, practising routines. Fortunately I got along very well with the other girls, otherwise we would have gone mad. We all slept in the same room the whole time we were touring, the three of us, one on a pull-out bed. We didn't have boyfriends. Mr Barrett was not keen on that. Family? Mr Barrett wouldn't hear of that. But then Fayette took a firm stand. She had met someone she wanted to be involved with. It didn't go down at all well with Mr Barrett so she had to leave. That was in 1976. In 1981, the Three Degrees as a group parted company with Mr Barrett. We had grown up a little bit and we were no longer intimidated by him. We were making money but unable to spend it, touring constantly. Even if we were ill, even if we were hospitalized, it didn't seem to stop the wheels. And we couldn't do anything about it, because we knew what he'd say: 'I have a quarter. I can call somebody to replace you at the drop of a hat.' But there came a time when we were all three of the same mind. Up to that point there had always been one or other of us hanging back. This time we were all in agreement, like triplets. We rebelled and there was nothing he could do. He couldn't replace all three of us at once; our faces were too well identified by then, and the record companies just wouldn't have bought it.

Despite these problems, however, Richard Barrett did have a major virtue as compared to the average girl-group manager. Says Valerie:

> We did get our money. I didn't have a complaint on that. We should have had more advice on how to invest our money maybe, because we

saved a lot of it, but I must say we did get what we were due. That was not the problem.

Things had obviously changed since the early sixties and the days of the Chantels.

Today, Valerie is back in action with the Three Degrees. Although her career has brought her comparative financial security over the years, she still has major criticisms to make of the way the music industry treats women in the eighties:

> They just don't understand the problems of having a family. I have a five-year-old. Suddenly they call me and change a recording date, and I'm expected to arrange everything instantly. What am I supposed to do, throw my kid in a suitcase and drag him with me? Sometimes you just get sick of it all. Even recording is a problem, let alone touring. Then there's the worry that you're not there for your child. That was why Sheila left the group in 1984; she wanted to be with her twins. Your conscience gets the best of you. You feel guilty all the time. I missed the day my son started school, I missed his class orientation and everything. I've got a parent meeting coming up next week and I'm just *not* going to miss that ... but you try telling them you've got a parent meeting. They say 'Oh come on!', as though you don't take your work seriously enough.

When I spoke to Valerie, she was having a particularly frustrating time, having just travelled all the way to Los Angeles to record, only to find that the studio equipment had packed up and possibly erased part of the tape she had worked on. However, in the long term she was optimistic about the new Three Degrees album:

> I'm glad that something's happening for us again. The album will be a very eighties sound; we've got some great producers, we're going for a new feel and introducing a new level ... but there'll still be those perfect harmonies that everybody knows the Three Degrees for. We will always work on that and maintain that pure sound as much as possible.

For all the Three Degrees' seventies' image of wealth, sophisticated glitter and siren sexuality, they were perhaps not in the end so far removed in terms of their sound from the poor innocent little Chantels of the fifties, with their white gloves, buttoned-up dresses and schoolgirl passions. The clothes had changed, the girls had grown up, got rich and become blasé, but when the Three Degrees sang, those high angelic harmonies of girls in the school yard re-echoed from their past.

* * *

First Choice was another girl group that emerged in the early seventies from Philadelphia. Rochelle Fleming, Annette Guest and Joyce Jones had been introduced to producer Norman Harris by a DJ in the city called Georgie Woods. Their first single, 'This is the House Where Love Died' was leased to Wand/Scepter in New York, and flopped; when the company turned down their second effort, 'Armed and Extremely Dangerous', the group signed to Philly Groove in their home town. Despite its alarming title, the song was actually a fairly innocuous bit of pop. Like Honey Cone, First Choice – or rather First Choice's songwriters such as Norman Harris, Allan Felder and Bunny Sigler – had a fondness for allegorical tales of love in terms of courtroom dramas, highway hold-ups and night-time robberies. It was in this spirit that 'Armed and Extremely Dangerous' was made; and its catchy hookline as well as its fast, funky-but-cool MFSB Philly beat – which by now was replacing Motown as the new sound of black pop – ensured it a place on the mainstream charts. The single made number twenty-eight in the US in April 1973, while in the UK it went up to sixteen, followed there in August by 'Smarty Pants' which hit number nine.

However, First Choice were unable to repeat their success in the pop world. This was largely because they appealed almost exclusively to black audiences. On the face of it, there was not much to distinguish the group from the Three Degrees, who had managed to achieve great popularity in the white bastions of the Las Vegas nightclubs. The actual singing style of the two groups was not very different; the Three Degrees and First Choice could both belt out gospel-styled 'woahs' when occasion demanded, but in most cases, they ended up singing carefully arranged formal harmonies over MFSB's orchestrated funk, in a style which usually complemented the smooth, polished sound of the music but could occasionally sound stiff and boring. It was not musical style that made First Choice an altogether different proposition from the Three Degrees; it was what they sang about.

Where the Three Degrees epitomized an upmarket sophistication in their music and went for a stylized, showbiz type of sex appeal in their image aimed primarily at white audiences, First Choice – although equally soph-isticated – were part of a very different cultural strand that had begun to show itself in black music and entertainment. At the beginning of the seventies there was, for a short time in the entertainment business, a general move away from ideas of black upward mobility and a mood of impatience with notions of integration that had previously prevailed. This was inti-mately connected with the political and social developments of the late sixties. In the wake of Martin Luther King's assassination in 1968 and the fragmentation of the black power movement, the idea of attempting to escape the ghetto, particularly through one of the most common routes – entertainment – was beginning to be seen not as an effort to better oneself, but as a way of denying the realities of black urban life. Or rather, the attempt to rise above the poverty and deprivation of ghetto life had been clearly shown to be an impossibility for most blacks in American society. The optimism of the recent past, which, in the entertainment world had been most clearly demonstrated by the rise of Motown, had proved false in a more general social context. The resulting disillusionment, not only with what black entrepreneurs would achieve for their community, but also with what a social upheaval led by the church and the more radical black leaders could achieve for its people, now showed itself in a return to images of black street life. There was a kind of radicalism in this; certainly, these images were on the whole anathema to white people, as threatening as the African robes and Afro hairstyles that were now also being adopted by hip black men and women. Yet this was clearly not in any way a straightforward political radicalism. 'Blaxploitation' movies like *Shaft* and *Superfly* glamourized the cool dudes and arcane games of the ghetto in a way that was essentially conservative, yet at the same time they pointed up submerged aspects of American life that many would have preferred to ignore. The movies also often sent out totally conflicting messages. In *Superfly*, for example, Curtis Mayfield's soundtrack, with songs like 'Freddie's Dead', spelled out the self-defeating nature of the hero's lifestyle, while the film itself glorified it. Nowhere were these contradictions between celebrating a very separate black culture and accepting its fundamental fragmentations, limitations and sorrows more pointed than in the context of the women who were portrayed as surrounding the new ghetto king.

First Choice sang about pimps and prostitutes, about a black urban lifestyle that was completely separate from, and unacceptable, to whites. Their songs were peopled by small-time crooks, pimps and gangsters like 'The Player' and 'Hustler Bill', characters who would never in a million years have made an appearance in the Supremes' or even the Three Degrees' songs:

> *Girls I'm telling you, he'll be knocking at your door*
> *If you let him in one time, you gotta come back for more*
> *He drives around at night, living in his fancy car*
> *Breaking hearts from left to right, he don't care who you are*
>
> *cos he's a player, he'll get next to you*
> *he's a player, this is what he'll do*
> *he'll shoot you down, right down to the ground*
>
> *girls, I'm warning you, he'll have you eating in the palm of his hand*
> *his loving is addictive, you'll never want another man*
> *he'll wine you and he'll dine you, say you're the only one*
> *he'll take your heart, tear it apart, then he'll be on the run*

cold-blooded son of a gun, yes he is,
he'll shoot you down, right down to the ground

'The Player' was more than a cute metaphor for a heartbreaking lover-boy; likewise the warning to 'Hustler Bill' that he would wind up 'dead in a ditch' if he continued his dangerous games did not sound exactly playful. Pimps, cardsharps and the victims of gang violence were hardly standard metaphors for errant lovers in the average girl-group song; neither did the lovelorn girl singer usually adopt the pose of the prostitute obsessed by the power and glamour of these men. A new realism was being invoked; yet, because of the strong fantasy element of the blaxploitation genre, it was not in any sense a serious political or social realism. The references to the ghetto in First Choice's songs were nothing to do with a real ghetto. Fundamentally, one allegory was being swapped for another. Now, instead of imagining white weddings and idealizing married life in the suburbs, the girl group was glamourizing the ghetto and romantic involvement with a flash hustler.

This was not as startling a departure as it may sound; firstly, the blax-ploitation craze in music was shortlived, and secondly, its significance was ultimately not very profound. First Choice were not, after all, in the business of seriously expressing the reality of life for a black prostitute; they were about celebrating her flamboyant lifestyle, or at least that of her pimp. This meant that the unpleasant undercurrents and disturbing aspects of portraying her life were altogether glossed over. No real attempt was made to do more than to latch on to some of the drama of the blaxploitation movies. The group themselves, in their pink-and-black satin trouser suits, all wide lapels, flares and platforms, looked cheerfully trendy and streetwise, and not in the least threatening. And indeed, they were not really threat-ening; under cover of the upbeat, smooth Philly sound they had managed to make the desperation of ghetto life seem like a fantasy of cool.

First Choice: fantasies of glamour and violence in ghetto life.

Ironically, however, even to create these dreams was to acknowledge a reality which was dark, sordid and dangerous. The women that First Choice sang about were, on the one hand, glamorous, with a proud independence that came from their status as the consorts of the Shafts and Superflys; on the other, they were prey to a humiliating world of sexual oppression. The illustration on the cover of First Choice's LP *The Player* summed up the image that the group, under the direction of their producers, were projecting through their music. The pose of the figures called to mind many girl-group publicity shots, from the Shirelles to the Supremes, in which a male hero is pictured surrounded by adoring girls, but there was also a distinct under-current of violence and masochism running through the visual image which was quite unique in girl-group history.

A more lighthearted image of the black producer as a corpulent sultan surrounded by his girl-group harem was played up by Barry White and his three-girl vocal group, Love Unlimited. Linda James and her sister Glodean, together with Diane Parson, had grown up in San Pedro, California, and had teamed up with maestro Barry White in the late sixties. I finally tracked Glodean down at the Holiday Inn in Birmingham to interview her, after many conversations with White's entourage, all of which were conducted with extreme politeness and some of which featured the deep bass voice of one Blanchard Montgomery, an ideal spokesman for White's Love empire. Now Mrs White, Glodean was accompanying her husband on his British tour. Although Love Unlimited had been temporarily disbanded, she was in the process of re-forming the group; she laughed as she remembered its earliest days:

> We started out as a group in the early sixties. We called ourselves the Croonettes! What a name! I don't know why, I suppose it was the crooners we liked. We were at high school at that time, and we were living in the projects in San Pedro. We all formed glee clubs and so on, and I put together this little group because I liked to sing. My mother used to sing, she was in a gospel group at the local baptist Holiness church. The Croonettes performed with a local band at graduation parties and weddings, that kind of thing, but after we left school, the group broke up. We got jobs and got married and kind of forgot about singing I suppose. But then a girlfriend of mine called me, her name was Andrea Sprewell, and she asked me to help her out with the background vocals on an album she was recording for Barry White. I told her that the group had split up, but then I thought, well, why not get back together again? So I called the others and we started rehearsing. When we were ready, Barry came over to Andrea's house to hear us sing. He liked our sound. We told him we didn't just do backgrounds, that we had our own group, but that we had broken up because we heard all the ghost stories about the entertainment business and had got scared to take the chance. Once we had finished Andrea's album, he suggested doing a record on us. So that was how we got the fever again.

In the early seventies, Barry White was beginning an extremely successful run of hits, adopting the pose of the romantic, wooing macho lover which befitted his breathy, seductive deep bass voice. Barry's lush musical odes to red-rose, chocolate-box, satin-sheets romance were gorgeous, if sometimes a little repetitive, and his vocal chords seemed capable of melting any heart, although occasionally his amorous remarks, such as 'There's only one like you, there's no way there could have been two' (in 'You're The First, The Last, My Everything') verged on the banal. Not that Barry's devoted female fans were deterred in the slightest; with that voice, he could have been reciting the telephone book for all they cared. Neither did the fact that his vocal range was rather limited seem to matter, for the production on his songs was brilliant; the plush, swishing strings of the Love Unlimited Orchestra combined with Barry's breathy murmurings were the aural equivalent of the romantic novel, and his passionate outpourings, such as 'I'm Gonna Love You Just A Little More Baby', 'Can't Get Enough of Your Love, Babe' and 'What Am I Gonna Do With You' sold in buckets throughout the seventies.

Like so many other male producers and songwriters, Barry White soon decided to add a girl group to his stable of performers, as Glodean recounts:

> After Barry signed Andrea to ABC Dunhill, he took us under his wing. I would say Barry was really the fourth member of Love Unlimited. He tailor-made all our songs for us. We had written a few of our own things, and Diane played piano. One of our songs was 'Are Your Sure?' and that was included on an album. But on the whole, everything was done for us; we were spoiled, and we got lazy. We left Barry to do all the arrangements, because he really was such a good writer. His first love is music, his whole creativity is writing and producing. He built up a whole orchestra, and he named it the Love Unlimited Orchestra after his favourite group – us. Our first record was for Uni, now MCA, and it proved that what Barry had had in mind for us was right; it went gold.

That record was 'Walkin' In the Rain (With the One I Love)', which in 1972 proved to be a big hit for Love Unlimited on both sides of the Atlantic. This early success was followed by a number of releases such as 'Oh Love, Well We Finally Made It' in 1973 and 'Under the Influence of Love' in 1974, but it was not until 1975 when 'I Belong To You' reached number twenty-seven in the US charts that the group had another major hit. Comments Glodean:

> I think we were successful when we came out because we sounded different from all the other groups. We had a nine-piece band behind us with a big horn section. We were compared to the Three Degrees, but other than the similarity of three girls and three voices, we weren't really like them. We enjoyed listening to the Three Degrees, and we were all in competition of course, but we were unique because Barry based the whole Love Unlimited Orchestra sound around us. I don't think that happened with any other female group.

Love Unlimited also had a major British hit in 1975. Perhaps it was the British weather that gave 'It May Be Winter Outside (But In My Heart It's Spring)' its UK appeal, but whatever the reason, the song charted to number eleven, as Glodean remembers:

Barry had had that song out with Felise Taylor, and on our first album we decided to include it as one of the tracks. We were very pleased when it did so well over here, because since 1972 we had been going through an awful lot of record company changes. There had been a lot of turmoil, turnover of executives and that sort of thing, and the group had suffered by becoming caught up in that aspect.

After the hits in 1975, however, the group slowly disintegrated:

My sister remarried in 1978 and moved to Switzerland. She's been there for the last ten years now. Sadly, Diane passed away with cancer in 1985. I did a duet album with Barry in 1980, and I was going to go on and do a solo album, but I decided to re-form the group instead. One of the new members is my daughter, Bridgett White, and the new group will be called Love Unlimited II.

Today, Glodean still travels with Barry White, although at present she is not performing. She and Barry married in 1974, at the height of his success. Was it, I asked her, the voice that won her heart, as it had his millions of female fans?

No! It was his mind. He is such a philosopher, so knowledgeable about life. That wooed me over. And every day has been wonderful with him. We have eight children between us, five from Barry's previous marriage and two from mine, and then the baby we had together. We used to travel all together when our children were younger, and my mother travelled with us. Then when they got older, both our mothers stayed home with the children. It worked very well, but there were a lot of long-distance phone bills!

Talking to Glodean, I got the sense that the world of Love Unlimited is one seen through rose-coloured spectacles, so heavily tinted as to block out any possible disturbance whatsoever to the beautiful scenario of universal love. I could hardly bring myself to raise the subject of whether perhaps Barry White might have exerted too much control over the members of Love Unlimited, but when I did I was told, quietly but firmly, 'We didn't want control. We were a family. Everything Barry did was in our best interest. He put all his energy and effort into us.' I then raised the distasteful subject of the criticisms that the group had sometimes received in the music press during the seventies; Glodean replied, again quite firmly, 'We never heard any criticisms; we have always had a very positive press throughout our career.' Despite the rather odd feeling one has talking to Glodean that here is someone who has decided, for whatever reason, to avert her gaze from the nasty realities of life, there seemed to be something genuine and

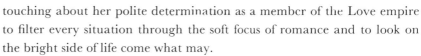

touching about her polite determination as a member of the Love empire to filter every situation through the soft focus of romance and to look on the bright side of life come what may.

Not surprisingly during the seventies, this attitude, as exemplified by the musical offerings of Barry White and Love Unlimited, was regarded with the utmost disdain by rock critics; but even soul aficionados detested this new strain of Mills-and-Boon romance in black music. Clive Anderson wrote in *The Soul Book*, published in 1975:

Love Unlimited (above) epitomized silk-sheets soul and chocolate-box romance in the seventies, while the Emotions (below), with their warm gospel tones and their natural Afro look, showed their allegiance to the 'black is beautiful' philosophy.

> Barry's extended monologues, his romantic street brother raps, are something else. Pure kitsch, embroidering on the worst in Isaac Hayes, they belong properly to the world of advertising and oversell. Mr White is a man of undoubted talent but this pop vulgarity is where his bread and butter lies and he has not seen fit to change the formula.

Love Unlimited fared worse; Anderson went on:

> Under the Svengali influence of White, Love Unlimited have provided the market with an antiseptic female choice, cellophane wrapped, and infinitely more bland than the Supremes or the Three Degrees.

Quite why Love Unlimited were seen as so much worse even than the reviled Three Degrees is hard to see today. In the 1980s, Love Unlimited records, far from being forgotten, are much sought after in Britain by DJs and collectors as rare groove classics of the early seventies. Fortunately, the line between so-called 'pop vulgarity' and serious soul is not being drawn quite so confidently these days.

If Love Unlimited were regarded during the seventies as the ultimate in commercial schlock, the Emotions, another seventies' girl group, were not so easy to dismiss. Originally from Chicago, sisters Sheila, Wanda and Jeanette Hutchinson first made their name as a soulful trio on the southern label Stax. After 1968, when Aretha Franklin from Detroit recorded so successfully in Muscle Shoals, Alabama, many northern black artists began to look to studios in the south to give them the authentic deep soul sound that was now, with Aretha and such artists as Otis Redding, beginning to prove commercially popular. The Emotions were amongst those to follow the trend in black music towards getting back to the warmth and honesty of the southern musicians, both black and white, in order to create the new roots sound of soul music.

Jeanette Hutchinson currently lives in California, where I spoke to her about the Emotions' early days:

> As young kids, we sang in a family gospel group, the Hutchinson Sunbeams. My father developed a particular style for us; we were kids,

and we couldn't do all those hard runs like the big gospel singers, so instead we used harmonies to create an emotional effect. In our songs, the lead parts were very often harmonized, as opposed to having one singer at the front and the others singing behind. That was unusual, and people used to tell my father how emotional they felt when we sang, which was why he later called us the Emotions.

To begin with, the Emotions were my father's concept. He had trained us to a very high standard from an early age. He was a jack of all trades, a self-made person; he had taught himself to read and write music, and he had a big ego about it. My mother was a very quiet, supportive, prayerful woman. As we were growing up, we became quite well known, singing with my father on TV gospel shows and that type of thing. Then when I was about seventeen, my father was approached by Pervis Staples from Stax records in Memphis, who suggested we should go down there and work with Isaac Hayes and David Porter. When we signed to Stax, Daddy decided not to sing with us any more, but to go into the management side of things.

The Emotions' output at Stax was in every way an artistic triumph, and established the group firmly in the black charts. With their sweet voices and high harmonies, the Emotions might have called to mind the candyfloss sound of the Supremes had it not been for the sheer musical sensitivity and range of their singing technique, which was breathtaking. The Emotions' vocal interpretations made the Supremes seem monolingual; the fine tuning of their harmonies combined with the soaring, free-flying passion of the lead singer, made the Supremes' wispy, insubstantial little coos and oohs behind Diana's tremulous voice sound positively clodhopping by comparison. It was not that the Emotions were pouring forth gutbucket gospel or sweaty soul in contrast to the Supremes' squeaky-clean pop; it was that they, like Darlene Love, were from a cool and sophisticated strain within gospel that gave them tremendous musical flexibility, eventually enabling them to make the transition from soul to pop without any difficulty. As Jeanette points out:

We were gospel singers, but our daddy had taught us all kinds of other music too. For harmony practice, we'd sing songs like 'The Blue Danube', 'Cool Water' and 'Ave Maria'. We were always comfortable singing secular music. To me, gospel is a style; to religious people, it means a certain lyric. The way I see it, gospel is a technique of colouring music – I even hear it in white people sometimes, like Sheena Easton. So because we had a real understanding of gospel technique, we had no trouble adapting to the material we were given at Stax.

At their new label, the Hutchinson girls' talent was showcased by some of the best writers, producers and musicians in southern black music. Isaac Hayes, together with David Porter, wrote and produced a number of scorching ballads for the group, contributing an inimitable atmosphere of brooding passion to the tracks. In true southern soul style, the songs were about the pain and conflict of a woman's adult life rather than about girlish fantasies; and the Emotions gave their material everything they had. Yet their sound was balanced and cool even at moments of intense gospel passion; this was true even on the most torrid of tracks, such as the pleading 'So I Can Love You', a song that the girls had written themselves which reached the top forty in 1969, and the Hayes-Porter number 'Stealin' Love':

> *Caught up in something I know is wrong*
> *but I can't help myself*
> *even mama told me, 'leave home'*
> *and I didn't cry when I left . . .*
> *I don't like thieves but now I'm one*
> *every time I take your kiss*
> *I only get to see you once a week*
> *other times I have to reminisce*
>
> *cos I'm stealin' love*
> *I know it just ain't right but I'm*
> *stealin' love*

The song could have been a sob story of the highest order, but the way the Emotions sang it, the situation sounded like a lot more fun than perhaps it should have been. In the same way, 'When Tomorrow Comes', although full of emotional vulnerability, re-echoed the tentative optimism of youthful girl groups like the Shirelles rather than the sad dreams of more adult, world-weary women:

> *oh please when tomorrow comes*
> *will the need still be there?*
> *I want to know*
> *will you still care?*
> *will your love for me be the kind of love I want to know?*
> *will you reach out to hold me tomorrow*
> *will you reach out?*
> *oh when tomorrow comes*
> *will your kisses still be hot?*
> *will you still want the love I've got?*

These were not the questions of a young girl on her first night of passion, however. A more mature, experienced – but not yet despairing – woman was speaking, demanding more than just fidelity: 'Will your love for me be the kind of love I want to know?' The fundamental need for reassurance was still there, but our heroine was now acknowledging the reality of life, that any old love – however romantic – would not do, and that her relationship with a man would require more than just dramatic vows.

In 1974, the Emotions' record company Stax sadly folded, and the group returned to earning their living as a live act. Says Jeanette:

> After we left Stax, we were free agents again, and we did a lot of touring. We always loved performing, and also we were more in control; that way, we were making our own money. After a year or so, we met Maurice White who was introduced to us by Ron Ellison from CBS. Maurice wanted to work with us, he was really a fan of ours, because by that time we were seasoned performers and we'd written a lot more songs. We were not little kids any more, as we had been with Isaac Hayes on Stax.
>
> We went to Maurice with our own sound already, and he really knew how to bring out the best in us. He used several of our songs for our first album with him, *Flowers*, adding a jazz feel to our work. He was also very into rhythm, and he introduced a dance sound to what we did. We really loved working with him because he respected and understood what we were all about, yet he was giving us something new in our music.

Maurice White was the moving force behind the black supergroup Earth, Wind and Fire, who during the seventies managed to introduce jazz-inflected funk into the pop charts with astounding success. Naturally, an association with White promised the Emotions, who up till then had had a following only amongst R&B fans, a new level of commercial success. Yet this did not mean that White was about to do a makeover job on the Emotions; as Sheila pointed out, their relationship with him was not the classic one of naive young women acting out the musical fantasies of a male producer.

The group's first two albums with Maurice White, *Flowers* and *Rejoice*, showed just what could be achieved when a producer let a talented girl group have their head. On *Flowers*, the sisters wrote five of the nine tracks, and throughout the album, especially on the title track written by White, the gospel sensibility evident from the Emotions' early days on Stax shone through. Yet the gospel feel was given an update and, in keeping with the mood of the times, was transformed into a happy, relaxed celebration of the 'black is beautiful' philosophy. With the Emotions, this was not merely a black version of the posturings, posings and hypocrisies of the love and peace generation, however. It seemed more like a genuine acknowledgement of the fact that by the mid seventies a significant number of black people – particularly those in the entertainment business – had shown that it was possible to become successful without surrendering ethnic cultural values entirely to the white mainstream. In the sphere of music, Earth, Wind and Fire themselves were proof positive of that. On the album *Flowers*, the Emotions appeared to be celebrating a contemporary feeling of hope, sharing a moment of pleasure and relief from the struggles and frustrations of life, without however ignoring the basic function of gospel – to acknowledge those struggles and to give spiritual comfort to the listener. Wanda's 'No Plans for Tomorrow' expressed the emotional strength needed to endure a hand-to-mouth existence, while her beautiful ballad 'How Can You Stop Loving Someone', which had the lead singer performing the feat of crying in tune, was more personal, a gentle reflection on the generosity that even a painful failed love affair can bring. The album ended, touchingly enough, with a true gospel flourish, two lines of a cappella harmony: 'Be not dismayed whate'er betide, God will take care of you.'

Although *Flowers* did well, it was not until the group's subsequent album *Rejoice* that the Emotions became known to a wider public. This time, the Emotions brought their gospel warmth to pop-flavoured numbers like 'Best of My Love', 'Love's What's Happenin'' and the title track 'Rejoice', creating a sound that was upbeat, optimistic and exuberant. 'Best of My Love' in particular met with immense success. With its catchy hookline and confident lyrics it was a beacon of hope for pop in what was often during the seventies a rather dismal sea of substandard chart singles. With its slick, tight backing and clever vocal harmonies, the track was a sophisticated production job, but it shared the same straightforward joyful spirit, if not the rough edges, of girl-group pop in the early sixties. Perhaps for that reason, it was a resounding success and stunned everyone, even the girls themselves, by becoming a number one hit and remaining in the pop charts for seventeen weeks.

There were several more tracks from the album that became popular, including 'Don't Ask My Neighbours' and 'Rejoice'. In the years that followed, the Emotions sustained their position in the world of black music with a tremendous album for an independent record company, the Red Label, and a less successful one for Motown, but their only subsequent big pop chart hit was 'Boogie Wonderland', recorded with Earth, Wind and Fire. Yet their contribution to mainstream pop was unique; their polished surface gloss and deep gospel warmth combined not only to recreate an atmosphere of flip high spirits but also to spell out a more serious message of comfort and hope. A track on the album *Rejoice* written originally for solo artist B.J. Thomas by Barry Mann and Cynthia Weil – the pair who had so perfectly captured the mood of hope and upward mobility in their songs for girl groups in the early sixties – perhaps best summed up the prevailing mood of performers like the Emotions in the seventies:

sisters, brothers don't you know
we've come a long way
we've got a long way to go

Today, Jeanette and her sisters are planning a comeback as a live act after many years out of the limelight. She explains,

For a long time we were doing big tours with Earth, Wind and Fire and the Commodores. My sister Pamela replaced me on tour for a while in 1977 when I was carrying my second child, so we managed to continue, but there came a time when we really had to stop. Wanda and Sheila wanted to have children, so we decided to take a break and put the major emphasis on our families for a few years. Also, there had been rifts in the family during our career when my father was alive – he passed away in 1985 – because Daddy was in charge of everything. He couldn't see that we had grown up, that we were three adults; he did all the accounting and he couldn't understand why we wanted to see all the books and so on. That was always a problem.

Right now we are all working in the field of music – I do commercials, I write songs and TV theme tunes and I'm also writing a book based on my father's life – but I think we all feel it's time to get back out there as a group again. I think we could still appeal to audiences today, because what people really liked about us was always our music. We especially appealed to women; a lot of women came to our concerts and bought our records. We'd get letters from women. Our music is what people remember about us, not our image.

We were never that hot on our image, anyway. In fact, we needed more input into how to appeal to women on that side. Our mother was a country woman who was involved in home things, so we knew nothing about fashion, lipstick and all that. When we first got out there, I guess you could say that we looked like country bumpkins! Also, we weren't what people expected personality-wise, ego-wise. We were so humble that people thought it was an act! I suppose it was because we had been used to singing in a church environment. But the main thing was, we were very comfortable with whatever kind of music we were doing. There were certain vibratos we made together, so it was not three individual voices you heard, it was a blend. We wanted to sound like one voice. We were not looking to feature just one girl, we were three sisters singing close. Ours was a real, true family sound.

*   *   *

Back in Philadelphia, a youthful vocal harmony group called Sister Sledge were breaking away from the grown-up, sophisticated image that had generally prevailed amongst girl groups since the Supremes. Joni, Kathie, Debbie and Kim were teenage sisters whose career, masterminded almost entirely by their female relatives, heralded a return to the teenage roots of the music. They started out as an infant combo known as 'Mrs Williams's Grandchildren', singing at school assemblies and church suppers. Grandma Viola Beatrice Hairston Williams was the matriarch of a large extended family, a former lyric soprano and social worker; her daughter Flo had performed in such venues as the Club Harlem with Joel Noble and Lorraine Knight's Dancers and had married Edwin Sledge of the dance team Fred and Sledge. When Flo and Edwin divorced, Flo began to work two to three jobs. She told *Ebony* magazine in 1980, 'That's one reason that the girls sang so much. They couldn't go out to play a lot. I didn't want them on the street while I was at work.' When a club owner heard the girls sing at a fashion show, he asked their mother how much she would charge to have them sing at his place; she jokingly replied, 'about $200 a night' and, to her amazement, he booked them. 'I couldn't believe my ears,' she told *Ebony*'s reporter. 'I wasn't making that much with three jobs.' The girls then began working the local night spots, under a series of names that included 'The Brand New Generation', 'A Group Called Sledge' and 'The Sledge Sisters'.

These days, the spokeswoman for Sister Sledge is usually Joni, but I spoke to one of the sisters who prefers to stay out of the limelight, Debbie, who takes up the story:

While we were growing up we admired Aretha Franklin and Gladys Knight. In fact, if you listen carefully to the way Kathie sings you'll notice the way she modelled her style on Gladys's. By the time we were in our teens, we were known a little bit locally as singers, and we got our first chance to record when we did a background for someone making a demo. The song was called 'Hot Pants Party' I remember! Then we met a member of the Stylistics, a friend of our older sister Carol's, who produced a demo for us. We then recorded a song called 'Time Will Tell' on a local label. It didn't do much but we were in seventh heaven to have a record out at all.

Sister Sledge, as their name finally became, had their first small hit with a single called 'Mama Never Told Me', produced by Tony Bell and Phil Hurtt at Sigma Sound. Despite this minor success, it was at first hard to convince anyone that the public would take more than a passing interest in a group of young teenage girls; the trend with girl groups at the time, particularly in Philadelphia – home of the Three Degrees – was towards a more adult, cabaret style. However, once the girls began working as backing vocalists with Kenny Gamble and Leon Huff, their potential became clear;

a major label, Atlantic, signed the group up and released 'Mama Never Told Me' again. This time, it reached the top twenty in Britain, where the group were to have a distinct following for many years.

As it turned out, there was a place for the youthful Sister Sledge in the pop world of the mid seventies. In 1969, The Jackson Five had burst into the charts with 'I Want You Back' and followed this up with an incredibly popular run of hits. Their brand of 'bubblegum soul' could not fail to impress even the most hardened critics of commercial pop; the phenomenal musical talent of the group, and particularly of its lead singer, the boy wonder Michael, could not be ignored. Moreover, the stranglehold that progressive rock was maintaining over the music industry had forced pop towards a teenybop market. A new generation was growing up who, at a much younger age now that pop music had been well established as a consumer industry, desperately needed their own dance music.

Sister Sledge emerged as the female counterpart to the Jackson Five, although they were nowhere near as successful. Their first LP, *Circle of Love*, was not such an earth-shatteringly danceable affair as the Jackson Five's – after all, the girls were part of the smooth, sophisticated sound of Philadephia rather than the big pop beat of Motown – but the songs were full of youthful high spirits. The uptempo tracks on the album bowled along at high speed with enough sudden halts and exuberant shouts to make them sound as though the four girls were having the time of their life on a joyride, while the ballads harked back to the innocent days of the Shirelles. Lines like 'Cross my heart, I love you, hope to die without you' were perhaps a little too close to the adolescent puppy-love paradise of teenybop groups like the Osmonds for comfort, but the ballads on the whole had more in common with the limpid, sweet sound of the Stylistics than with the syrupy cooings of Donny and his brothers.

However, despite the album's sparkle, it did not sell well, and Sister Sledge continued to make the rounds of the clubs without much interest from the general public until, in 1979, they teamed up with the ace dance music combo, Chic. Debbie describes that first meeting:

Nile Rogers of Chic was introduced through Atlantic to produce us. Our first encounter with him and Bernard Edwards was strange because we were not used to their way of working. They were very businesslike and we mistook this for rudeness. The other problem was that we couldn't understand what Nile wanted us to do. He had strong ideas, but he couldn't sing in tune and he didn't play the piano, so we had a hard time trying to work out what he meant! But over time, we came to respect him very much. He was the only producer who understood us and he created exactly the right sound for us.

By the time Chic came to produce Sister Sledge, they were already massively successful with dancefloor stompers like 'Dance Dance Dance (Yowsah Yowsah Yowsah)', 'Everybody Dance', 'Le Freak' and 'Good Times' to their name. With Sister Sledge, they worked their magic again and gave the group their first big hit, 'He's The Greatest Dancer':

One night in a disco on the outskirts of 'Frisco
I was cruisin' with my favourite gang
The place was so boring, filled with out-of-towners touring
I knew that it wasn't my thing
I really wasn't caring but I felt my eyes staring
at a guy who stuck out in the crowd
He had the kind of body that would shame Adonis
and a face that would make any man proud . . .

I wonder why he's the greatest dancer
that I've ever seen . . .

He wears the finest clothes, the best designers, heaven knows
ooh from his head down to his toes
Halston, Gucci, Fiorucci
he looks like a still, that man is dressed to kill!

He's not a rebel, no, no, no; and he don't wear those dirty old black boots no more; he's spinning round and round on a lit-up disco floor in a three-piece suit, and he's the greatest dancer.

The youthful toothy grins of the Sledge girls on their first LP (above) were replaced by more cautious, sophisticated smiles as the girls grew up; but their music remained incurably optimistic.

Sister Sledge's new collaboration with Chic proved highly successful, and the single shot into the top ten in March 1979. The song featured vocals that managed to be both cheerful and erotic, while Nile Rogers contributed a fast, bouncy guitar motif that defied the listener not to dance. Suddenly, Sister Sledge moved right into the limelight. Chic had landed them slap, bang in the middle of disco fever.

'He's the Greatest Dancer' was a paean of love to the figure that everyone in the late seventies now recognized as the pivot of the disco movement: the male dancer. The film *Saturday Night Fever* had, by 1979, introduced the general public to the mysteries of a disco subculture that had been going on in America's big cities for some years. Shot at a club called the 2001 Odyssey in Brooklyn, and starring the likeable, cheery figure of John Travolta, the film was a cleaned-up version of the disco scene which down-played the role of the black and Latin DJs and dancers who were such an important part of it, and ignored the gay element altogether, but it did capture the music's sense of optimism and excitement. For, whatever its faults, disco did re-establish the values of early rock 'n' roll that by the late seventies white rock music had strayed so far away from; it was entirely working class, it had no pretensions to being Great Art, and its primary aim was to get people to dance. Like rock 'n' roll, disco was also completely reviled, but this time by the older rock generation itself. So threatening to the established music industry was it that a 'Disco Sucks' movement was launched, and there was even an anti-disco rally in Chicago's Comiskey Park.

One of the features of disco was its pillaging of all kinds of music in search of the ultimate dance groove. There were the proto-disco forms of the Philly sound, of Barry White's bedroom symphonies and Isaac Hayes' rap marathons. From Europe, there were disco singles featuring orchestral sounds created by electronic studio technology. Giorgio Moroder in Munich produced Donna Summer's seminal 'Love To Love You Baby' in 1976; also from Munich came Silver Convention, and Cerrone hit in 1977 with 'Give Me Love'. On the dance floor, the monotony of the fast, foursquare disco beat was occasionally tempered by one-off classics like Manu Dibango's 'Soul Makossa' or the beautifully light, cool sound of George McCrae's 'Rock Your Baby', a record which had helped to break the disco scene on its release in 1974. In the clubs, the three-minute single was ditched in favour of the 12″, which allowed DJs to remix and extend tracks; 'disco versions' began to flood on to the market, as both soul and rock artists jumped on to the disco bandwagon. This meant that the club DJ could hit his dancers with a stunning variety of music tied down to a strict ration of steady beats per minute, and so induce the trance-like state they needed for the marathon task of boogieing all night long. However, the monotony of those standards beats per minute also had its drawbacks; if the track didn't work its magic, the music could be as miserably dull, and as long, as the boring parts in a Wagner opera. Disco music had to sustain an ambience in the clubs of collective enthusiasm and individual prowess, but it often failed dismally. And it wasn't just the DJ's fault if that happened; depending on one's mood, the disco dance floor could seem either a democratic mass of sweaty humanity united by the common cause of Dance, Dance, Dance (Yowsah Yowsah Yowsah), or a nightmare of introverted individuals isolated from each other by sound, parading themselves in a meat market.

Sister Sledge's disco singles emphasized the more positive, collective side of the scene; they were upbeat, fun and full of warmth. 'We Are Family', their second hit single, epitomized the spirit of optimism and community with complete strangers that disco could, at its best moments, cause to erupt on the dance floor. The single reached number two in the pop charts, and became well enough known to function as an anthem for a number of causes. It became a rallying cry at events as disparate as feminist marches and sports matches. In October 1979, for instance, millions of US TV audiences watched 70,000 fans of the Pittsburg Pirates carry their team to victory with a mass rendition of the song. Debbie comments:

'We Are Family' was written for us by Nile and Bernard. It summed up what they thought about us when they met us. It described our close relationship as sisters but it also spoke of bonding in whatever situation. I think it took off because that message of community was not said enough, and it needed to be said.

'We Are Family' also had a particular meaning for the black community; in a sense, the song was a celebration of the traditional values of family and church solidarity that underpinned the girls' career. Sister Sledge were held up as models of black upward mobility in magazines like *Ebony* at the time, and today continue to personify the clean-living, close-knit black American family. Conservative as this image may sometimes be, it is also one that conveys respect and pride for the achievements of black families held together mainly by women. In the same way, it confirms the value of supportive communities such as the church, which plays a large part in the Sledge family's life.

'We Are Family' was followed up with 'Lost In Music' from the album released in 1979. 'Lost In Music' returned to the more specific theme of the joys of the disco lifestyle and provided a fantasy for every young person who had ever wanted to pack their job in and try to make it as a pop star:

Have you ever seen some people whose everything
is to go with their mind?

responsibility to me is a tragedy
I'll get a job some other time
I want to join a band and play in front of crazy fans
I just like all that temptation
give me a melody, that's all I ever need
for music is my salvation

we're lost in music, caught in a trap
no turning back
we're lost in music,
feel so alive,
I quit my nine to five
we're lost in music

Coming from a bunch of disco girls, these were more novel and radical sentiments than those so often voiced by the rock heroes. Since when had ordinary young women proclaimed themselves to be in the throes of an abandoned, desperate passion for music rather than for love, and expressed the desire to throw up everything to 'join a band' or 'play in front of crazy fans'? Doubtless, however, the lyrics were not meant to be taken seriously; they expressed the momentary irresponsibility and hedonism of Saturday nights out on the town, that once-a-week reward for holding down a boring job. Like the film *Thank God It's Friday*, the song was a cry of gratitude for the ecstasy of weekend clubbing rather than an attack on the work ethic. Ironically, it actually seemed almost to confirm the necessity of the nine-to-five job with its weekend pay packet; how else could one finance a disco night out, underwrite those moments when caution could be thrown to the winds, and get lost in music?

Sister Sledge's disco episode was shortlived. With its initial roots in the gay clubs, the disco scene, after a period of general popularity, reverted in the eighties to a more exclusively male gay milieu. Here, Sister Sledge did not fit in at all; for, unlike disco divas such as Eartha Kitt and Miquel Brown, the group was decidedly orientated towards young women. 'He's The Greatest Dancer' had spoken of 'cruisin' with my favourite gang' in the disco, but in essence it had described a fairly standard social scene that was really just an updated version of the early sixties' gaggle of schoolgirl friends at the sock hop.

As if to emphasize their return to the traditional basis of support for girl groups, that of young female fans, Sister Sledge launched 'All-American Girls', a song that would have sounded patriotic if it hadn't been sung by four black girls asserting their desire as feminists to make real the promises of a democratic America:

We're not asking to reverse
Roles so long rehearsed
Give us an equal share
That's just fair
We're All-American girls
and we love the life that we lead
We're All-American girls
hear what we say, know what we mean

Debbie comments:

> We knew that we were role models for young girls. That was why we
> made 'All-American Girls', which was mainly a fun song, but it made a
> statement. It was about being proud of your womanhood and standing
> up for your rights and having confidence.

The year 1982 saw a Sister Sledge re-make of the Mary Wells classic,
'My Guy', followed by a self-produced album, *The Sisters*, in 1983. The
following albums, *Betcha Say That To All the Girls* and *When the Boys Meet the
Girls*, did not do particularly well, although the girls did have a surprising
hit in 1984 when 'I'm Thinking of You', the 'B' side to the single 'Lost In
Music' originally released in 1979, began to get played in the British clubs
and eventually made the charts. In 1985, 'Frankie', a lightweight, poppy
single with a 'girlie' sound became a big European hit, marking a move
from the group's natural connection with girl fans to a more manufactured
one. The song was a nostalgic story of innocent teenage love from the
vantage point of a grown-up woman who by chance meets her idol again
and asks him, 'Do you remember, Frankie?' Joni Sledge commented on the
'Frankie' album in *Blues and Soul* that year:

> We've built a strong and loyal following amongst girls and young women
> between the ages of thirteen and twenty-five. In fact, this album really
> contains material to which they particularly could relate. We decided to
> put songs on this record that reflect how teenagers feel, especially when
> they first fall in love. You know, forget about sex for a minute ... let's
> talk about the whole puppy love thing. A song like 'He's The Boy Most
> Likely' typifies that.

'Frankie' may have appealed to the general record-buying public because
it was genuinely and self-consciously nostalgic in a fairly unspecific way,
but the rest of the songs on the album – perhaps for that very reason – could
not, for the most part, sustain this appeal. They were based on a misguided
notion of what the fifties' and sixties' girl groups were all about; the anodyne,
pre-teen sentimentality of Donny Osmond's cleaned-up, puppy-love para-

dise in the seventies was mistaken for the songs of innocent sexual desire expressed by inexperienced but passionate young girls in the sixties. Most early girl-group songs did not 'forget about sex', even for a minute; they were full of the confusions and excitements aroused by growing up and encountering it, and that was part of their charm. Sister Sledge's teen songs of the eighties, like those of so many other girl artists, did not always recapture that charm but had an airbrushed pseudo-naiveté about them that failed to ring true.

Looking back on Sister Sledge's career, which is still in progress as the girls prepare to produce their new album, Debbie Sledge remarks:

Our rise to fame was very sudden. Actually, at the time of our first hit I was pregnant. By the time the tours began I was on maternity leave, so Carol stood in. To this day, my sisters kid me about not being on that first tour. They went all over the world and suddenly there was all this glamorous, star stuff. It hit them very hard. When they describe how wild the crowds were at the peak of our major hit, I feel glad that I missed it all and was at home relaxing! Later of course I had that experience too, and it was very strange. Suddenly there was access to money, there was more security, crowds trying to get at you, and so on. But Sister Sledge could handle that. Our values remained the same. It was partly our mother that kept us steady; I know for a fact now that she protected us from a lot of things.

Our business manager was initially our mother. Later on we hired accountants and financial advisers. I don't know if they did any better! We didn't make the money we should have and we didn't sustain the success we should have. After the success of 'We Are Family', we felt we had proved ourselves and now it was our turn to get some support. But we didn't get it. And the reason was that we were black and we were women. We didn't have the money, power or influence.

The industry is still extremely difficult for women. It hasn't changed, but I think women have got smarter. I have six children, which is unusual for a woman in a career. I look back and wonder how I managed, but I was lucky; I have a loving husband and family who have been very supportive. I used to take my babies on the road with me, and my sisters took theirs; sometimes we must have looked like a travelling nursery! And when they were school age, I was always able to leave them with someone who would love them and care for them, somebody I trusted.

Leaving Atlantic has been the first step for us in having our own say-so on our records. Right now, Joni does all our producing but it depends on whoever's most energetic with their ideas. One major change is that Kathie recently decided to go solo, and we wish her the best. The three of us left in Sister Sledge will be bringing out a message of Christianity, but we'll still be making dance music. Our voices have matured, but since our style has always been strong, uplifting music, that will only be a change for the better.

*   *   *

Whilst Sister Sledge were creating a teen dream of dance and romance in disco during the seventies, a group called the Jones Girls were building up a following at the more adult, sophisticated supper-club end of the girl-group spectrum. The Supremes had been the first to break into plush showbiz cabaret and the Three Degrees had followed their lead in making black women performers acceptable to white audiences. In a sense, the Jones Girls inherited this role, only by this time, things had changed; there was by now a sizeable black middle-class audience who wanted a slightly different kind of nightclub entertainment. A certain level of musical complexity coupled with specific references to black culture – for instance to a kind of feminism that had been a tradition within black music since the blues, or to notions of pan-Africanism that were in vogue at the time – could now be presented in a way that was thoroughly middle class. The Jones Girls were the group who perhaps best took advantage of this new opportunity for artistic development

Shirley Jones is now a successful solo artist living in Atlanta, Georgia. She is married to one of the Harlem Globetrotters and when I spoke to her, she was in an optimistic frame of mind; she was expecting her first baby in a month's time and was also busy negotiating a new record deal for herself and her sisters. She is an articulate, rather intellectual woman, with a crystal-clear idea of the Jones Girls' role as pioneers of sophisticated black pop in the late seventies and early eighties:

Technically, I would say we were the best singers out there at the time. We had all studied piano, chord structures and so on. We were into exploring difficult harmonies, minor sevenths and thirds; we enjoyed structures that most singers shy away from. I think the fact that we were sisters had a lot to do with it. Our voices were always very close; there's the same tonality, the same sound in the voice; in fact it's hard to tell our speaking voices apart. Also, we got along very well and we loved singing together because that had always been part of our life.

We had started out singing very young. My father was a minister, but my parents divorced very early on. My mother was left to raise us. She was a gospel singer, so she took us out with her; we were aged six, five and four when we started. We had to sing to earn a living! That's how we became the Jones Girls.

We lived in Detroit, and so naturally as girls growing up there we had always been fascinated by the Motown sound and the Supremes. We patterned ourselves on them. As teenagers, we began to get work as backing singers; we worked with Holland-Dozier-Holland, for example, and they also cut a couple of records on us as a group. After our contract with them expired we went to Curtis Mayfield's company in Chicago; I must have been around sixteen at that time. He recorded us as a group and wrote some songs for us. They were songs with a political message; he was doing *Superfly* around then.

In 1976, we got our big break. Diana Ross had left the Supremes and was looking for backing singers, so we auditioned for her and got the job. We were flabbergasted! I was only nineteen, in my second year of college, but suddenly we had hit the big time. We dropped everything, got our passports and off we went on an international tour.

Diana taught us a lot. She taught us how to organize a tour, how to travel on our own, how to make sure you get your money from promoters, how to get good accommodations, how to get the best of everything. She showed us how important it was to be a good businesswoman. As well as setting us an example, she also encouraged us as much as she could. She used to say we were far too good to be her backing group, and she gave us a song to do as a solo number on stage; it was 'If I Ever Lose This Heaven'. Whenever there was a big record producer in the audience, she'd call us down. That was how we met Gamble and Huff.

With the Jones Girls, it was no longer a question of green youngsters being exploited by the music industry; under their mentor Diana Ross, of whom Shirley has nothing but good things to say, the group were protected and groomed until they were able to go it alone.

Urbane feminism for the cocktail set: the Jones Girls.

The Jones Girls' first hit at Philadelphia International was a smooth dance track that had the girls giving out the warning, 'You gonna make me love somebody else, if you keep on treating me the way you do.' Like the Emotions, the Jones Girls proved on their first hit single that they could use rather than abandon their own unique style and impeccable musical pedigree to make satisfying dance music. The Jones Girls soon established themselves in the late seventies as the classiest girl group in black music and until 1982, they continued to hold this position. Gamble and Huff wrote songs for the group that gave them a distinct profile as sophisticated but progressive women; for example, there was 'At Peace with Woman':

There won't be peace on earth
till man's at peace with woman
there won't be peace on this ground
till man and woman sit down

There's always going to be fighting
there'll always be that push and shove
in this world there's too much lying
and there just ain't enough love

There could hardly have been a more obvious expression of the importance of women's struggle for equality than this, but once again the majority of commentators, feminist or otherwise, were deaf to anything that might suggest girl groups to be other than fluffy half-witted bundles of fun. The critics had their stereotype and they were sticking to it. Yet, as Shirley Jones remarks:

I think our songs always had a positive feminist theme. They were always about women standing up to various situations. Gamble and Huff talked to us a lot about our childhood, about the way we grew up in a very religious family with our mother raising us. They wrote songs for us with that in mind. They knew there were things that we would not sing. They also knew our audience was pretty much women. Men liked us too but at our concerts it would be the women yelling, 'Right! Right on!'

The Jones Girls came to epitomize for women an urbane, feminine independence, but they also had more general appeal. 'Nights Over Egypt' from their third album was an eerie, atmospheric track that combined middle-class sophistication with a notion of cultural autonomy to express a fantasy of Africa. This was something quite new, as Shirley remembers:

We were amazed when 'Nights Over Egypt' hit. We thought it would be too avant-garde, so we released it as the second single from our album, not the first. But everyone loved it, and the radio stations jumped on it!

I think it was because people were beginning to appreciate something different. The song had a haunting quality to it, and those harmonies were so unusual. Kenny had also given us a slightly African image; he was always into that, though we weren't. I think we would have been happier wearing mini skirts!

Once the Jones Girls moved to RCA, the image changed, and although the group put out an excellent LP, *On Target*, they lost popularity. Says Shirley:

I think the change was too drastic for our followers. Up to that time we had tended to sing songs with messages, haunting ballads. Suddenly we were in short dresses singing uptempo numbers. It didn't work.

By the mid eighties, the group had gone their different ways; Brenda married in 1982 and Valerie went back to college to study. Shirley, however, returned to Gamble and Huff and emerged as a solo star on their new label, this time with songwriting credits to her name:

I had always written songs, and as a group the Jones Girls had always contributed ideas. After our first hit, Gamble and Huff listened to our ideas and often used them; they were not rigid. But in those early days, we didn't get production credits or anything for what we did. We didn't know to ask for them! On my solo album, however, I took more creative control and the result proved very successful. Interest was resparked for the Jones Girls, so now I'm working on a deal for the group as well as for myself. It's tough, but I feel it's important for me at this stage of my career to get exactly what I need. I don't want a quick single, I want to build a solid career. I'm not in my twenties any more, so I want to be presented in a certain way. I want to be looked on as a woman, not as a kid or a teenager. There's a huge market out there for that now, I'm sure.

By the end of the seventies, the increasing professionalism of girl vocal harmony groups was beginning, paradoxically, to erode their distinct profile as a genre within pop music. The Pointer Sisters are perhaps the best example of a girl group whose eclecticism, whilst it brought them massive popularity, often led them far away from the 'girl talk' sound with its bedrock appeal to female fans. Ruth, Anita, Bonnie and June Pointer, daughters of a pastor in Oakland, California, began by singing in church, and early on in their career joined the Northern California State Youth Choir. Soon they began to sing at clubs and parties on the West Coast, and also found work as backing singers, for artists as varied as Elvin Bishop, Esther Phillips, Taj Mahal, Grace Slick, Dave Mason and Boz Scaggs. Around 1972, the group started to work as the Pointer Sisters in their own right, recording briefly for Atlantic. Ruth had been the last to join the group; as she told a *Black Music* reporter in 1974: 'It seemed like a good idea to me. They seemed to be having a good time and I sure wasn't. I was a key punch operator at the time.'

By 1973 the girls had developed a musical style, a pastiche of forties' singers like the Andrews Sisters that showed off their ability to scat fast and sing in tight harmony. They also adopted a retro style of dress; with their forties' platform sandals, feather boas and print dresses they stood out from the run-of-the-mill girl vocal harmony groups of the day. They first became popular with gay audiences, appearing at the Troubadour Club in Los Angeles to great acclaim; from then on, as their TV bookings and live shows increased, they became the darlings of the rock scene. On stage, the Pointer Sisters were first and foremost entertainers, their showbiz flamboyance and slick professionalism earning them a deservedly high reputation in the music business; they could and did sing anything from Allen Toussaint's 'Yes We Can Can', previously an R&B hit for Lee Dorsey and their first chart hit in 1973, to jazz standards like 'Salt Peanuts', to their own compositions like 'Fairy Tale', their country smash in 1974. They were tough, witty and seductive in the classic mode of the forties' vamp; they were also, unlike many rival girl groups, talented songwriters and arrangers. Their self-penned 1975 hit 'How Long (Betcha Got a Chick on the Side)', with its percussive, whispering chant of 'bet you got a chick on the side, sure you got a chick, I know you got a chick on the side' mined the classic girl-group

The Pointer Sisters' unique brand of forties' glamour and versatile vocal style made them the darlings of the rock scene.

territory of jealous love, but this time the heroine of the song made it clear that there were no flies on her; her lover could accuse her of suspicion and paranoia, but she knew damn well what was going on. There was, however, also a trace of romantic regret underlying her canny, hardheaded attitude, as the lead singer clearly expressed:

How long will this game go on, how long?
It might hurt for a while but of one thing I am sure
I'll get over you, yes I'll find someone new
every time I open up my heart, it seems to just get torn apart

In the late seventies and early eighties, the Pointer Sisters' extraordinary versatility enabled them to adapt quite happily to the pop rock, West Coast sound normally reserved for white groups. They were the first black vocal group to be given the opportunity to exploit the vogue for rock-based movie soundtracks; for example, the girls appeared singing a number in *Car Wash*, while their single 'He's So Shy' featured on the soundtrack of *Blues Brothers*, as did 'Neutron Dance' in *Beverly Hills Cop*. In the pop charts, the group had increasing success. In 1978, there was the smash hit 'Fire', a song written by Bruce Springsteen that betrayed a strong girl-group sensibility as it evoked the fumblings of suppressed sexual passion in the proverbial automobile; but the song had a gritty realism and adult sensitivity to it that showed just how much our heroine had grown up. Gone was the overblown romantic symbolism that the early girl groups had used to express their lust; here, sexual passion was real and imminent. 'Fire' was not about a youthful fantasy, but about the immediacy of a woman's struggle with her conscience, between what she ought to do and what she wanted to do.

The Pointer Sisters' subsequent big hits in the eighties like 'He's So Shy', 'Slow Hand', 'Should I Do It', 'I'm So Excited' and 'Automatic' almost always returned to this theme of a mature woman with a strong sexual drive looking for a way to find individual happiness and satisfaction without forfeiting respect from society in general. 'Slow Hand' in particular made a brave and forthright statement on the part of women's love rights; here was the heroine of the song demanding, in no uncertain terms, a bit of adroitness, expertise and patience on the part of her lover for a change. Clearly, the sexual revolution of the sixties and seventies had not altogether failed; in the eighties, it was now possible for a girl group to publicly demand a woman's right to good sex without resorting to any coy metaphors whatever. In their early days, the Pointers' camp forties' image had given them a licence to adopt the vampish poses of that era in a lighthearted way; eventually they were able to shrug off the caricature and speak frankly in favour of women's sexual liberation.

*　　*　　*

Besides the Pointer Sisters, there was one other girl group that managed in the seventies to make some inroads into the world of rock: Labelle, whose career also spanned the decade before. Labelle started out as the Ordettes, a group of teenage girls from Philadelphia and neighbouring Trenton. Sarah Dash and Nona Hendryx were recruited from a group called the Del Capris by a local promoter, who put them together with Patti Labelle and Cindy Birdsong. The group then became the Bluebelles and began to work the clubs. Cindy Birdsong, who later joined the Supremes, remembers:

> We worked very hard. I call those my pioneering days. We got a lot of gigs, even without having a hit record out. That was because we really were good singers. All the other groups liked us, we were very much singers' singers. And Patti had this unusual voice. When we started she was sixteen, and she could hit a high concert 'C'; she had a five-octave range. That's still unusual now, not many girl singers have it. She had such a pure, clean, beautiful sound, especially on ballads like 'People' or 'Taste of Honey'. We used to do a lot of old show tunes and ballads, and people were amazed that we could sing so well being such young teenagers.
>
> We were very fortunate in getting signed in 1962 to a record company in Philadelphia, Newtown Records. We got our first hit with them in 1962; it was a record called 'I Sold My Heart to the Junkman'. After that, we were never short of work.

'I Sold My Heart to the Junkman' was a pop standard, but Patti's voice made the Bluebelles' version unique, and it went up to number fifteen on the mainstream charts. Soon after the release of 'Junkman', the group became Patti Labelle and the Bluebelles, and in 1963 they scored their next hit with 'Down The Aisle', an ode to marriage in typically lunatic doo-wop style, with Patti's voice lurching between cutesy little-girl whisperings and deafening bawls. Other releases from this period, such as 'One Phone Call' and 'Where Are You', continued in this mode, treading a line between the ultra-conventional and the bizarrely avant-garde as Patti showed off her vocal acrobatics. At the end of 'Where Are You', for example, Patti swooped up through a few octaves on the final note until she hit the top, sounding more like a rogue fire engine than a lovelorn teenage girl.

After another hit, 'You'll Never Walk Alone' in 1964, the girls' record company was taken over by the pop label Cameo, who failed to see the potential of the group and took very little interest in them. However, by this time the group had become popular as a live act. They were now making regular appearances at some of the bigger venues on the chitlin' circuit like the Uptown in Philly, the Apollo in New York and the Brooklyn Fox. When Atlantic records came down in 1964 to record a Saturday night

Before and after: the Bluebelles were known as the sweethearts of the Apollo (above) before transforming themselves into space cadets of the seventies as LaBelle (below).

show at the Uptown, the Bluebelles were on the bill and so impressed the company that they were immediately signed up.

Unfortunately, the Bluebelles' stay on Atlantic was not as successful as they had hoped. It was not until 1969 that their fortunes began to change, when Vicki Wickham from British TV's Ready Steady Go came to the rescue. Vicki had first met the girls when she booked them on to the programme in the early sixties. At that time, Patti Labelle and the Bluebelles were hardly a household name in the States, but Ready Steady Go, prompted by black music aficionados like Dusty Springfield, had a habit of unearthing obscure black American R&B bands and showcasing them on the programme. Vicki had been very impressed by the group, who had appeared on the show twice running owing to their popularity, and had kept in touch with Patti over the years. When the Bluebelles obtained a release from their contract with Atlantic, Patti contacted Vicki to see what she could do to help.

By this time, Cindy Birdsong had left the Bluebelles to replace Florence Ballard of the Supremes. British producer Kit Lambert signed the remaining trio to his Track records and took the girls to England to record; he started to produce their first album but in the end it was Vicki who finished it off. She gave them completely different material to sing, re-named the group

LaBelle, and tried to dispense completely with their, as she calls it, 'flakey' girl-group image. As for the Bluebelles, they weren't complaining; they were up for anything that would revive their flagging career. 'They were nowhere at the time,' Vicki points out. 'They had been playing small dives, and they'd got involved with some real hoodlums for management. They were at a stage where they all realized they had to make a change.'

The first LaBelle album, on the Warner Brothers label that Vicki had signed the group to, showed them wearing jeans in an effort to copy the downbeat styles of dress favoured by white rock groups. This proved disastrous. The group simply weren't suited to looking ordinary, and ended up seeming just plain drab. However, in an odd instance of an audience providing an image for its performers, a solution was found. As LaBelle started to play clubs like New York's Bitter End, they drew a following partly made up of gay men. Amongst these were some talented designers, as Vicki recalls:

> There was a guy called Larry Lagaspie who used to come in with sketches and bits and would literally make things at home for the girls. Between them, they came up with a crazy, spacey glitter image and this was, of course, before the New York Dolls or Kiss had done it.

The outrageous image did the trick and got LaBelle noticed in the rock fraternity. The feathered headdresses, weird padded silver garments and metal bras that LaBelle wore may have looked ridiculous, but they gave the group a strong visual rock 'n' roll identity which had not been seen in black girl groups since the Ronettes. It may not have been an identity that reflected the individual personalities of the group's members – Patti in particular looked strange to say the least wearing a long spiked hat held on with a chinstrap – but it worked for the group. Moreover, in a sense, LaBelle's new pose retained the spirit of frivolity of the early girl groups; also, although their rock sound was a new departure, their on-stage presence together reflected their past as a girl group, as a close-knit group of girlfriends singing for the fun and excitement of it all.

By now, the group had been together for years; they had grown up together since the age of fifteen and their closeness showed in their inter-action with each other. In their stage act, LaBelle brought a new freedom and abandonment to what had in the past usually been a very guarded, staged and unnatural expression of sexuality amongst female performers. They took one of the fundamentals of the girl group, that sense of close friendship and shared experience which was so appealing, and took it one stage further; it was as though their membership of an all-female group allowed them to express an electric sensuality on stage that was far more explicit than any solo female performer could ever have got away with.

LaBelle's stage act entranced many audiences, who saw in it many different expressions of sexuality, and the group's following became very mixed. There was a large gay contingent, as well as a coterie of black artists and intellectuals such as Nikki Giovanni, James Baldwin and Alvin Ailey. There was also a sizeable following of young fans, male and female, black and white, gay and heterosexual.

Little by little, as they released a series of albums, the group began to meet with critical acclaim from the rock press. Their first LP – *LaBelle*, in 1971 – was followed by *Moonshadow* in 1972; then came *Pressure Cookin'*, and finally in 1974 *Nightbirds* appeared, which gave the group their first number one pop hit, the memorable 'Lady Marmalade'. *Nightbirds* was produced by Allen Toussaint, a highly respected black producer, and this gave the album credibility to an R&B audience; but also, the album featured the writing talents of Nona Hendryx, giving the group the singer-songwriter status so obligatory in the rock world.

However, after the promise of the first few years, LaBelle did not achieve the heights of success that Vicki Wickham had planned for them. Despite the group's evident talent, fundamentally everything was against them. They were sometimes given ecstatic reviews in the press, but they also regularly took a knocking. A 1975 issue of the British magazine *Let It Rock*, for example, devoted itself to the subject of 'Women: Rocking or Rolled' and contained an article by Robin Katz in praise of LaBelle; she pointed out that they were the first black female group to compete with the white boy rock bands on their own terms, which included mounting a theatrical, over-the-top image of the pop star à la Genesis or David Bowie. In the same issue, however, LaBelle was castigated by another critic, Jean Peters, who asked, 'What fantasies concerning the rampant black woman do LaBelle encourage? *Voulez vous couchez avec moi ce soir?* Do they even know they are singing a New Orleans *vodun mamaloi* song?' The condescension of Ms Peters' tone was typical of the mid-seventies' feminists, who, whilst encouraging what they called 'all-women bands' in theory, in practice denied female performers access to the same armoury of sex, glamour and glitz that male pop stars were particularly fond of using at the time. If male stars like David Bowie appeared on stage half-naked and covered in make-up, this was fashionable androgeny; if women performers like LaBelle did it, they merely reduced themselves to the level of sex objects. There were many understandable confusions about women and sexuality at the time, as there still are, but the unfortunate result of this was that many feminists joined in the racism and sexism of their 'radical' male peers. The fact was that during the seventies, at the height of the feminist movement, women performers, particularly black women performers, were accorded no place whatsoever in the world of mainstream rock.

The reviewer in *Let It Rock* had ignored the fact that LaBelle's pop hit, 'Lady Marmalade', was made in a spirit of high camp and that, musically, it was the exception on the *Nightbirds* album; the other songs, particularly Nona's, were much more serious in nature. Yet this selective deafness was common amongst LaBelle's critics, precisely because the group did defy the categories in popular music that had, by the seventies, reached an extraordinary level of rigidity. White radio stations in the US would not play LaBelle because the group were black; black stations saw the music as white. In England, black music fans wanted R&B and soul; white rock fans wanted boys playing macho guitar solos. Looking back, Vicki Wickham describes the LaBelle experiment as brave but 'impractical' given the industry's racist bias; but she adds, 'LaBelle were the guinea pigs. We always hoped that LaBelle clones would come along after us and force the stations to change their policies. But it just didn't happen.'

Today, Patti LaBelle, Nona Hendryx and Sarah Dash are pursuing separate careers, with varying success. Nona, still managed by Vicki Wickham, has continued to pioneer black rock, while Sarah Dash recently released a new album. As for Patti, she has emerged in the eighties as one of the great voices in black music. In 1975, Vicki had remarked; 'If it were up to Pat, she would really sing standards in a gown at Vegas'; over ten years later, that is exactly what she is doing – to tremendous acclaim. However, as Cindy Birdsong remarks,

> Patti has been around since she was sixteen years old and it's only now that she's been getting the recognition she deserves. It's taken years. And all of that time she was singing just as great as she is now. I'm glad that people realize now what a wonderful singer she is, but I wish they had taken more notice of her before!

The barriers that mainstream white rock had begun to erect in the music industry in the late sixties and which were maintained throughout the seventies had forced artists from the girl-group scene like Patti out of the critical limelight for many years. However, the girl groups had gone from strength to strength during the seventies, reaching new heights of musical sophistication and continuing to entertain a mass of mainly female fans. In the eighties as straightforward pop once more regained its credibility, new girl groups emerged from the undergrounds of punk, funk and hip hop and stood blinking in the glare of daylight once more.

⑥ marry me (if you really love me)

At the beginning of the eighties, the pop single came back with a bang. Michael Jackson was perhaps the artist most responsible for reviving it, but by the mid eighties he had been joined by the likes of Madonna and Prince. Madonna in particular accomplished the feat of putting girls back into pop and making sure that this time, everybody sat up and took notice. She was the first solo girl singer to become a superstar; in the UK in 1985, for example, she notched up more weeks on the charts with her singles than any female artist had done since Ruby Murray in 1955.

Like the girl groups of the sixties and seventies, whose upbeat dance sound and spirit of optimism she shared, Madonna appealed first and foremost to teenage girls and young women. She was the epitome of straight-forward, innocent, good-to-be-alive pop; but she also had an irony, wit and sophistication about her that was quite new. She was clever, too, using that irony and wit to protect herself: here was a young woman who exuded sexuality, who was determined to show herself off, but who seemed to be more interested in pleasing herself than in inviting male desire and approval. Madonna threatened rather than flattered the male ego because, for all her pouting and wriggling, she was quite evidently enjoying the power of her role. She was fundamentally a narcissist, a sexual subject rather than object. And thousands of young women looked with her at the beauty of her reflected image, seeing themselves there. The men were left out completely; or at best, they were invited to worship at Madonna's shrine too. If they were very lucky they might even be allowed to contribute to its financial upkeep. When it came to men, Madonna's Material Girl was a selfish, vain minx and a bit of a gold-digger; when it came to women, she was an inspiration, a clear example of being able to express one's sexuality and not pay the price for this traditionally male privilege; of having one's cake and eating it too.

Salt, Pepa and Spinderella: today's Ronettes of rap.

Madonna's self-conscious, ironic and blatantly manipulative stance became the trademark of girl pop in the eighties. However, whereas Madonna trod the thin line between sexual subject and object with confidence, many of those who followed were unable to perform such a delicate balancing act. A whole host of girl stars appeared in her wake who traded her youthful enthusiasm and ironic pragmatism for a ghastly, half-witted jolliness coupled with an entirely cynical commercialism. This horrible combination proved especially successful for the child and teenage market, with an endless conveyor belt of young starlets like Tiffany, Debbie Gibson and Kylie Minogue; in Britain it also, with a few modifications, covered the adult tabloid market, with seaside-postcard girls like Sam Fox, Sabrina and Sinitta; and then again, there were the straightforward Madonna clones, like Elisa Fiorillo and Taylor Dane. Yet despite this rash of substandard mutations and imitations, Madonna's overall success has had a positive side in paving the way for a huge variety of new female artists who now, for the first time in the history of pop, have begun to dominate the charts.

Madonna's influence has inevitably led to a higher proportion of solo female pop acts than girl groups. However, the girl groups who remain in the eighties – and who, with the new wave of hip-hop girl crews, look set to increase their numbers – share her extrovert, independent spirit; in addition, they continue a loyal tradition of schoolgirl friendship and dance-floor solidarity inherited from the girl groups of earlier decades.

*   *   *

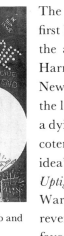

Debbie Harry: 'def, dumb and blonde'?

The beginnings of a self-conscious and highly sophisticated pop revivalism first became clear to the general public well before Madonna's success, with the advent of Blondie in the mid seventies. Blondie's star turn, Debbie Harry, had started out working as a waitress at Max's Kansas City, the New York hang-out of the city's avant-garde milieu. In the summer of 1970, the legendary Velvet Underground had played at Max's; although by then a dying flame, they had at one time been the musical arm of Andy Warhol's coterie, a group of artists who functioned under the principle of 'the Pop idea' which, as Warhol remarked in Victor Bockris and Gerard Malanga's *Uptight: the Velvet Underground Story*, 'was that anybody could do anything'. Warhol's great strength was that he combined a respect bordering on reverence for America's commercial artefacts, including pop music (Andy's favourite record was reported to be 'Sally Go Round the Roses' by the Jaynettes) with his esoteric and confrontational notions about art. In the same way, at the heart of the Velvet Underground's eccentricity was Lou Reed's loyalty to old-time rock 'n' roll, to the crazy doo-wop groups of the fifties, rather than to the more intellectually respected blues singers so adored by new rock idols like the Rolling Stones. Lou Reed explained to Bockris and Malanga:

> Some of the music we really like is records by the Eldorados or the Harpchords, all the really very nice, old records. The El Chords, the Starlighters, 'Valerie', Alicia and the Rockaways, Buster Brown, Bo Diddley. Everyone's going crazy over the old blues people, but they're forgetting about all those groups like the Spaniels, people like that. Records like 'Smoke From Your Cigarette' and 'I Need A Sunday Kind of Love', 'The Wind' by the Chesters, 'Later for You, Baby' by The Solitaires. All those really ferocious records that no one seems to listen to anymore are underneath everything we're playing.

In place of the intellectually inept and emotionally dishonest rock super-groups of the sixties and early seventies, with their non-committal peace-and-love chants and their pretensions to a music way beyond mere teenage rock 'n' roll, the Velvet Underground stubbornly persisted in reproducing the fury, incomprehensibility, and wickedness that early rock 'n' roll had represented to a generation of parents in the fifties, this time in such a way as to alienate the priggish sensibilities of their own peers, the Love generation.

If the Velvet Underground had tried to bring rock 'n' roll out of the dustbin of history in the sixties, Blondie succeeded in restoring the next phase, quality pop essentially that of the early girl groups and the British beat groups – to its rightful position in the seventies. The Velvet Underground had been the musical equivalent of one of Warhol's interminable art movies, attracting only a cult following; Blondie was the Campbell's soup can, immediately recognizable and accessible.

During her stint at Max's, Debbie Harry had formed her own vocal harmony girl group, the Stilettos. Although the Stilettos never made a record, they often performed live, and became known for their songs such as 'I Want To Be A Platinum Blonde', an ode to hitting the bleach bottle and to the life of glamour that could be pursued thereafter. When Debbie met up with Chris Stein and others to form Blondie, the song was included on their early demo, together with a cover of the Shangri-las' 'Out In The Streets'. The demo did the rounds of the New York record companies in the usual way and was rejected by several producers and A&R people. Ellie Greenwich, amongst others, found the group weak; 'they really weren't very good, and I was looking for more of a voice,' says Ellie today, adding ruefully, 'but little did I know!' Blondie finally found themselves a producer in Richard Gottehrer, the man behind the Angels' hit 'My Boyfriend's Back' in the sixties; their first hit single was 'Denis', a cover of a sixties' tune by Randy and the Rainbows; and the rest, as they say, is history.

In a sea of pompous rock albums, and at a time when disco was dying, Blondie went on to pioneer a series of intelligent, succinct pop singles that met with tremendous commercial success.

Yet the Blondie sound was not merely a throwback to the halcyon days of the sixties' girl groups, as bass player Gary Valentine explained to *Sounds* reporter Richard Cromelin in April 1977:

> It's not a nostalgia trip. We do original material. We're not like Sha Na Na saying, 'Hey, remember these songs?' We're saying, 'Do you remember when it sounded like this, do you remember when songs sounded like songs and you could turn on the AM radio and hear ten great songs in a row?'

Blondie were reported as talking 'like a graduate seminar in contemporary culture' but they had the intelligence to see that this kind of discussion could not successfully be put on disc; rather, they had grasped the essentials of the pop single and applied them to their own contemporary songs instead of attempting, as so many other groups were doing, to force the medium to accommodate more serious, complex issues than pop ever set out to deal with, thereby creating nothing but banal slogans.

Blondie's music was clearly the product of a sophisticated pop sensibility; the same went for the group's image. Whilst the boys dressed like a sixties' beat group, Debbie Harry provided a classic blonde sexbomb image with the vital ingredient that it was not quite perfect. There was a tackiness about her bleached blonde hair with its black roots, her cheap mini dresses, and her big sunglasses that was an ironic comment on the sex goddesses of the sixties; 'Brigitte Bardot on speed' was what one journalist called her. The fact that she was extremely beautiful meant that she could get away with this tawdry glamour. She was quite candid about her role as sex kitten in Blondie; when asked about it in a *Melody Maker* interview she replied, 'Yes, it's a cheap trick, isn't it?'

The fact that Debbie was well aware of what she was doing made her appear somehow impervious to the sexism of puerile male journalists who rushed to dribble all over her in print. The *New Musical Express* ran a double spread in April 1977 entitled 'Male Chauvinist Pigs' Corner' describing Debbie as 'a provocative blonde fox who drives frantic young boys with rapidly failing eyesight to lock themselves in the bathroom for hours'; and an article on 'yum yum slurp luscious Ronnie Spector' was thrown in for good measure on the opposite page. 'Mouthwatering' Debbie managed to rise above this schoolboy wit with characteristic cool, whilst Ronnie, ex-Mrs Spector desperately trying to make a comeback in her own right, did not come off so well. 'Take your hands off me – my heart belongs to Marshall McCluhan' ran the caption for Debbie's picture; Ronnie's only read: 'Mmmmmm. Eighty-eight pounds of compact yumminess on parade for all you heavy guys out there.' The game was the same, but the rules had changed; only this time, Debbie knew how to play, and Ronnie didn't.

These complicated games of sexual politics were played out very publicly over the next few years in Britain, where punk rock was becoming headline news. More because of their social milieu than their music, Blondie had been dubbed punks; but as girl-group expert and one-time Blondie producer Alan Betrock pointed out when I visited him in New York, the term 'punk' in the US described an essentially very small and insular coterie:

> There was a punk scene here in New York. Max's Kansas City had fallen off since the late sixties, but then groups like the New York Dolls came along and started off a revival of live music at places like the Mercer Arts Centre and CBGBs. There were independent labels and magazines, and quite a few interesting bands were doing the rounds. Things were quite lively, but it wasn't what you would call a movement. It was nothing compared to what happened in England.

Malcolm McLaren, who had managed the New York Dolls, brought the New York art/rock scene over to Britain; like Warhol, he was one of the great style entrepreneurs of his day. Together with partner Vivienne Westwood, McLaren's clothes shop on the New King's Road – variously entitled 'Let It Rock', 'Too Fast to Live, Too Young to Die', 'Sex', and 'Seditionaries' – soon became a mecca for the embryonic punk movement. But British punk was not just a question of style; teenagers flocked to buy McLaren's New York-inspired T-shirts at his shop, but they were also looking for some action. Just as 'punk rock' (a term initially used to describe the flood of garage bands that appeared in America after the British Invasion) originated from an upsurge of interest in do-it-yourself live music, British teenagers now were beginning to find a way to bring rock 'n' roll back to its roots. The New York punk scene had been cliquey, arty and elitist, steeped in sophisticated notions about America's rock 'n' roll heritage; the British scene was quite the opposite. British teenagers did not know or care about the American rock 'n' roll of the fifties and sixties; all they saw were the monstrous, bombastic rock supergroups from both sides of the Atlantic who had taken on the mantle of the music.

By the mid seventies, bands like Yes, Emerson Lake and Palmer, and Pink Floyd were busy cultivating the idea that rock was a matter of tremendous intellectual profundity, extraordinary technical skill and big speakers. Rock was now a music that only electronic wizards could play and that required banks upon banks of complicated electronic equipment. The supergroups played enormous stadiums and went on and on for hours; dancing was quite out of the question of course, and doping oneself up to the eyeballs to avoid being bored to tears became a positive necessity rather than a leisure activity. Though its diehard fans would never admit such a thing, rock had become a lot of pompous, pretentious rhetoric spouted by rich, indolent kids masquerading as the messiahs of the counterculture.

Punk was a response to this sorry state of affairs. It was as much a cry of outrage against the shibboleths of established hippiedom as it was a violent reaction to 'the system'. Against a dull grey background of co-opted liberalism, middle-of-the-road consensus politics and a failing British economy, the punk movement was a completely unexpected eruption of optimism, excitement and enthusiasm. Instead of denying the mediocrity of everyday life, as the hippies had done, punk turned its apathy and dullness into a DIY drama of glamour and violence. Billing itself as thick and boneheaded, mainly to annoy people, punk at its best had a level of iconic sophistication, humour and irony undreamed of within the bastions of the establishment, which now included the heroes of mainstream rock.

The Sex Pistols, a band that McLaren had formed with the express aim of showing the rock industry just how gross it was, became the focus of punk's raw energy; and in Johnny Rotten, the band's flamboyant leader, punk found its most articulately inarticulate spokesman. Yet despite all the revolutionary posing, it soon became clear that the Sex Pistols had 'joined the system' too, signing to EMI for an advance of $40,000. Whatever the Sex Pistols' role in this, McLaren's bizarre experiment had paid off; the rock establishment had fallen for his little trick. With the Pistols' subsequent break-up, the whole affair might have been quickly forgotten, yet punk persisted; for despite what the tabloids claimed, punk rock was more than just the Sex Pistols. What had started off as a cynical joke became a genuine movement, which took off at top speed right across the country.

One of the many attractions of punk to Britain's teenagers was that the rock ethos of artistic excellence went out of the window. In its place was the notion that anybody could play music. 'I don't understand why people think it's so difficult to learn to play guitar,' Sid Vicious told *Sounds* laconically in October 1976. 'You just pick a chord, go twang, and you've got music.' This blasé attitude, which was after all closer to the true roots of rock 'n' roll than were the esoteric pretensions of the rock idols, encouraged numerous new bands; and for young women in particular, playing rock 'n' roll music now became an irresistible challenge; suddenly, all those dreams of being the Beatles at last became real.

There were other factors besides punk's 'anyone can do it' philosophy that encouraged young women to take to the stage. For one thing, the movement de-emphasized sex. This was in part done to shock; nothing could have outraged the tabloids more than to learn that punk rockers didn't even like what sold their papers every day; they were horrified to learn that Johnny Rotten considered sex to be no more than 'three minutes of squelching noises', a view which prefigured Boy George's remark in the eighties that, given the choice, he'd 'rather have a cup of tea'. In reality, of course, punks had no less interest in sex than anyone else; but the fact that such a pose could shock not only the establishment but the remains of the counterculture as well, made it clear how complacent the liberalism of the sixties had become. But not only did punks appear to dislike sex, they actually had the nerve to ridicule it as well. Girls like the notorious Jordan, who worked in McLaren's shop, caused extreme commotion as she travelled up to London on her commuter train wearing suspender belts, rubber dresses, see-through macs and the like all topped off with an elaborate hairdo and plenty of ghoulish make-up. Punk was turning conventional immorality on itself and having a good laugh about it all; the accoutrements of commercial sex – whips, rubber dresses, schoolgirl uniforms – were now being used to threaten men in public. Punk enabled women to protect themselves by flaunting their sexuality in a highly threatening, disturbing way – one which, in the eighties, Madonna was not slow to emulate.

In the sixties, the Beatles had spawned hundreds of copycat beat groups, but there had been surprisingly few girl bands amongst them; those such as the British Liver Birds or the American Goldie and the Gingerbreads remained fairly obscure. Punk changed all that. Several influential girl bands arose, like the Slits, the Raincoats, the Modettes and the Dolly Mixtures. Even more influential was Siouxie Sioux, whose first public appearance with the Banshees included a rendition of the Lord's Prayer, cut in with fragments of the only other party pieces she knew, 'Twist and Shout' and 'Knocking on Heaven's Door'. Her performance earned her the instant adoration of her fans and the disgust of A&R men everywhere; but finally, she did manage to bring the record companies round, and became one of the biggest female stars to emerge from the punk era.

Punk's first wave burnt out quickly; by 1981 key groups like the Buzzcocks, the Slits and the Adverts, to say nothing of the Sex Pistols, were long gone. However, a new wave of groups soon sprang up who were inspired by punk's DIY philosophy but whose musical approach was very varied. 'New Wave' ranged from the skinhead ska of the Specials to the sensitive bedsitter material of Everything But The Girl, from the ironic glossy pop of ABC and the Human League to the retro rock of the Stray Cats. Amongst the most successful of the new groups was a tacky all-girl vocal trio who first appeared in the summer of 1981 at London's West End clubs, singing their repertoire of one solitary song over a backing track. Nobody would have been at all surprised if the group had lasted less than eight months; but eight years later they are still almost permanently in the British charts. Their name: Bananarama.

I spoke to Keren Woodward the day after Bananarama's appearance at the Royal Variety Show, and she traced the journey from the group's early days as a bunch of girls going out clubbing to their current status as the Beverley Sisters of today's pop world:

I met Sarah Dallin at secondary school in Bristol, and we used to get involved in musicals there. I remember we did 'Guys and Dolls' and 'South Pacific'. I always loved singing, and I was in the choir at school. When Sarah and I left school, we moved to London; I got a job at the BBC because I wanted to go into entertainment, but I ended up in an office. Sarah went to the London College of Fashion and she met Siobhan Fahey there. We all went round together; I suppose we had a pretty rough lifestyle because none of us had much money, but we were having a great time. Sarah and I were living above the Sex Pistols' old rehearsal room. We met Paul Cook, who was the Sex Pistols' drummer, and he let us use the room; we used to go down there and fool around. We were also going out every night, so we started to ask bands we knew if we could do back-up singing and dancing for them. Paul thought we were really good; he liked our attitude. Back then, the punk idea was that anyone could have a go, and that inspired a lot of people, especially women. There was no showing off about how brilliant you were; we felt we could be natural, be ourselves and just do what we enjoyed doing on stage.

The first thing that got us noticed was a song we did called 'Aei A Mwana'. We got it off a record from Siobhan's singles collection; it was by a group called Black Blood, and it had had a lot of percussion and chanting on it. People at that time were listening to a lot of African music and reggae as well as punk. We liked the song, so we just used to go out and sing it in West End clubs over a backing tape whenever anyone would let us. Then we met someone who paid for a demo for us, and the next thing was that Decca records – now called London – picked it up and released it.

The single, which had a similar home-made feel to it as the Dixie Cups' 'Iko Iko', did not sell much, but it was popular in club circles. Terry Hall of the successful group Fun Boy Three was one of the people who picked up on it, as Keren explains:

Terry heard 'Aei' and he liked it. He liked the way we were so unpretentious. He phoned and asked us if we'd sing on his album. We were terrified! We told him that we weren't session singers; we could sing in tune and everything but that was about it. He said that was why he liked us; he'd got sick of using more sophisticated people and was going back to basics. So we agreed to do the album, and of course it was a fantastic break for us.

Bananarama's original line-up, with (left to right) Keren Woodward, Siobhan Fahey and Sarah Dallin: 'three jolly bimbos'?

In 1982, 'It Ain't What You Do It's the Way That You Do It', a cover of a song written in 1939 by trumpet-player Sy Oliver, hit the charts and reached number four. It was credited to Fun Boy Three with Bananarama, but by the next single, 'Really Saying Something', it was Bananarama who were headlining. The song was a remake of the Velvelettes' sixties' classic but Hall's production gave it an offbeat charm that was altogether original; the rhythm section shuffled and shambled behind the group's echoing schoolgirl voices in a way that seemed oddly sophisticated, almost calculatedly naive and simple. Bananarama's image matched the music, as Keren recalls:

We had no money and we were very scruffy. Our hair was a bird's nest style left over from punk. The clothes we bought were very cheap; we had some tie dyed dresses from Kensington Market that we wore all the time I seem to remember. Otherwise, we made our own clothes; I still get the machine out occasionally. We did look a mess I suppose, but in a way it was quite good because we were different from everybody else. Nobody ever decided for us what we should wear, nobody ever dressed us. It was all our idea. We do look better now, I must say, and perhaps we're more sexy, but I think that's just because we've grown up.

Bananarama's success in the charts with their second single, which reached number five, had made them hot property and they began to look around for a new producer. They were keen to make dance music and one of their favourite groups was Imagination, so they asked Imagination's producers, Tony Swain and Steve Jolley, to step in. Swain and Jolley produced a string of hits for Bananarama, including 'Shy Boy', 'Cruel

Summer' and a cover, 'Na Na Hey Hey Kiss Him Goodbye', whose sing-song chant became something of a theme tune for the group. There were also several hits that Bananarama co-wrote with their producers; says Keren:

> We always liked doing covers. Basically when we started, that was what we were known for; we'd fish out one of our favourite records and just get up there and do it. But we also wrote quite a lot of stuff, which is one thing most people don't seem to notice about us. We wrote 'Robert de Niro's Waiting' which was one of our biggest hits, and then there was 'King of the Jungle' and 'Rough Justice'. 'Rough Justice' was inspired by a friend of ours that died in Northern Ireland.
>
> We went through a stage when we really wanted to be taken more seriously as a group. But it didn't work out. I think maybe we laboured over our songs too much. Whatever the reason, people didn't want to see our more serious side. We were really at a low point, we hadn't had success for a while, so we decided to make an intentional move back into pop dance music. We'd heard Dead or Alive's single 'You Spin Me Right Round Like A Record' and we knew that was the kind of sound we wanted, so we got their producers Stock Aitken and Waterman in. SAW were the biggest factor in turning the group around, and I like to think we helped.

With their new team behind them, Bananarama shot into the charts with 'Venus', a cover of Shocking Blue's 1970 hit. The song was a favourite from Bananarama's early days, and it was now given the SAW treatment with a businesslike disco beat that knocked spots off the group's earlier dance tracks; for the first time, the girls really belted out their vocals, and the whole effect was one of exuberant high spirits in the best girl-group tradition. More hits followed, with Bananarama co-writing almost all their material with the SAW team; but as time went on, as Keren admits, the music began to stick more and more to a safe formula:

> To begin with, we were very involved in everything that went on. And together with SAW we made an album that was classic pop; it was just packed with singles. But then SAW had a lot of success with acts like Kylie Minogue and Rick Astley, who just came in and did what they were told. Slowly, it became clear that SAW wanted us to work like that too. We'd go in to see them and we'd be expected to choose a backing track off the shelf. They had a whole little production line going there. But we don't work like that; we don't want to sound the same as all their other acts, so we've come to a point where we're not going to go along with that idea at all. Pete Waterman has been quoted as saying we're the

most difficult group he's ever worked with; I take that as a compliment.

We have always made sure to keep control of everything that goes on; we managed ourselves for years. The press make out that we are the puppets of someone or other, I'm not quite sure who, and they have been representing us as three jolly bimbos for years. But the truth is we've remained very close to how we were when we started.

In those days, we were just three friends, girls going out clubbing and having a laugh. We didn't play instruments and we couldn't be bothered to learn, so we never pretended to be 'a band'. Since then, we've improved a bit, but we've never tried to make out that we're the greatest singers or dancers in the world; that's not what we're all about.

So what are Bananarama all about? Keren:

The most important thing to us is our friendship. We value that over everything else. When we go out on tour, we still take along people that used to help us in our early days, like our choreographer Bruno Tonioli. When Siobhan left the group to live abroad, we got Jacquie O'Sullivan in because she was a mate of ours; if we hadn't known anybody we liked as a friend, we would have just continued as a duo. But we knew she would be fun to travel with, we knew she had the right outlook. Those things still matter to us, because we have never got carried away with our success. We've always kept our feet on the ground and I think people can see that we're not just put together; that's our appeal. We have become more professional over the years, but I think our basic thing is still that we're good mates.

In many ways, Bananarama embody the spirit of extrovert self-confidence and unpretentious, straightforward good fun that characterized the pop girl groups of the early sixties. Yet, as Keren comes close to admitting in her criticism of SAW, the group's music has not always lived up to that spirit. Bananarama's efforts to retain their image of youthful optimism and naivete begin to look a little tired, not to say cynical, when processed through the SAW conveyor belt and served up for mass consumption. Perhaps too the problem is that the girls themselves emphasize the downside of their undoubted appeal; they may want to keep the image of three girls larking about and having a laugh, but that doesn't mean they have constantly to reiterate their incompetence. After eight years, the jokes about not being able to sing or dance very well, bumping into scenery and getting drunk in clubs are not as funny as they used to be. Because for women in pop, things have changed; as Madonna has shown, it is possible to look like a fun-loving airhead and at the same time be respected, both by the industry and by the public, as a complete professional.

Towards the end of our interview, Keren hints that in future, Bananarama will be working with a new producer. 'We still want to do dance music,' she says, 'but it won't be as lightweight as what we've done recently.' It remains to be seen whether Bananarama will come up with new songs and a new sound that do justice to their genuine sense of pop romance, irony and humour or whether they will continue to function as 'three jolly bimbos' who have more in common with the British music-hall tradition of the Beverley Sisters than with that of the American girl groups.

Stock Aitken and Waterman, the production team behind Bananarama, has had a tremendous impact on the British charts in the mid to late eighties, particularly with its teen girl acts. The 'hit factory' is almost entirely geared towards the teenage market and has a high turnover of artists in a way that is reminiscent of New York's Brill Building in the early sixties; as Alan Betrock pointed out to me, the SAW modus operandi is something uniquely British, a kind of cottage-industry throwback to the early days of the US pop industry, when ephemeral teen idols rather than pop megastars ruled the day:

I think the way they work is very British. You've had that kind of thing in Britain since the sixties, since George Martin, and then Mickie Most, and Mike Chapman. It happens every couple of years. First it was glitter rock, there was T. Rex and Sweet, Gary Glitter, all those kind of groups. Then it dies down and happens again. That's a very British phenomenon. Usually, very few of those groups have staying power. Some of them may break through in America on one single like Rick Astley did here, but I don't think they have careers. It's very Brill Building. There are hit records, but I don't know how many hit careers there are.

'Get Fresh at the Weekend': Mel and Kim showin' out.

To find out more about London's mini Brill Building, I visited the Waterman empire, which is situated in a dingy, as yet unfashionable area of London; from the outside, the building looks like a run-down warehouse, but inside it is palatial, its walls shining with gold records. Pete, a blond man in his forties with a suntan, ushered me into a vast living room with palm trees and an open fire and began to expound his theory of pop to me:

> It's always been girls who've bought pop records. Those New York and Motown girl groups, they really brought an element of feminism into pop; girls were singing the songs and girls were buying the records. In the seventies, the whole industry went into a decline, they were going for an older market, students – but they weren't selling enough of those albums. Because pop isn't about being intellectual, about slashing your wrists and telling everybody how awful it is. It's not about politics either. Politics is too serious a business to discuss on a three-minute single. No, it's about teenage romance, about boys and girls, about going out and having fun and falling in love. Nowadays, there's an upturn in the business – a small upturn, but it's there – and that's because we've regained our audience again: teenage girls.

Certainly, Pete has a clear understanding of and sympathetic feeling for the history of black pop, particularly of the girl-group phenomenon; and his own track record confirms that he does have a secure grasp on the dynamics of teen pop appeal in the eighties, at least in Britain; his female stars like Princess, Hazel Dean, Bananarama, Mel and Kim and Kylie Minogue have met with great popularity in the UK. However, his analysis of pop is a little too glib; he ignores the fact that an element of genuine and often disturbing originality also sells records, even commercial teen girl records. Sex, death, radical politics, violence and slashing your wrists are highly appealing topics to many a teenager, as the cult death records and broken romance epics from groups like the Shangri-las have shown in no uncertain terms; and after all, it was punk that threw up Bananarama, one of Waterman's best examples of safe, happy pop.

Pete Waterman's protégées Mel and Kim, two mixed-race sisters from London's East End, were an exception to SAW's routine bland anachronisms. They first came to public attention with their hit single 'Showing Out (Get Fresh at the Weekend)' in 1986. Of all SAW's girls, Mel and Kim were the most stylish and talented. Their clothes, and particularly their hats, set a whole new fashion style. Yet the duo were not designer heroines, like Sade; their look was pure chain store, but they managed to carry it off with an extraordinary flair. For Mel and Kim, high fashion was not *haute couture*; looking distinctive did not mean looking rich. The fact that both of them were very beautiful helped; but they were also great dancers whose neat stage routines made them a cut above the others. Moreover, they genuinely caught the prevailing mood in pop. 'Showing Out' seemed to express the teen dream of the eighties: having a good job, with enough money to go out and have a good time at the weekend. Their next single, 'Fun Love and Money', spelt out the ideals of a new generation of young women in simple, direct terms; it was a milestone in girl pop because for the first time it romanticized the notion of financial independence for young women in a totally explicit way; 'boyfriends are boring' chanted the girls; having your own pay packet was, they seemed to be saying, a lot more fun than sharing his, and might even lead to new and more exciting things than monogamous romance. 'Fun Love and Money' summed up pop's progression from the fifties, at least in terms of the fantasies created by the girl groups; fun – the excitement of being young, buying and making hit records; love – adult emotional life in pop soul; and money – being able to buy fun, love, independence . . . having power.

*   *   *

The punk movement in the late seventies and Madonna's presence in the eighties has meant that today girls in pop – or the producers and songwriters who work with them – need to acknowledge a general awareness of feminist issues such as economic and sexual independence if they are to sustain credibility amongst a predominantly female set of fans. However, well before these developments on the pop scene, US girl groups working in the field of black music had been expressing the strongly independent and sexually uninhibited sentiments that Madonna made so familiar to mainstream pop audiences. Paradoxically, it was in the macho strongholds of funk and hip hop that the new girl groups made their most powerful statements.

Since the sixties, there had been girl groups in the world of funk and R&B, but they had tended to play a minor role, mostly as backing vocalists whose producers would occasionally release separate tracks for them. Taking their cue from Ray Charles's Raeletts, Ike and Tina Turner's Ikettes had two major hits in their own right in the sixties, 'I'm Blue' (also known as the Gong-Gong Song) and 'Peaches 'n' Cream', both numbers that had more to do with the very real bump-and-grind of a sweaty dance floor than with adolescent fantasies of chocolate-box romance. Later, in the seventies, the maverick George Clinton released albums for a curious duo called the Brides of Funkenstein, who were also backing singers for his group Funkadelic; he did the same for Parlet, the singers behind his other combo, Parliament. George Clinton's protégées, however, did not make much mark on the pop charts, and remained very much a sideshow attraction in the Clinton circus. It was not until the eighties that a new breed of young black producers working in the area of funk began to put together girl groups who had a distinct image of their own.

The Brides of Funkenstein: sideshow in the George Clinton circus.

In the early eighties, Motown's wonderboy young funk star Rick James, a highly talented and innovative artist who pioneered a brand of music he called 'punk funk', put together a new girl group called the Mary Jane Girls. The Mary Jane Girls were extremely successful in the black charts; in 1983 they also had two hit singles in the British pop charts, 'Candy Man' and 'All Night Long'. Rick James told the magazine *Blues and Soul* in July 1984:

> I am very happy with what's happened with the group. You see, I'm really an old fan of the Shirelles and the Ronettes and I felt that since the sixties we haven't really had a strong girl group. I knew it was time for us to have a group of women that combined today's reality and sexuality.

In a sense, the dynamics of a situation in which a male producer used a girl group to express his personal musical ambition – in this case, perhaps, Rick James's desire to create a poppier kind of funk – had not really changed since the sixties. It seemed that the Mary Jane Girls were not really about Candi, Cheri, Jojo and Maxi as the group's members apparently called themselves, but about Rick James. At the same time, however, it was perfectly clear that the group were not merely a form of self-indulgence for their producer. Contrary to appearances, male producers had never really been in a position to create girl groups on a whim, simply to fulfil their own fantasies; in order to succeed, the groups had first and foremost to appeal to women fans. Time had moved on since the heyday of the girl groups in the early sixties, and James himself now acknowledged that women's adult sexuality had become an issue that needed to be addressed. Like the male girl-group producers of the past, James was trying to write to a female audience, and to do that he had to grasp the preoccupations of women whose aims and ambitions had changed since the sixties. James realized that, in order to be truly contemporary, the Mary Jane Girls had now to be concerned not just with women's desires as sexual subjects, but with the fulfilment of those desires.

The Mary Jane Girls' songs could no longer be about a new romance that promised vague sexual bliss, a big engagement ring, a white wedding and a down payment on the mortgage. The modern independent woman demanded less, but she did expect her man to actually deliver the goods. She did not ask to be transported to undreamed of heights of ecstasy and everlasting love – well, not often anyway – but to love a man who understood her sexual needs, who cared about what she wanted; she did not ask to be kept – unless money was all she could get out of a selfish lover – but to have a relationship with a man who could keep himself, who had money in the bank, and who was not going to be too mean about sharing it.

The songs on the Mary Jane Girls' album released in 1983 ranged over all these topics. 'Candy Man' spoke of love, affection and sex in a domestic setting:

When I wake up in the morning
you bring me breakfast in my bed
and when I need a little sugar
that's when you go to my head
you're the sweetest man I know
And I'll never let you go
Just say you'll stay with me forever
And our love will surely grow

The mood of 'Prove It' was somewhat less warm and contented, however:

I don't want no man who doesn't work
sittin' back at home like a stupid jerk
Readin' all the funnies
Spending all my money
And then at night he wants some sugar honey
Talking all that trash about his fantasies
And all the nice things he's gonna do for me
I don't need that rap, you silly sap
just give me some money honey

The Mary Jane Girls: women of the world, but with a healthy dose of adolescent pop sensibility.

The Mary Jane Girls' songs, whether of sexual contentment or of hard-headed realism, were unmistakably those of the experienced woman. Yet the group also managed to catch something of the excitable, optimistic spirit of their predecessors, the sixties' girl groups, without trying to fake a youthful naivete. It was partly that with the Mary Jane Girls, Rick James had managed to combine a satisfyingly sparse, bass-driven funk groove with a bouncy, happy pop feel that made the group's records irresistibly danceable. But also, there was the sense in his songs that for a woman, age and experience did not dull the excitement of falling in love, but gave her new confidence in meeting the sexual challenge it offered. 'All Night Long', one of the group's best-known singles, was particularly successful in re-creating the youthful thrill of a new romance; and this time, our heroine knew exactly what she wanted:

Something's got me so excited baby
A feeling I've been holding back so long
You got me shook up, shook down, shook out
on your lovin'
And boy I can't wait to get started

loving you
Cos all night long
I've waited for your love to come
It's you that I love, I love
And now that I can feel you comin'
closer to me I'm not runnin'
Boy may I say I can't wait to get it on
All night long

Girl groups had come a long way from the wild fantasies of adolescence; now, one sensed, anticipation would be met with delight and fulfilment; and if sex was no longer a mystery, neither was it likely to come as a rude shock and an awful disappointment.

Whilst Rick James was working with the Mary Jane Girls, another enlightened young producer, Prince Rogers Nelson, came up with a girl group named Vanity 6, whose album appeared in 1982. Much to the annoyance of arch-rival James, through Vanity 6 Prince presented the public with a set of confusing, disturbing sexual images that made the Mary Jane Girls look positively conventional. Vanity 6 were nasty girls, who terrorized men with their voracious appetites for money and sex; as the group's name suggested, they were concerned only with their own selfish, narcissistic pleasures. The group's three members, Vanity, Susan and Brenda were depicted on the cover of the album in a typically alarming pose; Brenda and Susan in the background wore lacy underwear and suspenders while Vanity, the star of the group, dominated the foreground, wearing a baggy three-piece suit and staring arrogantly at the camera. All part of Prince's sexist male fantasy world perhaps; only there was something so revealing, humorous and honest, yet complex and frightening, about the songs on the album that in the end Vanity 6 seemed not to distinguish between male or female sexuality; in Prince's eyes, the sexual subject had become a shadowy human being slipping between the two dark, taboo worlds of both.

'Nasty Girl' was the most popular track on the album, in which Vanity began her narrative:

That's right, pleased to meet you
I still won't tell you my name
Don't you believe in mystery, don't you wanna play my game?
I'm looking for a man to love me, like I've never been loved before
I'm looking for a man who'll do it anywhere even on a limousine floor
Cos tonight we're living in a fantasy
our own little nasty world

Tonight don't you want to come with me
Do you think I'm a nasty girl?

Prince's Vanity 6: 'nasty girls' with a taste for trash.

The story became steamier as the track progressed, with Brenda and Susan joining in and exhorting, 'Ooh, it's time to jam, nasty girls, dance, dance, dance'; but finally, Vanity was less than satisfied with the general outcome, asking as the music died away: 'Is that it? Wake me when you're done. I guess you'll be the only one having fun.'

Not surprisingly given its lyrics, 'Nasty Girl' did not make the pop charts, but Vanity 6's hard, bitchy image did influence a whole new generation of girl pop stars. Janet Jackson for example reproduced it in a sanitized form on her 1986 album 'Control', which featured tracks such as 'Nasty' ('No my name ain't baby, it's Janet; Ms Jackson if you're nasty') and 'The Pleasure Principle'. The other tracks on the Vanity 6 album, all credited by Prince to members of the group, further explored the world of insatiable females and inadequate males, as in 'He's So Dull'; another track, 'If A Girl Answers (Don't Hang Up)', crossed gender lines in classic Prince style. It was a heated conversation over a thumping beat, in which Vanity traded insults over the telephone with her lover's boyfriend, played with perfect camp petulance by Prince himself. The dialogue began:

'Brenda, how are we going to get to the party?'
'Call up Jimmy, he's got a car.'
'And what if a girl answers?'
'Hang up.'
'Hang up nothing, Jimmy said I was his girl . . .'
'Honey, don't you know everyone's Jimmy's girl?'
'Brenda, I know better than anybody.'
'Well, if a girl answers, don't hang up, just talk *about it.'*
(rrring ring)
'Hello, this is Vanity. Is Jimmy home?'
'Yes, but he's taking a shower.'
'Oh I see, did he just take out the trash?'
'No, that's something he used to do, now he's taking out me.'
'Oh I see, well tell him he left his pants over here last night.'
'That's OK you keep them, he won't be needing them tonight . . .'

And so on and so forth; the insults became more and more lurid until Brenda grabbed the phone and did battle; but in the end the girls gave up, agreeing, 'There's two things we can't stand, one's a jive talk man; the other's a jive talk man with no money.' Such an undignified tale of jealous squabbling over the affections of a bisexual man was hardly the usual subject matter for a girl group, yet for all its worldly sophistication, 'If A Girl Answers (Don't Hang Up)' was pure soap opera in the best Shangri-las' tradition.

Vanity 6's album proved popular on the black charts, but the group was shortlived; Vanity herself soon left the group to pursue a solo career on Motown records. She was replaced by Italian-American Patty Kotero, renamed Apollonia. Patty starred in Prince's film *Purple Rain* and the group dutifully became Apollonia 6. Unfortunately, however, the group's new lead singer was not up to the Vanity mark; where Vanity had had a convincing raunchy arrogance about her, Apollonia's attempts to look vampish only seemed rather foolish. The effect of Apollonia's failure was to make the whole group seem a cheap, sexist commercial act. It became clear that there was a very thin line between expressing female sexuality and parading oneself for the benefit of lecherous men, and that unless played with conviction, the camp role of powerful, man-eating siren could collapse into just another over-familiar stereotype.

As much as Rick James and Prince tried, with their girl groups, to explore women's sexual fantasies in an honest way, their perspective was bound to be limited by the fact that they were men. When Bernadette Cooper, one of the very few women producers on the scene in the eighties, put together a girl vocal group called Madame X, the scene was set for something completely new. I spoke to Bernadette at a time when she was extremely busy and rather tired, but she still projected a formidable sense of ambition and determination that had obviously been with her since her earliest days, as she told me:

I grew up playing drums in a Baptist church. It wasn't unusual to play drums in church – in the black church you often have some musical accompaniment like that – though it was very unusual to see a girl play drums! But I wanted to do it, and my mother had instilled in me that I could do anything, that there was no man's way or woman's way of doing things. She was a very strong person, and it rubbed off on me. My parents were divorced when I was young, so my mother brought me and my brother up on her own. We lived all over, we moved a lot; she was the kind of person who would always move around, who was always trying to better herself.

As a teenager I liked listening to Aretha Franklin, Janis Joplin and the Rolling Stones . . . all kinds of music. I started playing in different bands. Then in the early part of 1980 I had this idea. Sometimes I have these ideas that come into my mind and I just have to follow them through to the end, I can't tell you why. Anyway, I decided to form an all-girl band. It wasn't that I was particularly interested in working with women. I just saw a way to do something different. And I consider myself a businesswoman, so that was the way I looked at it.

Bernadette's first group was Klymaxx, an all-girl funk outfit in which all the members played instruments; Bernadette herself mostly played drums. To begin with, the group adopted a feminine version of the rebellious, macho rock-band pose, as on 'Never Underestimate the Power of a Woman', the title track of their debut album in 1981. But as time went on, their songs began to focus on aspects of women's social life together. 'Girls Will Be Girls' on Klymaxx's next album, began with the heroine 'on the phone, calling up my girlfriends, 'cos tonight is ladies' night', and went on to celebrate the pleasures of getting dressed up and going out; it also covered the same territory as the Shirelles' 'Tonight's the Night', in which the heroine anticipates the outcome of a new budding romance. This time, however, there was some hardheaded realism in evidence as the lead sang 'want to know if he's charming, if he's witty, has he had success?' and the backing vocalists retorted, 'Wonder if he's got some cash?' 'All Turned Out' on the same album made a witty musical comment on the story of a woman whose life is overturned by a man with 'devilish charms'. The end of the track is interrupted by the sound of an organ playing 'Here Comes the Bride'; the singer stops and laughs, 'Hey, wait a minute, I'm not that turned out! You'll have to change your tune, hear it sisters.' The organist obligingly switches to a funk mode and plays her out.

By 1985, the group's members, particularly Bernadette, were taking more and more control of production and songwriting, and Klymaxx put out what Bernadette considers to be the group's best album, *Meeting in the Ladies' Room*; she says,

> I think it did make a big difference having woman producers. On *Meeting in the Ladies' Room* we said things that a male producer writing for us wouldn't have known about. The album was about that feeling of working five days a week and then going out with a new dress on, looking good. A song like 'The Men All Pause' brought out that side of things, when you go into a room and all the men look around and you say, 'I know I look good ... I've just spent two hours in there putting on my make-up!' It allowed the silly side of us to come out.

Frivolous as it may have been, 'The Men All Pause' was also a wry description of male behaviour in the disco: 'the men all pause when I walk into the room, the men all pause and they all sing the same old tune.' The title song, 'Meeting in the Ladies' Room' was another disco drama, this time of revenge; the ladies' room was the place where girls passed on information and warned each other about what was happening on the

Madame X: their producer Bernadette Cooper is one of the few women to have expressed a fantasy of femininity through the music of her own girl group.

dance floor. Meeting there could also, however, be the female equivalent of going outside for a good punch-up. There was evidently nothing remotely sentimental about Klymaxx's description of a feminine social world; the conflicts and jealousies that arise there were very much part of the picture. 'Meeting in the Ladies' Room' was hardly an ode to feminine solidarity, but it did introduce the idea that a tough, all-girl funk band could broach the emotional dramas that go on between women in private. Klymaxx, like the girl groups of the sixties, made sure that female preoccupations, whether of solidarity and friendship with each other or of competition and rivalry, became part of pop's vocabulary.

In 1986, Bernadette decided that she needed a new challenge:

I left Klymaxx because I found it very difficult working with such a large group of women. We all had very different personalities and ideas. To me, five or six individuals' opinions are too much; you start to feel stifled in that situation. Everybody wanted something different. I was the focal point of the group, which put a lot of pressure on me; and because I have a strong personality, everybody we met latched on to me. That also caused problems. Eventually it got to the point where I wanted to write and create on my own.

I created Madame X in the same way that I created Klymaxx. It was an idea, the same force within me over which I have no control. I wasn't influenced by any other girl groups or producers. I didn't want to be like them, I wanted something totally different and wild. I don't copy. My initial idea was that at first, no one would see the girls. You'd hear the music first and then one day, the public would be allowed to see Madame X. I thought it would be great, but my record company didn't really like the idea.

Madame X was to be a girl vocal harmony group rather than a band, and this time, Bernadette decided to remain outside the group, taking the role of producer, one usually assigned to men. She assembled three singers, Iris Parker, Valerie Victoria and Alisa Randolph. Bernadette:

> I met Iris in a store. I used to go to this store where Iris worked and she would help me pick out nice things. I'm not addicted to drugs, I don't drink and I don't smoke, but I do have one addiction: shopping. There, I'm not under control at all. So I got to know Iris quite well, and after a while she said, 'I know who you are. I'm a singer but I don't want to give you a demo tape because I'm sure you get hundreds of those all the time.' So I said, 'Why don't you give me one?' I listened to the tape and thought she had a great voice that would be even better with the right production so I took her on. Valerie auditioned and I knew she was right immediately because she looked so wild, and her vocals also were very good. Alisa I chose out of fifty-five girls who auditioned. From then, I directed and produced the whole project; the girls didn't have any say in what happened.

Here, for the first time, was a vocal girl group on the standard model that had persisted in pop since the late fifties, whose whole concept, sound and image had been entirely created by a woman.

When the first album, *Madame X*, appeared in 1987, it became obviousthat as a producer, Bernadette had a talent to match the best in the field. The album was stripped-down funk of a type comparable to Prince's, and showed a similarly inventive turn of musical phrase. There were fast stop-start rhythms on 'Just That Type of Girl' and 'Flirt', cool, jazzy touches on 'Madame X' and 'I'm Weak For You' and even a classical, operatic track, 'Cherries in the Snow'. Lyrically, the album expressed the no-nonsense feminine sentiments whether of love, lust or hardheaded realism, that had make Klymaxx so distinctive. However, there had evidently been something of a change in Bernadette's perspective. The Klymaxx girl had been a fiercely independent, straight-talking, headstrong young woman; Madame X, as her name suggested, was more of a mystery. She was flirtatious but serious, giggly but clever, romantic but calculating; she was the sort of girl who got her way but was not well liked for it, particularly by other women; she wanted limousines and diamond rings, she wanted to eat caviare in Paris and Rome; she wanted to drink champagne in bed and go out on shopping sprees; and the only excuse she had was that she was 'just that type of girl'.

'Marry Me (If You Really Love Me)' was one of the most revealing songs on the album. Where Klymaxx had earlier poked fun at marriage, using the tune of 'Here Comes the Bride' to end one of their songs, now it seemed that things were a little different, as Madame X told her lover:

I realize boy that I wasn't right to say
you could move in with me
I thought it would be cute to have a live-in lover
to share responsibility
But five years have passed and you're still on your ass
walking round in your fruit-of-the-looms
And every time I talk about husbands and wives
you get up and leave the room
I don't want no disrespect
Marry me, if you really love me
Just marry me oh oh yeah.

This time, the wedding march played the singer out triumphantly at the end of the track, without any musical sabotage from the girls.

Clearly, in Madame X's eyes, experience had shown that living together as an alternative to marriage was not quite all it was cracked up to be; the adoption by a woman of a 'live-in lover' simply let the man off the hook. Paradoxically, in Madame X's song, marriage was now being demanded as a woman's right in much the same way that it had been in girl-group songs of the early sixties. This time around, however, there was no romanticism whatsoever attached to the idea.

After the staunchly feminist pose of Klymaxx's early songs, the sentiments of Madame X's 'Marry Me' obviously had something more to them than met the eye. 'Marry Me' turned the clock back and asserted a woman's demands for a committed relationship in marriage once again; to this extent, its sentiments could be taken as part of the moral backlash of the eighties. However, the song did not simply proclaim a return to traditional values; it did in fact chime with a new realization on the part of many women that the relaxation of the social convention of marriage over the preceding decade had not fundamentally changed their domestic relationships with men. The song voiced a woman's aspiration, not simply to have a husband to rely on, but to have an equal partnership in which the man really pulled his weight. After the years of hidden domestic, emotional and sexual subservience that women had undergone in the name of free love since the late sixties, this was in its own way a radical demand, even if it was not, practically speaking, much of a solution to the problem; quite why marriage should suddenly have transformed Madame X's lazy live-in lover into a bustling, houseproud husband was not altogether clear. However, in a sense, the unlikeliness of the scenario was irrelevant; the business of girl-group pop was never to advance coherent political solutions, but to create and reflect the changing fantasies of women.

Bernadette says of the songs she wrote on the *Madame X* album:

Yes, I think I did have a different image of women from the one that came over with Klymaxx. It has changed. But I don't just write songs for women. Maybe I write from a woman's point of view, but I try to say something hard and real about what is going on. I don't write songs that just say, 'I love you, I need you, I can't live without you; take care of me because I don't know what to do on my own.' I really don't like those kind of songs. Women are always supposed to take whatever from men and justify it by saying, 'I love you', but my songs are more likely to be, 'I love you and I'll be yours but I'm my own person and I want to do what I want to do': or 'I'm sick of this relationship and I don't need you.' That offends men. I've had quite a few complaints about my songs; there was one DJ who said, 'That's too harsh coming from a woman.' Well, I suppose some people just don't want to deal with reality.

But is reality for women a matter of limousines, diamond rings and shopping sprees? Bernadette:

Music is about what you feel. Those songs are about moods, and that was the mood I was in when I wrote them. Not all of my songs are materialistic. But they are realistic. I don't think people want to hear about the harder side of women, and that's what I'm giving them.

I'm not a materialistic person. I'm a nice person. It's just that I don't feel comfortable unless I have half a million dollars in the bank!

Bernadette Cooper is a tough young woman on her way up in a very male-dominated world. Not surprisingly, she is defensive about her position; she has obviously been hard on herself to get where she is today, and consequently she can seem harsh, authoritarian and unsympathetic to others less powerful and able than herself. However, one has to remember that if she were a man, her attitudes would be accepted as normal; as it is, her ruthless and unapologetic determination comes as something of a shock. Also, one has to bear in mind that unlike many of the other women interviewed in this book, her career is currently in full swing, so that her remarks in this respect are inevitably guarded. One senses that as a woman passionately committed to gaining success, money and respect not only through her talent but through sheer force of willpower, Bernadette has sometimes upset her peers and made her fair share of enemies; yet one also senses that for a really ambitious woman in the music industry, the situation could not possibly have been otherwise.

*　　*　　*

The newcomers to girl-group pop, have, in the eighties, been the girl crews of hip hop. Their sharp, quick-witted boasting and bragging style has brought a completely new dimension to girl-group music, but they are undoubtedly part of the same tradition. In hip hop, history comes full circle; shades of doo wop, the teenage streetcorner harmony craze of the fifties which produced early girl groups like the Chantels, can be seen in the street styles of today's rappers. Like its precursor, hip hop is in essence simple: just as the doo wop group sang a cappella, hip hop's central vocal style, rap, in its most basic form requires no more than the human voice; just as the doo woppers sang anything from old spirituals to Tin Pan Alley novelty tunes, today's hip hoppers mix the rhymes of black folklore with tunes that range from advertising jingles to rock 'n' roll standards; and just as the Chantels broke into the male world of the streetcorner groups in the fifties, hip hop girl crews like Salt 'n Pepa in the eighties have made their mark in an almost entirely male-dominated sphere. Moreover, like the Shirelles and the Supremes, Salt 'n Pepa have been able to take the music further, right into the middle of the pop mainstream.

Salt 'n Pepa's rap style comes out of a submerged black male culture that has only recently become part of our everyday musical language. Hip hop culture derives from a period in the early seventies, when New York DJs in clubs, at block parties, and in open-air parks began to use new techniques of playing records to entertain the crowds. The standard equipment for a DJ consisted of two record decks, a mixer and a microphone, on which the DJ could chat to the crowd. Gradually, instead of occasional rallying cries like 'to the beat y'all, ya don't stop, that that that body rock' to lift the dancers' enthusiasm, DJs began to deliver a fast patter, concocted from rhymes they knew or made up on the spot; or perhaps there might be someone in the crowd who would be passed the microphone for an impromptu performance. So as to get a long enough instrumental break to talk or 'rap' over, the DJs would put two copies of the same record on each of their decks and cut back and forth between each one, using the fader on the mixer, in such a way that a short instrumental section on the record could be extended indefinitely. Obviously, the difficulties involved in cutting from deck to deck and at the same time making witty remarks in rhyme over the microphone proved too much for most people, and soon the functions of the DJ and rapper, or MC as he was called at that time, were split between two people. This enabled the DJ to experiment further; by spinning the record backwards and then slowly letting it come forward, controlling its speed with his hand, he could find a spot where, just before the music came back, the needle on the groove made a gravelly scratching sound. This sound could be used to create rhythmic variations, which, combined with those of the MC's increasingly complex rhymes, could result in a virtuoso display of ingenuity and skill.

The basic idea of talking over records was familiar to many black New Yorkers through hearing 'toasts' performed by reggae MCs over huge sound systems at West Indian parties. However, when non-West Indian, urban American blacks came to copy this idea, talking their own New York street rhymes over funk rather than reggae beats, the result was very different. What came out was the extraordinary hybrid of poetry, rhyme and sing-song that made up the very rich and varied oral tradition of ghetto life.

First, there were traces of playground rhymes that children learned for circle and skipping games, often very ancient bits of patter and chatter mixed with constantly changing snippets of rhyme picked up from the TV, from pop songs or adverts. Such rhymes are a part of every child's life, but in each culture there are always strong historical and local variations. Amongst these in black culture are games known as signifying and the dozens, which continue from the playground, with increasing sophistication and skill, into the male teenage and adult hang-outs of pool-rooms and bars. 'Signifying' comes from reciting 'The Signifying Monkey', a folkloric narrative tale which tests the speaker's imaginative skills as he recounts his personal version of it, describing the antics of a clever, resourceful monkey baiting a strong but usually rather dim-witted lion in the jungle. 'The dozens' is a game in which two men trade insults with each other, reaching a crescendo as each player tries to outdo his opponent, usually with ever more complicated and inventive jibes directed at the other's female relations.

Such verbal battles have traditionally thrived in an all-male environment, especially in prisons or in the army, as a means of whiling away the long hours. In 1976, Dennis Wepman, Ronald B. Newman and Murray B. Binderman collected many of these poems and rhymes in a book called *The Life*, which showed how, through the prisons, the traditional 'toast' had come to refer specifically to an underground part of black ghetto life. This subculture was known as 'the Life', and the authors described it thus:

> People in the Life engage in petty crimes like shoplifting or in victimless crimes – those in which people's desires are exploited, in which the criminal is approached with a request to supply some non-lawful product or service; sex, narcotics, gambling ... This pattern characterizes pimping, the favored game in the Life.

The pimp was the central character in toasts describing the Life. He was known for his sharp dressing, his fast jive talk, his sexual prowess and his ability to gain the loyalty of his women. Like the signifying monkey, he had no real power or strength but lived only by his wits. His lyrical and imaginative skills, replicated in those of the narrator, were considered admirable, but, like the monkey, he was in essence a loser. He was characterized as a weak, vain, hedonistic, dependent ladies' man who constantly courted and met disaster, and who relied on the brains and resourcefulness of the more strongminded and potentially treacherous women who supported him. He craved the high life; as king of the crock, he could flash his fine clothes, control his women and retain an icy detachment towards them; but more often than not, he was left standing in the shadows of the street or in a prison cell, watching or imagining his women pass by, dressed in furs on the arm of a richer, more powerful and successful gangster business-man, whose money he had hoped, through them, to win.

By the sixties, the Life was dying out in the ghetto, replaced, as the authors of the book put it, by 'organized crime and black militancy'. In the early seventies, the fleeting blaxploitation culture that had arisen in the wake of political disappointment revived some of the images of the Life. Characters from the Life appeared in commercial blaxploitation films about the world of organized crime, of narcotics rings and diamond smuggling. In popular music, which often provided the soundtrack to these films, the same images of players and hustlers cropped up, as in the 'sound of Philadelphia' groups like First Choice. Less commercially and more genuinely, political black militants like the Last Poets re-told stories of the Life in recordings such as Jalal's 'Hustler's Convention', released in 1973. Today in hip hop this phase in black music is being re-explored by DJs who seek out certain types of now-deleted rare groove records that date from the early seventies.

It is hard to see how women in hip hop fit into this picture at all. The rap styles that evolved in hip hop's early days, before it burst into the mainstream of popular music, were almost entirely based on the bragging and boasting routines of the male denizens of the Life, immortalized in informal prison toasts. There was the minute detailing of clothes and jewellery, derived from toasts like 'The Pool Shooting Monkey':

> *He wore a herringbone jacket with Hollywood slacks*
> *And a raglan benny with slits in the back . . .*
> *. . . An Elgin ticker with a solid gold band*
> *And an egg-sized diamond flashed on his hand . . .*
> *. . . A pocket full of money and a head full of herb*
> *A cadillac coupé parked at the kerb . . .*

There were the tough-guy boasts that came from southern, rural badman stories of legendary heroes like Jody and Stagger Lee that had slipped in to northern, urban stories of the Life:

> *I was born in a barrel of butcher knives*
> *Raised between two .45s . . .*
> *. . . I eat raw polar bear meat, and needless to say*
> *I swim to the North Pole three times a day . . .*
> *. . . Human blood is my food, poison is my wine*

When I wake up evil, I dare the sun to shine . . .
. . . I've handcuffed lightning, shackled thunder
Walked through a graveyard and put the dead to wonder

There were incredible tales of luxury, based on accounts of the high Life at its best, such as this description of a restaurant meal:

We ate hummingbirds' hearts and other rare parts
topped off with a seven-inch steak
Grand à la king with butterfly wings
And a salad that took three chefs to make

We had bumblebee legs and peacock eggs
Steamed over leaves from Peru
An hour was spent over crème de menthe
As we sat admiring the view

Most of all, there were endless scatological and misogynist stories of sexual conquest, revenge and treachery, all designed to bolster the male ego.

In such a context, it is not surprising that few women came forward to wage verbal battle with the men. However, there were some who had the courage to join the fray. Spoonie Gee, nephew of Sylvia Robinson who ran Sugarhill records, one of the first black, independent New York labels to pick up on the new hip hop craze in the seventies, was noted for his marathon 'badman' raps which mostly revolved around his sexual exploits, all described in the graphic language of the Life. He was backed by a three-woman crew, the Sequence, who also recorded in their own right.

Blondie, Cheryl the Pearl and Angie B were originally a singing group from Columbia, South Carolina, but had hooked up with the Sugarhill label and Spoonie Gee when they attended a concert in New York. When they sang over the stripped-down funk beats that were becoming popular at the time, they sounded professional but unremarkable; their rap style, however, was something new. Their best-known rap track was 'Funk You Up', in which the three of them showed off their very different styles of rap attack. Blondie's hard-edged voice was followed by the smooth tones of Cheryl the Pearl, while Angie B finished up with a bouncy, rocking rhyme. Like the men, Sequence's boasts were mainly concerned with their sexual magnetism; Blondie claimed:

You can ring my bell all through the night
and you can rock my body till the early light
but don't ring my bell saying please
if you cannot fulfil my needs
I don't mean to brag, I don't mean to boast,

but my name is known from coast to coast
from the coast of Philadelphia to the shore of Maine
everybody loves the way I play my game
I said I got more rhymes in the back of my mind
than Angie B she got lovers
I got style, and I got class
I don't talk my stuff too fast
I'm cold as ice, and twice as nice
And I get more sex than a cat chase mice
Blondie, hey that's me
and I'm rapping in the key of R and B

The first wave of women rappers in hip hop, as the style came to be called some time later, were quite prepared to counter the mens' sexual boasting with their own. Besides women like Sequence who proclaimed their erotic prowess, there were those who recounted stories of their skills as fighters and tricksters, like Lady B who told of winning a fight against Superman; evidently, there was a place in rap for female braggadocio after all.

As hip hop was taken up by a new generation of black American teenagers, many of the images taken from stories of the Life and used in raps over the new music became anachronistic. However, for young men, boasting about money, cars, clothes, jewellery and sex still had great resonance. The pimp of black folklore had basically depended for a living on, amongst other things, his verbal skills to recruit women; he had needed to develop 'sweet talk', which involved a tremendous amount of boasting, in order to get by. For a rising generation, these considerations had changed; the economic necessity for developing such skills in a sexual context was no longer there. However, the insecurities of the Player's life in the Game now became a metaphor for the difficulties of life in the modern-day urban ghetto; the Player's attempts to manipulate circumstances from a position of relative vulnerability through a combination of verbal skill and pure personal charisma were still fascinating to people who, in a more general context, were struggling to succeed and who had nothing to fall back on but their own skills and talents.

Many commentators on the new hip hop craze misunderstood what was going on and could not understand why teenage men insisted on all this boasting and bragging about cars, money and girls. They saw the so-called 'hotel/motel' raps that focused on these as so much reactionary, boneheaded machismo and pointed to the more overtly political 'message' raps that had arisen from the black power movement as a more acceptable form of expression. Where the 'hotel/motel' raps were performed without any of the imaginative lyrical skills of the traditional prison toasts, as they often were, the critics had a point; after all, the whole idea of the Player's patter to a woman, and of the prison toasts themselves, was to entertain and impress listeners with a display of verbal dexterity and skill, rather than to convince people that one really did have a gold-trimmed Eldorado parked outside by a dull repetition of the claim. However, people who appreciated the talent of a new generation of rappers in hip hop but regretted the content of their rhymes were being a little shortsighted. Why on earth should young, penniless teenagers raised on America's city streets boast about their fabulous wealth if not to somehow conjure their fantasies into being by means of their only tangible material asset, their own talent?

For the young women who began to emerge as part of the new wave of rappers in hip hop, taking the anachronistic imagery of the Life and using it as a metaphor in raps designed to boost their own status proved more of a problem. In the same way that many upwardly aspirational black teenagers in the fifties had rejected the earthy, bump-and-grind styles of R&B in favour of the more upmarket, romantic sensibilities of doo wop, some of the early girl rap crews tried to find a way of making their image more sophisticated and ladylike than that of the old-style, adult crews like Sequence who boasted – albeit in a rather more restrained way than the men – about their sexual conquests.

In 1979, Lisa Lee from the Bronx met Sha Rock, the girl member of the crew Funky Four Plus One More. She told Nancy Guevara about how she decided not to 'battle' with other girls on the microphone but to join forces, in an interview for *The Year Left 2* in 1987:

> Sha Rock was also rapping. Back then, it was more like competition. Other people would always compare me to her. They wanted us to battle. She wasn't into it and I wasn't into it, 'cause I don't like that kind of stuff. So, we got on the mike together.

A third rapper, Debbie Dee (also known as Sparky Dee), was then recruited to form one of the first all-girl teenage rap crews, Us Girls. The crew became well-known on the scene and starred in the feature film *Beat Street*, one of several movies that presented a cleaned-up version of the hip hop cult for general public consumption. Us Girls also contributed a song to the film's soundtrack, 'Us Girls Can Boogie Too'. In live performance, Us Girls tried to present a ladylike image, wearing dresses and high heels; the language of their raps tended to be romantic rather than sexually explicit. Where the men got down to basics in rap competitions, tearing off their shirts to roars of approval from the crowds, the girls had meekly to stand by and watch, prevented from doing the same. Lisa Lee commented:

How are we going to take off our skirts? . . . If they do it, if a male does that, the audience will say, 'Man they're crazy. I like that.' If a girl does it, they'll say 'Oh my God! They're disgusting and nasty.' That's how they judge it. I don't know. That's how it is out there.

Us Girls had wanted to gain the respect and admiration of the crowd by presenting themselves as respectable, attractive girls in the traditional way. However, their inhibitions made them seem weaker rappers than the more forthright and adult Sequence. Young teenage girls who, understandably, did not want to go around shouting about their sexual lives or making a public display of themselves seemed trapped by a double standard in hip hop which demanded, on the one hand, that young women appear fairly sweet, innocent and likeable, and on the other that they should brag, boast and show themselves off as sex machines like the men.

One way of dealing with the double standard was to confront it head on. Lolita Shanté Gooden, a fourteen-year-old from Queens, realized at a young age that the possibilities for a battle of the sexes on the microphone, using the classic methods of 'dissing' (disrespecting one's opponent) derived from the dozens, were literally endless. When UTFO, a male crew, put out a sexist rap in which three characters (the Kangol Kid, the Educated Rapper and Doctor Ice) tested their skill at chatting up a new girl on the block, claiming her to be 'all stuck up' when they failed, Lolita got her chance to sling some mud back and recorded 'Roxanne's Revenge' in 1984. UTFO, realizing that Roxanne Shanté (as Lolita now called herself) was on to a good thing, found another girl rapper and wrote her a rap which contained a convincing and humorous put-down of each boy as he tried his luck. To distinguish her from Roxanne Shanté, they called her The Real Roxanne:

Yo Kango!
hey what's up girl?
I'm the Real Roxanne and I'll rock your world
But you're all stuck up!
Well, you say that
cos I wouldn't give a guy like you no rap
I was walking down the street in the afternoon
I gave you a smile, so you assumed
that if you said hello, I would be flattered
but I kept walking and your ego was shattered
cos I'm Roxanne, the lady devastator
I'll make you feel hotter than it is in Grenada
the R-O-X-A-N-N-E
Roxanne is who I be

The Roxanne saga began a spate of 'answer' records with such names as 'Roxanne's a Man', 'Roxanne's Doctor' and 'No More Roxanne (Please)'. The battle of the sexes had begun, and teenage girls had finally found a natural base to operate from in hip hop.

As hip hop gained popularity at the beginning of the eighties, studios in New York began to churn out hundreds of 12″ hip hop records which featured, as well as rapping and scratching techniques over instrumental break beats, a clever mixing, cutting and splicing of sounds. In its most basic form on the turntable, mixing and cutting meant taking two different records (usually with the same beats per minute) and, using the fader on the mixer, switching between the two, cutting one tune in over the top of the other. In the studio, using more complicated equipment, this technique could be multiplied, and an array of drum machines and synthesizers could replace the simple break beat. Also, a huge variety of sampled sound effects such as speeded-up voices, dogs barking, snatches of TV theme tunes and so on could be added. The resulting cacophony came to be known as electro, a name everyone hated but which in retrospect seems to define that period in hip hop quite well. Like the early DJs, the electro producers raided every form of popular music they possibly could, jamming everything together in a strange musical collage over a solid dance beat. Many of these producers had come out of New York's Latin disco scene, and so there was a very strong disco feel to many of the new electro releases, with their fast, relentless, pounding beat.

Several girl rappers and singers featured on these releases. At the hip hop end were MCs like Two Sisters, whose 'B Boys B Ware' and 'High Noon' became cult classics. On 'B Boys', they proclaimed:

> *Got a degree in rapology, got a PhD in rhyme*
> *we rap so nice if you ask us twice, we'll do it double time*
> *Sisters gonna rock you sisters gonna shock you*
> *when B girls do that we just can't stop*
> *we rhyme on time and that's a fact*
> *we're gonna funk you up with our rap attack*
> *there's only two in our crew*
> *and B boys can't do what we do*
> *if what you hear you don't believe*
> *we'll do it for you in harmony*

At which point, the Two Sisters burst into song, bringing them closer to the disco end of the electro sound. In 'disco electro' there were singers rather than rappers, such as Xena, Shannon and Lisa Lisa. These girls were part of the Latin disco scene that Madonna emerged from, very close in style to later Latin pop girl groups like the Cover Girls and Exposé, and at the time, they represented the more commercial end of hip hop. Xena's 'On the Upside' was a girlish tale of the joys and miseries of love; Shannon's smash hit 'Let the Music Play' was a typical story of dance floor romance and was followed by 'Give Me the Night', which sounded almost exactly the same with its huge, dramatic synth crashes over a bubbling disco pulse. Lisa Lisa's 'I Wonder If I Take You Home' was a big pop hit in the summer of 1985; lyrically, the song was sheer teen girl group, full of adolescent angst and repressed desire as the heroine tried to make up her mind what to do:

Baby, I know you're wondering
why I won't go over to your place
cos I'm not too sure about how you feel
so I'd rather go at my own pace
and I know and you know
that if we get together
emotions will go to work
and I may do something I might regret the next day
and then the hurt

oh I don't know the way that I feel
I'm so afraid of a one-night deal
I wonder if I take you home
would you still be in love, baby
because I need you tonight
yes I need you tonight

lately you've been expressing to me
just how much you want to make love
you know I want it just as much as you do
but will you still keep in touch?
you say I'm teasing but I do have a reason
don't let your feelings fade
cos you will have me, and sooner than you know it
if you can only wait

Not a lot had changed in the world of teenage romance since the fifties, it seemed.

Lisa Lisa, who made her hit single in conjunction with a crew called Cult Jam, was the protégée of a group of black male producers and artists known as Full Force. Like the girl-group producers of the sixties, Full Force had a knack for writing songs with girl-teen appeal; The Real Roxanne, as well as Lisa Lisa, was one the the team's finds. Full Force, as it turned out, had written all the words to The Real Roxanne's sarcastic rap attack on UTFO, a fact which caused Roxanne Shanté, her biggest rival, to regard her with the utmost disdain. The feeling was mutual. The Real Roxanne, despite her title, was not a street rapper like Roxanne Shanté, who genuinely ad libbed all her rhymes and could produce a torrent of insults at the drop of a beat as occasion demanded; she was more a talented and attractive front person for Full Force's clever musical ideas. The Real Roxanne had dreams of becoming a film star, a torch singer, a clothes designer ... anything but a hard street rapper like Shanté. Unlike Shanté she dressed up in glamorous clothes like a lady ('a lady of the night', as Shanté put it) and seemed keen to escape from the confines of hip hop into the big, wide world of pop as soon as possible. In 1986, she got her break. 'Bang Zoom Let's Go Go' was a smart little pop single which featured all sorts of bits and pieces filched, in the usual hip hop mode, from here and there; Roxanne rapped over Washington-style clattering go-go beats and sang girlie choruses and the voice of a cartoon animal played the record out. 'Bang Zoom' went to number eleven on the pop charts and The Real Roxanne achieved her moment of fame at last.

The girls of hip hop, whether singers or rappers, were crossing over into mainstream pop on the heels of the boys. Run DMC, LL Cool J and the Beastie Boys had already taken hip hop into the charts, largely on a rock ticket. Def Jam records, run by heavy metal aficionado Rick Rubin, had introduced a hard form of hip hop into the world of mainstream rock; the macho MCs met the macho guitar heroes and everybody loved the joke. However, after a while the joke stopped being funny as scores of crews rushed to jump on the hip hop cock-rock bandwagon, in the process turning the music into one long, bleak ode to the tedium of machismo. In its next phase, hip hop stopped being boring and became frighteningly violent, expressing the intense frustration and nihilistic rage of a new generation growing up in a climate of Reaganomics.

The female element in hip hop appears to date to have steered well clear of this territory. We have yet to see a flygirl bragging about blowing people's heads off with an Uzi, although the possibility is not unthinkable. In fact, there have been very few references whatever amongst women rappers – on wax at least – to the gun culture of the USA. In 1986, Ice Cream Tee delivered an unusually forceful rap in an 'answer' record to a duo called Jazzy Jeff and Fresh Prince; 'Guys Ain't Nothing But Trouble' told the story of Ice Cream Tee's escape from a bunch of shady types by pulling a gun on them. However, the rap was hardly a gloating glorification of violence; nobody got shot and most of the interest of the tale revolved around the intricacies of the plot and the good-humoured banter between the heroine and her pompous male companions. Ice Cream Tee's innovative rapping style was also a major attraction of the record.

If the B boys of hip hop latched on to rock to launch them into the mainstream, the B girls have most definitely moved towards pop. Naturally, there already were a lot of pop sounds in hip hop, lurking amongst all the other musical debris that makes up the music; however, the girl crews have further developed these sounds. The most successful to do so are a rap duo named Salt 'n Pepa, with their DJ Spinderella.

In April 1988, I arrived at the offices of Next Plateau records in New York, just a stone's throw away from the legendary Brill Building on Broadway, to find Salt, Pepa and Spinderella –alias Cheryl James, Sandy Denton and Dee Dee Roper respectively – sitting in a row waiting for me, all wearing identical striped pillbox hats. At the time I interviewed them, the girls' first album, *Hot, Cool and Vicious*, had just gone platinum and they were in the process of making their second, entitled *A Salt with a Deadly Pepa*.

In 1985, Cheryl and Sandy, both from Queens, were working part-time in a New York department store, Sears Roebuck, and were set on becoming nurses, when suddenly their plans changed. Cheryl begins the story:

> We knew this guy called Hurby at work, and he used to rap in his neighbourhood. He was also going to a music school and he had to do a project for his Media Arts course. He had to actually make a record, go to the disc makers and all that, as a project. He chose us two as the artists because we worked at the same job as him and we were the loudest, rowdiest ones there. He decided to do an answer to 'The Show' by Dougie Fresh, so we did a rap and called it 'The Showstoppa'. He knew a DJ in New York here who played the demo tape and it used to get quite a few requests. Then a couple of record companies called us and asked us, could they put it on wax. We finally went with one and they put it out, and from there we made 'I'll Take Your Man'. Then we came over here to Next Plateau and did our album, *Hot, Cool and Vicious*. Now we're working on the next one, which we hope will go triple platinum.

Hurby Azor, now better known as Hurby Luv Bug, is a young musical entrepreneur whose behind-the-scenes mode of operation as A&R man, producer and songwriter for Salt 'n Pepa – he wrote almost all the songs on the girls' first LP – is very similar to that of the producers behind the sixties' girl groups. The way the crew's line-up has changed since it was formed also reminds one of those early days. Sandy continues:

> Spinderella joined us in June '87. We previously had another girl, Latoyah, but she got married and had a baby. We kept the name when Dee Dee joined us, because we liked it. The first Spinderella left because she got married and had a baby. She got with us when we were just coming up and things were hard. The money wasn't good, the shows

weren't good, we were having a lot of problems with management and record companies and stuff. She couldn't stay with it, she couldn't believe in it. I guess in the end she thought a married life was more important than a career.

However, Salt 'n Pepa, like some of the tenacious and ambitious members of girl groups before them, decided to stick out the hard times. Sandy:

When we first started, it was very difficult. There were hardly any girls around, you never really saw a girl on the mike. All the guys thought we'd just make one record and disappear. They'd look at us, and we'd be sitting in a corner, and they'd go 'Huh, Showstoppa! Now what?' The other thing was, we weren't really rappers in those days. We weren't down on the scene. We were more into club music, house and stuff. I used to dress in a punk style, with spikey red boots. We'd heard rap, but we weren't into it. It was Hurby that got us into it. But for us, it wasn't that difficult to do. If you're born and raised on the streets of New York, there's always rap at your block party, in your neighbourhood, and you kinda get to know how it goes. Well, we practised, and when we showed we was good, things changed. And now . . . like, it's time for a little respect here! The way they treat us these days, we're just like one of the guys.

If in the early days, Salt 'n Pepa had a difficult time getting respect from the men, 'I'll Take Your Man', the crew's second single, hardly endeared them to women either. It started:

Salt and Pepa's back we came to outrap you
so get out my face before I smack you
don't you know, can't you understand
if you mess with me, I'll take your man

and went on to deliver a stream of outrageous threats against a female rival. A black women's organization publicly condemned the record, and several DJs stopped playing it on the radio, as Sandy remembers:

They thought it was too harsh for women. They found it offensive. Other people loved it. They thought, 'The nerve!' Well, as a girl crew we spent a lot of time dissin' guys. We didn't see why we couldn't break on girls as well. Anyway, we didn't just say, 'I'll take your man', and that's all; if you listen to the record, there's a justification there. I'm sure if a guy had made a similar type of record – you know, 'I'll take your woman' – nobody would have even noticed it. If people found it offensive . . . well, we didn't really care. We'd do it again. We were kidding around. It's bragging, it's like a witty type of thing, that's all it is. That's the fun of it.

'I'll Take Your Man' revealed Salt 'n Pepa as a new breed of girl MCs who were not above playing dirty on the mike like the men. Their voices, too, were different; there was plenty of bass there, which, they argue, got people listening to them; they didn't come out with the high-pitched squeaking that made some young girls sound ineffectual. Moreover, their messages were direct and clear; there was little coy femininity about them. And although 'I'll Take Your Man' was a hostile rap addressed to a jealous girlfriend, it was clear that Salt 'n Pepa were talking girl talk, speaking to women in the audience rather than men about the private female world in which such conflicts arose.

In 'Chick on the Side', Salt 'n Pepa quite consciously referred back to the girl-group tradition. The track took its name from the Pointer Sisters' 1975 hit 'How Long (Betcha Got a Chick on the Side)' and retained the original chorus of the song; the Pointers' percussive chant now became rap, pure and simple: 'Betcha got a chick on the side, sure you got a chick, I know you got a chick on the side.' In the verses, however, the words had changed. Where the heroine of the Pointers' song had mused 'How long will this game go on?' and openly expressed her vulnerability ('Every time I open up my heart it seems to just get torn apart'), Salt 'n Pepa were in no doubt whatsoever as to what to do. Their response to Mr Wrong was short and sharp:

> *Whatever game you play, I play the same*
> *so if you wanna go mess around and cheat*
> *and you wanna romance between another girl's sheets*
> *go ahead, swinger!*
> *I expected that*
> *cos you're nothing but a cheap little sucker brat*
> *wherever you're at you want this and that*
> *you dirty rat I'm not a welcome mat*
> *I got another lover*
> *and I know he cares*
> *don't smile child, wipe your crocodile tears*

The girls had no qualms about taunting the abandoned lover with tales of a new boyfriend's tender loving ways:

> *He sets the table for his and hers*
> *and while the dinner simmers he serves the hors d'oeuvres*

nor of detailing the romantic fireside scenes of passion that ensued. Salt 'n Pepa's rap finally ended with a cheery goodbye:

I'm makin' it clear
See ya later 'gator
I'm gettin' outta here!

The simpering female had become a tough nut; but the link between the B girls and the Pointer Sisters was still there. Clearly, hip hop with its eclectic raiding of all types of music had made it possible for girls like Salt 'n Pepa to use, comment on, update and celebrate a specifically female tradition in pop, that of the girl groups.

'Tramp', a stinging attack on the sexist double standards of most men, was a classic example of Salt 'n Pepa's new tough-girl style. In it, Salt 'n Pepa 'broke on' promiscuous men, calling them the same name that such men would use towards girls:

Homegirls, attention you must pay
so listen close to what I say
don't take this as a simple rhyme
cos this type of thing happens all the time
what would you do if a stranger said 'Hi'
would you diss him or would you reply?
if you answer, there is a chance
that he will think you want what's in his pants.
Am I right fellas? Tell the truth
or else I'm a have to show you proof
you are what you are, I am what I am
it just so happens that most men are tramps

As much as their words, it was Salt 'n Pepa's sound that got them noticed. On 'Tramp', Hurby used a sixties' soul hit of the same name for the backing beats, and the girls sounded comfortable as their low voices settled into the grooves and prepared to attack. 'My Mike Sounds Nice', another single from the LP, reflected this sense of aural satisfaction; and by the time 'I Am Down' came out, it was a celebration of the crew's success as much as a boast about their prowess on the microphone.

With 'Push It', released in 1988, Salt 'n Pepa returned to the more complex territory, for women, of asserting their sexual desire. But here, they stressed, there were definitely limits. Cheryl explained:

I don't think you should go too far in this area. I wouldn't be embarrassed, it's just that it's not allowed. Society sets it up that way. You would be looked down upon, and that's the reason we have to be careful and judge it right. If a woman wanted to do that kind of bragging, I'd just say go ahead. But I know what she'd have to deal with after. If we did go too far, people would say, 'Salt 'n Pepa flipped. They lost it. They're crazy!'

Salt 'n Pepa had managed to gain a stronger foothold in rap than earlier crews like Sequence or Us Girls by shifting the emphasis away from sexual bragging or romantic lyricism towards insults contests, which worked well in the context of the battle of the sexes. Yet the erotic innuendo always present in the music, which came to the fore again with 'Push It', meant that the girls had to tread a fine line between being outrageous and, as they put it, 'losing it'.

The fact that Salt 'n Pepa could now return to the old style of rap, exemplified by Sequence, where women boast about how sexy they are, was proof of their growing confidence. Yet, as with Roxanne Shanté, who was not above proclaiming her physical attractions when the mood took her, this style amongst women rappers was often mistakenly perceived as a sign of their willingness to be treated as sex objects, perpetuating female stereotypes. In fact, it was no such thing; it was a courageous attempt to challenge the double standard which prevents women from competing with men on an equal basis. If occasionally female MCs lost their verbal balance, either by being too cautious and therefore playing up to male fantasies, or by being too outspoken and therefore alienating their female as well as male audience, that could be put down to the difficulty of the task as much as to their lack of judgement.

The same could be said in the context of how Salt, Pepa and Spinderella dress for their role as the top pop girl crew of rap. Pepa:

> Our style is changing. In the beginning, we wore shorts, sports clothes. Now, we dress up more. You start out with a street audience, so you dress street; now, our style is a bit more refined. But we're not leaving the street behind. They're gonna follow us. We wear something, like these hats, and some girls compliment us, others say, 'Nah, it's not street enough.' Then we find everyone on the street wearin' 'em. We do it first, and then it becomes street.

By the time the crew appeared in Mandela's birthday concert in July 1988, which immediately pushed them into the mainstream UK charts, their style had already changed from how it was when I saw them in New York in April. The big gold earrings and gold chains had got bigger; the girls were in leotards not chunky sweaters, and the hats had gone. Salt had dyed her hair blonde like Pepa, and all the girls were wearing big, bright jackets. The style was glam hip hop, street clothes customized for smart girls on their way up. But how far were the crew prepared to go along this road? Salt had assured me back in April, 'As long as we don't get into sequins, evening gowns and pumps to do rap, we'll be all right.' By the time Salt 'n Pepa released a cover of the Isley Brothers' 'Twist and Shout' in late 1988, however, there they were cavorting about on video, imitating the Supremes.

But the image was a clever, tongue-in-cheek one; here was a retro fantasy spelling out a new message: that Salt 'n Pepa were now up there in the pop charts with the best of the girl groups of the past.

Spinderella, however, as the DJ for Salt 'n Pepa, has had to forge an entirely new role for herself, one that has no models in the past. There are even fewer women DJs in hip hop than rappers; Jazzy Joyce and Wanda Dee are amongst the small group who, besides Spinderella, have achieved a name for themselves. Quietly spoken and looking very young, she was surprisingly confident in her new role, as she told me:

> I'm a good DJ now. I know, 'cause all the men want to take credit for teaching me! Then they can go and tell everybody, 'I taught Spinderella'! I picked up on it 'cause I used to watch other people. I looked at how they used their equipment. My ex-boyfriend, he used to do it and I would watch him for hours. But I never thought I'd get up there and try it. So one day I did, and he said, 'You're good.' And that's what pushed me 'cause he kept complimenting me. That's what I needed to hear. If he'd have said, 'You ain't good, get outta here,' I probably wouldn't be Spinderella today. When Salt 'n Pepa asked me to join them, I was still at school. My family weren't too keen. They thought the whole thing was a big crock. But then the money started coming in, and I guess that changed their mind ...

Salt adds:

> Her father was very suspicious at first. He allowed her to join us, but on condition that she went back to school after the vacation. He kept yelling 'Dee Dee's going back to school! Dee Dee's going back to school!' So we did some shows, and then it came back around for her to go back to school, so we said, 'Okay, you gotta go back to school, you can't do any more shows for now.' By this time, we were quite successful, but we did what Dee Dee's father wanted and let her go. And then her father calls me and he's really mad, and he says, 'Hey, what's the matter? You don't want Dee Dee in the group?!' We laughed so much over that one.

Salt, Pepa and Spinderella appear to be level-headed and sensible, but they, like the girl groups before them, have had to learn the hard way about the business side of their work. Salt remembers:

> When we started we were young, we were dumb, we were new to the business, we didn't know anybody, we didn't have anybody to audit our books – we didn't know books could be audited. We didn't know anything, we were just like newborns. People didn't pay us. Point blank. We had no money to take them to court, we didn't have anybody to tell, they knew they could do this to us, so they did it.

Yet unlike many of those early girl groups, they have apparently managed to manoeuvre themselves into a position of relative control over their careers, so that they now at least reap the benefits of their record sales. They are now well aware of the pitfalls of the music business, as Pepa's advice to would-be artists shows:

> You have to have an accountant that's really interested in you and makes sure you get what you deserve. You just have to have someone that knows what they're doing and knows how to audit books and keeps on top of your business. And you have to keep on top of the accountant! That's the mistake that's made, when you have John taking care of your books and Paul that handles your bills so you don't worry about it . . . and then when it's time to come and get your money, they tell you they had to pay for this, and that money went out for that, and then you're only left with $1,000 when you were supposed to have $100,000!

But quite clearly, whatever the problems, at the time I met them, the girls were in fact seeing some of the money due to them. When asked about what magazines they read, Salt replied shyly, 'I like *Good Housekeeping*, 'cause I'm getting ready to buy a home.' 'Oh no!' groaned Spinderella. 'It's good,' insisted Salt, rather embarrassed. 'It shows you a lot of nice things to do with ya house.' There was a silence and then the girls burst out laughing, tickled at this image of themselves as housewives, Pepa adding, 'I just bought a condo! So! I must purchase this housekeeping book!'

Artistically, it appears that Hurby Azor is still very much in control, although the girls emphasize that their tracks are often a collaborative effort. In the studio, Salt says, 'I'll throw a word, she'll throw a word and a lot of the time, if we don't like something Hurby's written, we compromise. We have other people writing for us too.' Yet it does seem that, despite the girls' increased financial control and their apparent freedom to adopt their own styles of dress, as well as to choreograph and present their own stage act, their contribution to writing and producing material is still minimal. The shadowy figure of the sixties' Svengali producer has not altogether died away with the advent of the new, hardheaded pop girls of hip hop.

As the crew's pop success increases, they insist that they will retain their street roots; says Salt, "Since 'Push It" we got a lot of pop stations, an audience we've never had before. But we're always gonna keep that hardcore hip hop, as well as going into pop. We're versatile.' However, she adds that there is a difference between pop rap and the street styles displayed by rappers like Roxanne Shanté: 'Anybody can go pop rap. It's good that different races get into it. But street rap is different. Only black teenagers from New York can do that.'

Salt 'n Pepa are convinced that a wave of new female rappers will follow

Pioneers of female rap on the UK hip hop scene: the Cookie Crew.

in their wake. In April 1988, they cited their favourite young female rap artist as Sweet Tee, who like them has had pop chart success, and labelmate Antoinette, who they say, 'sounds like a female Rakim, smooth' . . . but with an attitude'. At the time, there were other solo girl rappers in New York they did not mention, like MC Lyte, whose single 'I Cram To Understand You Sam' was attracting attention as a serious and sensitive exploration into the problems for girls raised by men's attitudes towards drugs. There were also other rap duos like Salt 'n Pepa coming up in the city, such as Finesse and Synquis. In London too, a new wave of girl rappers was breaking; these included the Cookie Crew, who were on the UK hip hop scene from the beginning, She Rockers, and the Wee Papa Girl Rappers, whose 'Wee Rule' later hit the UK pop charts. Increasingly the UK crews are proving that they can hold their own against those of the US; not merely by imitating black American styles of rap, but by drawing on elements of their own culture such as West Indian toasting and British cockney patter. As the Wee Papa Girls have proved, British girls can 'go pop rap' like Salt 'n Pepa; but they can also add their own street styles too.

*   *   *

The journey from the doo wop of the fifties to hip hop in the eighties has been a long one for the girl groups. Throughout, pop girl groups have created fantasies for their girl fans that, however contradictory, have been a clear expression of female aspirations for over three decades. Undoubtedly, those fantasies have changed as women's aspirations have moved towards notions of independence, both sexual and economic.

In the music business how real the fantasies have become is not altogether clear, however. Today girl crews like Salt 'n Pepa may seem to have got a better deal for themselves than girl groups like the Chantels – young black New Yorkers with a background not so very different to theirs – were able to command in the fifties; yet, in fact, it is difficult to assess their position. Until their popularity has waned, like the middle-aged women I spoke to who were stars in their teens, they cannot afford to bite the hand that feeds them, and will remain circumspect about their business affairs. Moreover, for every Salt 'n Pepa there are countless others who, without the weight of a platinum disc behind them, are well and truly ripped off – as Salt 'n Pepa were in their early days. The reality is that the music business still regards young women as the most pliant, vulnerable type of artist available, as well as the most sexually saleable; the industry is still grossly immoral, buying its girls at knock-down prices whenever it can and selling them at a profit however it can.

Yet the fantasies that the girl groups have offered their fans still remain. Whatever its treatment of girl stars, the industry's hands have been tied by public taste, and this has been its saving grace. The market for pop singles has, over the years, been dominated by young women, and pop has tended to reflect the preoccupations, however absurd, of this section of the public. In particular, the girl groups have supplied the fantasies women want. Reality may not have kept pace with the aspirations expressed in these fantasies, but there has been one major change. The actual girls who make the records have stepped forward into the limelight.

The girl crews of hip hop are no longer nameless, faceless voices on a pop single; in true rap style, they proclaim their identity loud and clear. They speak, not only for themselves, but for all the shadowy anonymous ghosts of girl groups past whose identity they now reclaim. They have made sure that they themselves are part of the fantasy of pop, part of what every girl fan wants to be. Salt sums it all up like this:

> The guys are in love with us, and the girls are proud of us. The guys may think we're sexy or whatever, but the girls think, 'Those are my girls. They're my homegirls!' They come up to us after the shows just to tell us they love us. Because they're proud. They're just bursting with pride.

BIBLIOGRAPHY

Note: asterisks denote books that have been particularly useful in my research. Special mention should be made of Alan Betrock's pioneering study of girl groups in the sixties, which was an invaluable source of information for chapters 1–3.

* Alan Betrock, *Girl Groups: The Story of a Sound*, Delilah, New York, 1982.

Victor Bockris and Gerard Malanga, *Uptight: The Velvet Underground Story*, Omnibus Press, London, 1983.

Nik Cohn, *WopBopaLooBopLopBamBoom*, Paladin, London, 1972.

* Tony Cummings, *The Sound of Philadelphia*, Methuen, London, 1975.

Mike Davis, Manning Marable, Fred Pfeil and Michael Sprinker, eds, *The Year Left 2: Towards a Rainbow Socialism*, Verso, London, 1987.

Barbara Ehrenreich, Elizabeth Hess, Gloria Jacobs, *Re-making Love; The Feminization of Sex*, Fontana, London, 1987.

* Peter Everett, *You'll Never Be 16 Again: An Illustrated History of the British Teenager*, BBC Publications, London, 1986.

Rob Finnis, *The Phil Spector Story*, Rockon, London, 1975.

Paul Gambaccini, Tim Rice and Jo Rice, *British Hit Singles*, GRR Publications, London, 1987.

Rochelle Gatlin, *American Women Since 1945*, Macmillan, London, 1987.

Nelson George, *Where Did Our Love Go? The Rise and Fall of the Motown Sound*, Omnibus, London, 1985.

* Charlie Gillett, *The Sound of the City*, Souvenir Press, London, 1970.

Philip Groia, *They All Sang on the Corner: New York's Rhythm and Blues Vocal Groups of the 1950s*, The Edmond Publishing Company, New York, 1974.

Gerri Hirshey, *Nowhere to Run*, Macmillan, London, 1984.

Tony Jasper, *The Top Twenty Book: Thirty Years of Hits*, Javelin, 1986.

* Marty Jezer, *The Dark Ages: Life in the United States 1945–1960*. South End Press, Boston, 1982.

Ian Hoare, Clive Anderson, Tony Cummings, Simon Frith, *The Soul Book*, Methuen, London, 1975.

* Greil Marcus, *Mystery Train*, Omnibus, London, 1979.

Bill Millar, *The Coasters*, Star Books, London, 1974.

Bill Millar, *The Drifters*, Studio Vista, London, 1971.

Jim Miller, ed., *The Rolling Stone Illustrated History of Rock & Roll*, Picador, 1981.

Michelle Phillips, *California Dreamin': The True Story of the Mamas and the Papas*, Warner Books, New York, 1986.

Mary Quant, *Quant By Quant*, Pan Books, London, 1965.

* Michael Shore with Dick Clark, *The History of American Bandstand*, Ballantine Books, New York, 1985.

Sue Steward and Sheryl Garratt, *Signed, Sealed and Delivered: True Life Stories of Women In Pop*, Pluto Press, London, 1984.

David Toop, *The Rap Attack*, Pluto Press, London, 1984.

* Dennis Wepman, Ronald B. Newman, Murray B. Binderman, *The Life: The Lore and Folk Poetry of the Black Hustler*, Holloway House, Los Angeles, 1974.

* Joel Whitburn, *The Billboard Book of US Top 40 Hits*, Billboard Pubs, 1983.

* Mary Wilson, *Dreamgirl: My Life as a Supreme*, Sidgwick & Jackson, London, 1987.

Richard Williams, *The Sound of Phil Spector: Out of His Head*, Abacus, London, 1974.